WAR STORIES

WAR STORIES

★

OPERATION IRAQI FREEDOM

OLIVER L. NORTH

Since 1947
REGNERY
PUBLISHING, INC.
An Eagle Publishing Company • Washington, DC

Library of Congress Cataloging-in-Publication Data

North, Oliver.
 War stories : Operation Iraqi Freedom / Oliver L. North.
    p. cm.
 Includes index.
 ISBN 0-89526-037-9 (paperback)
 1. Iraq War, 2003. 2. Iraq War, 2003—Television and the war. 3. Television broadcasting of news—United States. I. Title. DS79.76 .N67 2003
956.7044'3—dc22

                             2003024431

Published in the United States by
Regnery Publishing, Inc.
An Eagle Publishing Company
One Massachusetts Avenue, NW
Washington, DC 20001

First paperback edition published 2005

Visit us at www.regnery.com

Distributed to the trade by
National Book Network
4720-A Boston Way
Lanham, MD 20706

Printed on acid-free paper

Manufactured in the United States of America

10 9 8 7 6 5 4 3 2 1

Books are available in quantity for promotional or premium use. Write to Director of Special Sales, Regnery Publishing, Inc., One Massachusetts Avenue, NW, Washington, DC 20001, for information on discounts and terms or call (202) 216-0600.

For Betsy,
Who waited and prayed once again –
and this time got to watch

CONTENTS

ACKNOWLEDGMENTS

Whoever said "No man is the whole of himself. His friends are the rest of him," had it just about right when it comes to projects like this book. It couldn't have been done, to paraphrase the Beatles, without "a lot of help from my friends."

Most important to this book has been the support and encouragement of my best friend, Betsy, who once again managed to hold everything together at home as I went off to yet another war. While I hung around with heroes in Iraq and then buried myself in writing about them, she prayed for my safe return, planned a wedding for daughter Sarah and husband Martin, helped daughter Tait and husband Tom when Elizabeth St. Claire was born, did the same for son Stuart and his wife Ellen when James Stuart arrived, and still found time to attend every equestrian event in which daughter Dornin competed.

This book would never have happened had Roger Ailes, Jack Abernethy, Dianne Brandi, Kevin Magee, and John Moody at FOX News not sent me to cover the heroes of Operation Iraqi Freedom—and then decided to team with Regnery Publishing to chronicle their courage in this work. As he has for so many years, my colleague, collaborator, and friend Joe Musser helped organize this narrative and turned my military shorthand and jargon into comprehensible English.

Griff Jenkins, my field producer, cameraman, and friend, was by my side throughout our assignment in Iraq, requiring the understanding and patience of his wife, Kathleen, and two-year-old daughter, Madeline, who spent months without her daddy. They missed him, but I got to witness his competence, perseverance, and bravery.

Our incomparable FOX News team also deserves special thanks for making this project possible. In New York, senior producer Pamela Browne and our *War Stories* staff had to reschedule two months of production for our series, then rush to turn out the TV special on Operation Iraqi Freedom included with this book. In Kuwait, Don Fair and Gary Gastelu built a bureau from scratch; they and their team never failed us in the field. My colleagues Greg Kelly and Rick Leventhal, friends and fellow "embeds," managed to shoot some of the most dramatic war footage ever recorded. Brian Knoblock's foreign desk staff and Sharri Berg's technical team made sure that what we shot made it on the air for the world to see.

At Williams & Connolly, Bob Barnett and Kathleen Ryan had the vision to see how this collaboration between FOX News and Regnery Publishing could work, and made it happen.

Regnery president and publisher Marji Ross, my incredibly patient editor Miriam Moore, and art director Amanda Elliott had to bear the stress of being unable to reach me as deadlines approached and passed—and still managed to get this tribute to these young American heroes into print. Regnery's marketing and promotion guru Stephanie Marshall succeeded in getting this work out to booksellers so that the American people could see and read just how good these soldiers, sailors, airmen, Guardsmen, and Marines really are.

This is, after all, a book about them. Lt. Col. Jerry Driscoll, the CO of HMM-268, and Col. Joe Dunford, the commander of RCT-5, are two of the bravest men and finest Marines I've ever met. Lt. Col. Larry "Pepper" Jackson, CO of 3rd Battalion, 66th Armored Regiment is a great soldier. My sincere thanks to them and their valiant warriors who got us home in one piece. The men and women of the 1st Marine Division, the 3rd Marine Air Wing and the Army's 4th Infantry Division let us live with and follow them from late February through late April 2003 in pursuit of the most up-to-the-minute, and inspiring war stories—theirs.

Semper Fidelis,
Oliver L. North

THE LAND BETWEEN THE RIVERS

In one of our last broadcasts prior to leaving Iraq, I was asked by my friend Sean Hannity to predict what Baghdad will be like in a few years. "A thriving economy and a robust democracy in three years—if we stay the course," I replied.

What gives me the confidence to make such a bold forecast? The history of the place. The land between the rivers has been home to risk-takers and innovators for at least five millenia. From the Mesopotamian merchant who carved the first written word into a clay tablet; to Hammurabi's code and the foundation for our concept of laws; to Abraham and Sarah, parents of the world's three monotheistic religions; all the way to Saddam Hussein—and his removal from power by an invading army; all part of the history of the land we now call Iraq.

Understanding who the Iraqi people are—and who they aren't— is essential to comprehending the victory in Operation Iraqi Freedom. Herewith then, an epilogue that is in reality prologue for all that has happened since: a short history of the land between the rivers. It is this history that gives me hope for a better future.

★ Ancient Eden
Iraq, between the Tigris and Euphrates rivers
5000 B.C. to the twentieth century

Viewing Iraq today, the land along and between the Tigris and Euphrates seems an improbable place for the start of civilization. A few hundred miles north of where the two rivers merge, treacherous mountains rise to snow-covered peaks more than ten thousand feet high. Less than fifty miles west and south of the fertile land that lines the rivers are stark, unforgiving deserts. To the east, inhospitable malarial swamps and marshes make travel and navigation all but impossible.

Yet, if archaeologists are correct, this is the place where it all began at least five millennia ago. Here, an ancient Sumerian first carved written words onto clay tablets with a stylus. In the verdant terrain close to these riverbanks, seasonal planting of crops, animal husbandry, astronomy, irrigation, wheeled transportation, metallurgy, stringed musical instruments, pharmacology, masonry, ceramic engineering, brewing, algebraic mathematics, and warehousing of harvests were all invented or begun by the Sumerian, Akkadian, and Assyrian founders of Mesopotamian culture.

The place, also described as the Garden of Eden in the Book of Genesis, is thought to be near the site of present-day Al Qurnah, where the Tigris and Euphrates meet to form the Shatt al Arab water-way, less than fifty miles north of modern-day Basra.

Abraham and Sarah, the patriarch and matriarch of the world's three monotheistic religions—Judaism, Christianity, and Islam—are widely believed to have begun their long journey west to Canaan from the ancient city of Ur, on the west bank of the Euphrates, around 1850 B.C. Less than a century later, a Babylonian king named Hammurabi, the world's first emperor, decreed a code, prescribing punishments for infractions of his edicts that were less harsh than the practices of his day, but draconian in modern-day eyes. His code—and the determination that the law should apply equally to all—is the foundation of the whole Western legal system.

In 586 B.C., another Babylonian king, Nebuchadnezzar, descended on Jerusalem with his army, torching the city of David, leveling the temple, and driving the people of Israel into bondage in that same space between the Tigris and the Euphrates. Some believe that Jewish slaves, during their seventy-year Babylonian exile, built the Hanging Gardens of Babylon, acclaimed as the second wonder of the ancient world, with irrigation canals, terraces, and bridges over the Euphrates. A towering ziggurat in the center of the city, which came to be known as the Tower of Babel, was probably erected to honor the Babylonian god Baal.

Less than 250 years later, Babylon fell to the Medes and Persians under Cyrus the Just. He dispatched the Israelites back to Jerusalem to rebuild their temple, thus earning favorable mention in the Old Testament even though he worshiped the Babylonian god Marduk.

Next came the Greeks. In 331 B.C., Alexander and his disciplined army of Macedonians seized the city-state between the rivers on the way to Persia. Eight years later the young king returned only to die—from poison, some say—in Nebuchadnezzar's crumbling palace.

For the next half-millennium the land through which the Tigris and Euphrates flow was ruled by a succession of invaders—Romans, Seleucids, Parthians, and Sassanids—all seeking dominion over the region. All brought their own tongues and religions, yet by the end of the sixth century, Christianity was probably practiced by more people in Mesopotamia than any other faith. But then came Islam.

According to many of his biographers, Abu al-Qasim Muhammad was an orphan raised by a grandfather and then an uncle near Mecca, in present-day Saudi Arabia. Consigned to life as a camel herder, the young man was fortunate to marry a wealthy widow. One day, at the age of forty, he returned from meditating alone on Mount Hira with a message from the angel Gabriel.

Proclaimed as a prophet by many in Mecca, Muhammad began to preach that there was only one God, and admonished his tribal, nomadic, Bedouin countrymen to reject idolatry and greed and to submit to the will of Allah. Thus, Islam, meaning "submission to God," the world's third major monotheistic religion, began. By 630 A.D., Muhammad was in effect the political and spiritual leader of an Islamic state that encompassed most of the Saudi Arabian peninsula. When he died on June 8, 632, his successor, Abu Bakr, was appointed caliph. He resolved to spread Islamic theology, with its message of equality and strict rules for behavior, throughout the world by force of arms.

Two years later, a poorly armed but zealous Islamic army was on the attack against Christian Byzantium and Zoroastrian Persia throughout the area that we now call the Middle East. In 637, at the small town of Qadisiyah on the west bank of the Euphrates, ten thousand Islamic warriors defeated a force of eighty thousand Persians.

The land between the rivers would thereafter have no god but Allah.

The new rulers of Islamic Mesopotamia encouraged Bedouins from Arabia to move their herds of cattle, goats, and camels to the fertile river plains. They did so in a series of massive migrations, displacing the previous occupiers and destroying much of the ancient art and cultural treasures that had accumulated in the area.

History wasn't finished with the land between the rivers. The great schism in Islam that divided the religion between the Sunni and Shia sects was also played out here.

In 656 A.D., a bitter dispute over the leadership of the religion started by Muhammad broke out in the small town of Kufa, on the west bank of the Euphrates, about forty miles south of ancient Babylon. Ali, Muhammad's cousin and the first convert to Islam, was named caliph that year, and took up residence in Kufa in an attempt to avoid the enmity of other Islamic leaders in Medina and Damascus. It didn't work.

As Ali made his way home from prayers one night in the late summer of 661, an assassin felled the unsuspecting holy man. Nineteen years later, Ali's son, Hussein, the grandson of Muhammad, claimed the mantle of Islamic leadership as a familial right of succession. The rulers of the Islamic empire in Damascus rejected Hussein's claim and his accusations that they were using their power to amass great personal wealth while the people suffered.

In 680, Hussein and seventy-two of his family members and followers were confronted just west of the Euphrates, at Karbala, by four thousand soldiers dispatched from Damascus by the ruling Islamic elite. Hussein and all of his entourage, including women and children, were slaughtered. The severed head of the grandson of the prophet Muhammad was delivered to Damascus by horseback. Since that day, Islam has been divided between Sunni Muslims—supporters of consensual leadership—and the Shi'ite followers of Ali and Hussein.

Despite the internal split and three successive Mongol invasions, Islam continued to spread. By 1553, a century after the Ottoman Turks captured the Orthodox Catholic capital of Constantinople and changed its name to Istanbul, the Arabic language and the Muslim religion were both being taught and practiced in Asia Minor, the Balkans, the periphery of the Caucasus, northern and east-coastal Africa, southern Spain, and throughout what we now call the Middle East.

As Europe foundered through the Dark Ages, flourished during the Middle Ages, and began its Renaissance, Sunni sultans in Istanbul, espousing a pan-Islamic ideology, attempted to unify their dynastic holdings through religion, language, education, and common law. Where appeals to common philosophy failed, military coercion was employed—a strategy that prompted repeated bloody uprisings in Shi'ite controlled areas of Mesopotamia and Persia.

If not for corruption, costly military suppression of dissenters, and forays of European colonialism, the Ottoman Empire might still exist; and the country known as Iraq might never have arisen had the "Young Turks" who seized control in Istanbul in 1908 not chosen the wrong side in World War I. Infatuated by the Kaiser's militarism and feeling threatened by Orthodox Russia to the east, they opted to join the Central Powers in hopes that the alliance would help check both the czar's ambitions in Persia and British and French colonial expansion in the Middle East and Africa.

It was a costly mistake. The Young Turks found themselves having to contend with rebellions fomented by Shi'ite religious activists and Arab nationalists seeking independence from Istanbul while simultaneously trying to protect their fraying empire from the Triple Entente.

Though threatened from the outside and weakened by internal dissent, the Turks still fought back. In January 1916, conscripts recruited throughout the remnants of the Ottoman Empire, including Mesopotamia, inflicted a devastating defeat on British troops at

Gallipoli. While London was still reeling from the collapse of the Dardanelles campaign, a British expeditionary force attempting to advance from Basra to Baghdad was cut to pieces. On April 26, 1916, more than thirteen thousand starving British troops surrendered after enduring a 140-day siege at Al Kut, on the banks of the Tigris.

But these bloody victories were fleeting. Eleven months after the disaster at Al Kut, British troops occupied Baghdad, and when the "war to end all wars" finally ended, in 1918, so was the Ottoman Empire. In the aftermath of World War I, the Ottoman Empire was dismantled, and British and French forces and civil administrators moved into Arab capitals to take over as "trustees" under the aegis of the League of Nations. British army regiments occupied Basra on the Shatt al Arab, and Royal Engineers started building roads, railways, and canals to Baghdad and beyond.

What the British could not build was a firewall against the glowing embers of Arab nationalism and the Shia-Sunni animus that they had helped to foment during the world war. T. E. Lawrence, the legendary Lawrence of Arabia, had played to both and had wooed Arab Bedouins to revolt against Ottoman rule with pledges of postwar self-determination. But neither Lawrence nor any of the other advocates for local sovereignty could deliver. By January 18, 1919, when the victors sat down in public at the Palace of Versailles, British and French mapmakers were already secretly redrawing the boundaries of Syria, Jordan, Lebanon, Saudi Arabia, Kuwait, and the Palestine and Mesopotamian Mandates. In accord with the secretly concluded Sykes-Picot Agreement, all of these would be administered not by those who populated these lands but by British and French civil and military officers.

In the land between the two rivers this was a formula for disaster. On June 2, 1920, in a taste of things to come, Sunni nationalists in Baghdad and Shi'ite religious leaders in the south decided that as much as they hated each other, they hated the British occupiers even more. The ensuing jihad against British rule took nine months to suppress—at a cost of more than 2,200 British casualties and forty million pounds sterling.

In the aftermath of the "Arab Revolt," Winston Churchill, then secretary of state for colonial affairs, convened a conference in Cairo to determine the future of Britain's Mesopotamian Mandate. Without consulting with a single person who lived between the Tigris and Euphrates, the participants, including T. E. Lawrence, redrew the borders once again, renamed the territory "Iraq," and selected Faisal, the son of the sharif of Mecca, a Hashemite and a friend of Lawrence, for the throne of the newly minted "kingdom."

The British might have conceived of Faisal as their puppet, but they quickly learned that he had a few ideas of his own. Within months of his August 23, 1921, coronation, the new king convinced the British to send aircraft and motorized troops with machine guns to drive marauding Wahhabis back into Saudi Arabia. Though the operation required Faisal to acquiesce in yet another redrawing of the map—this time the creation of a "neutral zone" along the border of Saudi Arabia, Kuwait, and Iraq—security in the south meant he could start consolidating his authority over his new kingdom. By 1923 Faisal had expelled the Shi'ite mullahs and imams from the holy cities of Najaf and Karbala and sent them packing to Iran. A year later he handed down what he called the Tribal Disputes Regulations, suborning the rural Shi'ite sheikhs to his Sunni-dominated administration in Baghdad. In March of 1925, the oil-rich Sunni Kurdish enclave of Mosul was annexed. The British helped to make this move official by supporting the so-called Organic Law, which gave Faisal the right to convene and adjourn the Iraqi Parliament.

By 1930 the king had withstood an attempted coup and forged sufficient consensus among his fractious, multi-ethnic, multi-communal people to permit suffrage for men, implement universal public education, create a national army, institute a system of law, and commence a program of rural electrification. The 1930 Anglo-Iraq Treaty, granting independence and commonwealth status to the kingdom in 1932, reflected not just British fatigue and the effects of the Great Depression, but the Hashemite king's skills as an administrator as well. And though the treaty granted the British rights to military bases in Iraq, it made Faisal the first head of state of a sovereign Arab country and a member of the League of Nations. He didn't live to enjoy the fruits of his labor. A heart attack felled Faisal in September 1933.

The day after Iraq's first monarch was laid in his grave, his twenty-one-year-old son, Ghazi Ibn Faisal (meaning "victorious son of Faisal"), assumed the throne. The playboy-turned-potentate proved predictably inept and virulently anti-British. When the Shi'ites in southern Iraq complained, he ignored them. When they rebelled in 1935 and 1936, Ghazi sent the Sunni-led army to brutally repress the uprising.

As London warily watched Hitler's rise to power in Germany and Stalin's purges in Russia, Ghazi began making regular radio broadcasts laced with anti-British propaganda. In 1936, with the monarch's acquiescence, Bakr Sidqi, an army commander with a reputation for cruelty, led a coup against the pro-British elected government.

For the next two years, the regime in Baghdad conducted a quiet flirtation with Axis fascism, inviting emissaries from Rome and Berlin to Baghdad. By the time Ghazi killed himself in a drunken automobile accident on April 4, 1939, the British were glad he was gone. But much of what his father had tried to do in the way of uniting a dispirit country had also been undone.

Ghazi's son, Faisal II, was only three years old when he ascended the throne, so Emir Abdul al Ilah—a pro-British Hashemite—was appointed as regent. But just two years later, in April 1941, he was forced to flee for his life by yet another nationalist military coup. That was enough for the British, who were now fighting for survival against Hitler. On June 1, 1941, the British army landed in force at Basra, marched unopposed into Baghdad, and reinstalled Abdul al Ilah as regent.

The end of World War II brought an end to British occupation, but not to Iraq's internal discord. In January 1948, Communist agitators aligned with nationalists to create a series of street protests against a new treaty with Britain. Distrustful of the army, whose senior officers were predominantly Sunni nationalists, the regent called on the police to open fire. Hundreds were killed. The government collapsed, and even though the Treaty of Portsmouth was abrogated, those who hated the monarchy and the British had a grievous wrong to remember. By the end of the year, they would have another: the defeat of the Arab armies—including a twenty-thousand-man Iraqi contingent—at the hand of Israel in the Jewish state's war of independence.

By May 1953, when the eighteen-year-old Faisal II appeared before the Iraqi parliament to swear an oath to "safeguard democratic principles" and become Iraq's third constitutional monarch, the days of British influence—and the Iraqi monarchy—were numbered. Despite growing oil wealth, a commensurate increase in the standard of living, and a burgeoning intellectual community, the country was increasingly torn by internecine conflict and a potentially violent nationalist movement fueled in large measure by external forces.

In February 1955, Faisal II agreed to join the so-called Baghdad Pact, an anti-Communist alliance that also included Turkey, Pakistan, Iran, and, of course, Great Britain. The king was immediately branded a "lackey of Western imperialism" by the communist press, as well as by Shi'ite opponents of the regime, and Gamal Abdul Nasser—the Egyptian army colonel who had overthrown King Farouk in Cairo. It was the final straw for the anti-imperialist nationalists in the Iraqi army officer corps. They began to plot in earnest—not only against the pro-Western administration in Baghdad but against the monarchy as well.

Early on the morning of July 14, 1958, General Abd al-Karim Qasim ordered the army out of the barracks and to surround the palace. Before noon, Faisal II, Abdul al Ilah (the former regent), and the palace guards were all dead. Iraq's thirty-seven-year-long experiment with constitutional monarchy was over for good.

For the next decade (1958–1968), those who ruled from Baghdad described themselves to the world as an "Arab republic." But with the exception of a brief period under civilian governance in 1963, the country was run by a succession of military dictatorships. And since the process of electing deputies to parliament had died with Faisal II, the preferred methods for changing governments became assassinations and coups.

General Qasim barely survived the first such attempt at a change of government when a Baath Party hit team, which included a low-level party *apparatchik* named Saddam Hussein, tried to gun down the dictator on October 7, 1959. The second time around the Baathists were better organized. On the evening of February 9, 1963, in a scene foreshadowing what would happen forty years later, the new leaders of Iraq broadcast footage of General Qasim's bullet-riddled body on national television.

Nine months later, on November 18, 1963, the Baathist National Council of Revolutionary Command was itself thrown out in yet another coup. This one was led by a junta headed by General Abd al-Salam Arif, a friend and admirer of Egypt's Nasser. Al-Salam survived two Baath-inspired countercoup attempts in September 1964 and in 1965 only to die in a helicopter crash on April 13, 1966.

General Abd al-Rahman Arif succeeded his elder sibling as the head of Baghdad's military government. He fared even worse than his brother. Humiliated by Israel's defeat of the Arab armies in the 1967 Six Day War, in which Iraq's contingent never even engaged the "Zionist enemy," the resurgent Baathists tried again. This time it worked.

On July 17, 1968, a decade and three days after the military had destroyed Iraq's constitutional monarchy, the Arab Baath Socialist Party, a highly disciplined and secretive political entity of no more than eight thousand members, threw out the military dictatorship. General Arif was allowed to flee. In his place the Baathists installed the machinery that would eventually be seized by the most brutal ruler the land between the rivers had ever seen—Saddam Hussein.

✪ Modern Eden
Iraq, between the Tigris and Euphrates rivers
July 1968–September 2002

If the land between the Tigris and Euphrates is an unlikely place for the start of human civilization, then Saddam Hussein is an equally improbable person to become its head of state. Born on April 28, 1937, to a dirt-poor, illiterate family of shepherds, Saddam was apparently raised by a stepfather, his biological father having either died or run off before his son was born. By the age of ten, Saddam was attending school in Baghdad and living with his mother's brother.

Lacking the social contacts to get an appointment to the military academy in Baghdad, and too poor to attend a university, Saddam decided, at the age of twenty, to join the outlawed Baath Party. Two years later, in 1959, he was part of the hit team that tried to assassinate General Abd al-Karim Qasim. Though slightly wounded in the encounter, he managed to flee Iraq and spent the next four years on the run—first in Damascus and eventually in Cairo, where he studied law on a stipend and scholarship provided by Nasser's government.

In 1963 the budding Baath revolutionary dropped out of school, returned to Iraq, married his first cousin, Sajida Tulfah, and helped to plot another abortive coup later that year. Jailed in the aftermath, Saddam was released after signing an oath promising never again to participate in antigovernment or Baath Party activities. He immediately went underground and rose rapidly within the clandestine Baath organization, establishing a reputation for two qualities: intelligence and brutal ruthlessness.

On the seventeenth day of July 1968, when the Baathists took over in Baghdad, Saddam Hussein was the enforcer for the tightly organized party—a post for which he was uniquely suited. As the head of the *Jihaz Haneen*—the Baath security apparat—Saddam had the job of imposing discipline within the party's regional cells and to intimidate, coerce, or "remove" obstacles to consolidating control over the machinery of government. Immediately after seizing power, the governing Revolutionary Command Council (RCC) authorized Saddam to employ "terror and coercion" to "remove enemies of the revolution," and he bent to the task with zeal.

Two weeks after the coup, Baath Party leader Ahmed Hassan al-Bakr, the acting president of Iraq, gave his cousin Saddam the privilege of escorting Abd al-Razzaq al-Nayif, the head of Iraqi military intelligence and a potential rival for power, into exile and out of the way. Saddam immediately set about organizing a new intelligence service, the *Mukhabarat*, and staffed it with thugs from the Jihaz Haneen—many of them clansmen from Tikrit, the impoverished city on the banks of the Tigris that was hometown to both al-Bakr and Saddam.

In a matter of months the terror and killings were well under way. By January 1969, his security service had "discovered" seventeen "spies." Thirteen of them just happened to be Iraqi Jews. Saddam attended their public hanging.

The following month, the entire politburo of the Iraqi Communist Party was jailed. By the end of the year, thousands of Persian Shi'ites had been rounded up and expelled from the country in a Stalinesque deportation.

At Saddam's insistence, the new Iraqi leaders established a "watch system" similar to that employed by Lenin, Beria, and Stalin in consolidating Bolshevik control over the whole of Russia. Every neighborhood, newspaper, mosque, school, factory, oil field, and refinery, and particularly every unit in the military, had its own cell of loyal Baathists. The senior official in each cell acted as the commissars in Russia had, indoctrinating the uninitiated into the rules of the party and reporting any infractions up the line to officials in the Mukhabarat. Military officers who voiced concerns about the new regime in Baghdad were purged from the ranks. Any who continued to express reservations about the RCC or the policies of the Arab Baath Socialist Party agenda soon fled for their lives, were thrown into jail, or simply disappeared.

All of this worked well for controlling the levers of power in Baghdad and most other major cities in southern and central Iraq. But in the north, the Kurds were marching to the beat of a different drummer.

Along the northern frontier, intelligence agents from Syria, Turkey, and Iran incited the perpetually restive Kurds to begin a new campaign for an independent Kurdistan—one that would be carved not from their own territories but from Iraq.

Saddam devised a workable solution: divide and conquer. On March 11, 1970, with the full support of the RCC, he presented a

"Manifesto of Kurdish Autonomy" to Mustafa Barzani, the head of the KDP (Kurdistan Democratic Party), the most militant of the Kurdish factions. The deal was simple: In exchange for autonomy four years later, Barzani would immediately stop his fierce pesh merga fighters from attacking Baath Party offices, government posts, and police stations.

Barzani swallowed the deal and signed the manifesto, and Baghdad immediately went to work destroying all the other Kurdish groups. In a move reminiscent of Stalin's forced migrations in the Soviet Union, Saddam orchestrated the movement of tens of thousands of Arab settlers into the oil-rich Kurdish enclave of Kirkuk. And more than forty thousand Faili Kurds were expelled and pushed across the Shatt al Arab into Iran. Duplicity and deceit had bought time. In Baghdad, the Baath Party was on a roll and Saddam's star was ascending.

Internationally, the regime employed the same divide-and-conquer strategy. Denied access to Western arms, they concluded a "treaty of friendship" with the Soviet Union. When Moscow demanded payment for the tanks, artillery, and aircraft they were delivering, the regime devised a unique solution: On June 1, 1972, the RCC nationalized the British- and American-owned Iraq Oil Company and began using revenues from the wells to pay for the Russian ordnance.

The timing of the move was impeccable. On October 20, 1973, in the midst of yet another Arab-Israeli war, the oil-producing nations of the Middle East slapped an embargo on crude exports to any nations supporting Israel in the conflict. Iraq ignored the embargo and continued to ship. By the time the Western oil consumers convinced the other members of the Organization of Petroleum Exporting Countries (OPEC) to turn on the spigot again, the cost of a barrel of crude had risen to more than $11.50 from $3.10.

Suddenly the land between the rivers was swimming in money. A massive building campaign was under way in a matter of months. By mid-1975, new schools, hospitals, water treatment plants, cultural centers, public buildings, irrigation canals, athletic centers, and electrical generation and transmission facilities were under construction.

But that wasn't all the Baath Party erected with its newfound wealth. Archaeologists, funded by the RCC's Ministry of Antiquities, probed ancient Mesopotamian ruins for evidence of Iraq's unique place in world history, all in an effort to build a national identity among the nation's disparate people.

But all of these public expenditures notwithstanding, there was still more money left on the table than the RCC had imagined when they seized power in 1968. By the mid-1970s, Saddam was first among equal vice presidents in the Baath hierarchy, and using billions of dollars to erect a labyrinth of competing intelligence and security organizations—all aimed at suppressing any form of dissent inside Iraq, and eliminating any threats posed by the increasing numbers of Iraqi exiles living overseas.

The RCC also went on an international arms shopping spree. At the Ministry of Defense in Baghdad, Baath Party officials—not military officers—decided among competing bids from Soviet, Yugoslav, French, Belgian, and Italian arms brokers.

By 1974, the Iraqi military was, on paper, one of the most powerful in the world. When the Kurds began to agitate for the autonomy promised in the 1970 Manifesto, Saddam, as the Baath government official responsible for internal security, unleashed the army. Instead of self-rule, the Kurds were given brutality. The carnage among the pesh merga fighters and their families in the Kurdish highlands was horrific. By March of 1975, nearly one million Kurds had fled to Iran, Syria, and Turkey.

Fearful of growing internal discord in his own country, the shah of Iran, who had covertly supported the cause of militant Kurdish nationalism for years, suddenly abandoned his highland allies. In exchange for an agreement ending a long-standing dispute over the Shatt al Arab waterway, he went to Algiers, embraced Saddam, and closed the border. Betrayed by Tehran and besieged by Baghdad, the pesh merga were crushed. Mustafa Barzani fled into exile, and Saddam was lionized for eliminating yet another "threat to the revolution."

By 1978 Saddam Hussein was, in all but name, the head of state in Iraq. His cousin and mentor, Ahmed Hassan al-Bakr, might have borne the title of president of the republic, but the leaders of the RCC made certain that every decision was approved by Saddam. He had, he seemed to think, everything under control. Then came the ayatollah.

Even though they deeply distrusted each other, Saddam and Shah Muhammad Reza Pahlavi—sitting ruler of the Peacock Throne in Tehran—had come to an accommodation. In Algiers, they had settled their countries' dispute over the Shatt al Arab, reached an odious agreement on the fate of the Kurds, and even ended several disagreements over competing claims to oil deposits along their common border. So in October 1978, no one thought it particularly unusual that Saddam would acquiesce to a request from the shah to evict a sixty-three-year-old Shi'ite imam, the Ayatollah Ruhollah Khomeini, from Najaf, where he had resided beside the Tomb of Ali since November 1964. Saddam gave the old man twenty-four hours to get out of Iraq. He saw the ayatollah's departure as a returnable favor to the shah—and a good way of ridding a potential Shi'ite opponent from the neighborhood. But the white-bearded ascetic with the severe visage and furrowed brow wasn't gone long.

From Paris, Khomeini continued to incite his Shi'ite followers to overthrow the shah and replace the monarchy with an Islamic theocracy, one that would be led by imams and mullahs who also happened to be his devotees. On January 16, 1979, besieged by student riots and suffering from the cancer that would eventually kill him, Shah Pahlavi stepped down and departed Iran for a wandering exile. Fourteen days later, Khomeini returned to Tehran and proclaimed an Islamic revolution.

The rest of the world watched with dismay as the Iranian *pasdaran*, inspired by the mullahs and imams close to Khomeini, purged the Iranian armed forces, ripped up international agreements, and sacked Western libraries, hospitals, Christian missions, and, eventually, consulates and embassies. And while Iran's neighbors didn't shed many tears over the destruction of the American embassy in Tehran or the seizure of fifty-three American hostages, they were horrified to hear Khomeini now advocating a worldwide Shi'ite uprising and preaching regularly about the need to replace secular regimes in all Islamic nations with clerical governments.

By the summer of 1979, the Syrian strongman Hafez al Assad, feeling vulnerable, sought to find some common ground with his Iraqi neighbors and flew to Baghdad. When Assad arrived at the airport on June 16, 1979, Saddam refused to meet him.

A month later, Khomeini started broadcasting appeals directly to the Shi'ite population of Iraq to "bring an end to the infidel Baath regime." Saddam ordered the army to crack down on Shi'ite terrorist groups like the al-Dawah and the al-Mujahedin, which he believed were operating out of mosques in Karbala and Najaf. Senior army officers, concerned that their Shi'ite conscripts might mutiny, refused to act. Saddam decided he'd had enough.

On July 28, Saddam announced that the Interior Ministry had discovered a plot to overthrow the Iraqi government—not by Iran but by Syria. Eleven days later, at a meeting of the Baath Central Committee, Saddam watched impassively as twenty-one members of the Baath Party leadership were hauled from their seats, denounced, marched into the hallway, and shot by members of the Amn Al Khass, part of his Hydra-headed security organ. When the carnage of

August 8, 1979, was over, President al-Bakr was "retired" and Saddam Hussein was president, prime minister, chairman of the RCC, and chairman of the Baath Party. Within thirteen months, and with much of the world distracted by the Soviet invasion of Afghanistan, Saddam would plunge his country into the bloodiest military confrontation since World War II.

On the night of September 17, 1980, Saddam Hussein went on Iraqi national television and tore up—literally—the Algiers agreement on the Shatt al Arab that he and the shah had so carefully negotiated in 1975. Everyone knew that the act meant war. But no one imagined that it would last more than seven years and consume more than a million lives.

When Saddam attacked along a 750-mile front on September 22, most of the world expected that the Iraqi army would make short work of the heavily purged and demoralized Iranian army. Khomeini and his zealots had decimated the Iranian officer corps. Not only that, the United States had cut off the supply of parts and ammunition to the American-built Iranian military. Most of the West had done the same. Within a matter of weeks, the Iraqis had captured the Iranian port of Khorramshahr and surrounded the oil fields and refineries at Abadan. Saddam predicted an end to the war before the end of the year. He couldn't have been more wrong.

By the end of the year, instead of victory, Saddam had a stalemate, as the carnage continued. And though the war was being fought mostly on the Iranian side of the border, Iraqi casualties mounted—as did public disaffection, principally among the Kurds in the north and the Shi'ite population in the south.

While both sides were supposedly subject to the same UN-imposed arms embargo, Saddam convinced his neighbors that Iraq was fighting for them. He told them that his cause was their cause, against a radical theocratic regime that was a threat to every Islamic country. Consequently, Saudi Arabia, Kuwait, and Jordan became conduits and suppliers of every kind of weapon and ammunition. And they weren't alone. Ordnance from the Soviet bloc continued to be delivered to Iraq via Egypt and Libya and, most of it, through Jordan.

NATO turned a blind eye to Italian land mine shipments. The Germans sent explosives and chemicals. Belgian-made machine guns were delivered by the thousands. And until June 7, 1981, when the Israelis bombed the reactor at Osirik, the French provided parts and know-how to Saddam's nuclear program.

Yet despite the volume of weaponry, the Iraqi army could advance no farther. In early 1982, the Iranians started sending human wave attacks through the minefields east of Basra—killing tens of thousands of youngsters, thirteen, fourteen, and fifteen years old—and drove the Iraqis back. Al Faw Peninsula fell to Iranian assaults, and Basra was left little more than a bombed-out wreck.

By 1987, the war had degenerated into what had come to be called "the tanker war," with Iraqi and Iranian air and naval units targeting oil tankers leaving each other's ports. To keep the sea lanes open, the U.S. Navy began patrolling the Persian Gulf. Then, on March 17, an Iraqi pilot flying a French-built Mirage F-1 fighter fired two French Exocet AM39 missiles into the side of the USS *Stark*, killing thirty-seven U.S. sailors.

Suddenly Iraq was back on the front pages of American newspapers, and it soon became apparent that Saddam had been regularly employing chemical weapons against the Iranians and had begun using them against his own people as well. In April, he ordered Ali Hassan al-Majid, the secretary-general of the Baath Party's "northern bureau," to use chemical weapons against a Kurdish guerrilla stronghold in the mountains of northwest Iraq. By February 1988, chemical weapons—including mustard gas, hydrogen cyanide, and sarin, a nerve agent—were being routinely used against not only the Iranians, but also the Iraqi people.

By the time Saddam and Khomeini agreed to a UN-brokered cease-fire on July 21, 1988, as many as one million Iranians and Iraqis were dead, with hundreds of thousands of Iranians and tens of thousands of Iraqis killed by Saddam's weapons of mass destruction. More than 1,200 entire Kurdish towns had succumbed and 250,000 of the surviving Kurds were forcibly disarmed and relocated. When the killing was over, every single Iraqi who survived knew the name of someone who had been killed in the prior eight years of carnage.

A year after the war ended, Saddam Hussein, resplendent in the dress uniform of a field marshal and mounted on a white stallion, led the Iraqi army beneath Baghdad's newest monument. Called the Victory Arch, it comprises two massive forearms rising up from the ground at each end of the parade ground. Each hand holds an enormous sword, said to be replicas of the sword carried by Saad ibn Waqas, the leader of the outnumbered Islamic force that beat the Persian cavalry at Qadisiyah in 637 A.D.

The symbolism was inescapable. Saddam didn't want the war seen as a draw so he simply declared it to be an Iraqi victory. Yet not an inch of Iranian territory had been permanently taken. Ayatollah Khomeini was still in Tehran, exporting terror and fomenting threats. There were nearly half a million Iraqi casualties—many dead at the hand of Saddam, not Iran. Despite all of this, Saddam reinforced his "victory" by telling his people that they had stopped the Iranian revolution inside Iran. Saddam had won! That's how the man on the white horse presented himself to the world—not as a man who had barely survived stalemate and defeat, but as a victor. Before all the dead could be counted, before his shattered cities were rebuilt, Saddam began thinking of other victories. In the land between the rivers he had a million-man army, 4,000 tanks, chemical weapons, missiles, and long-range rockets, and he knew how to use them all. The only question was where and when.

✪ The Gulf War Legacy
   Baghdad
   August 1990–February 2003

Shortly after midnight on August 2, 1990, more than 150,000 Iraqi troops, accompanied by 350 Soviet-built tanks and five hundred armored personnel carriers, swarmed across the northern border of Kuwait. Thirty-five hours later, the last Kuwaiti army unit had either surrendered or been driven south across the border into Saudi Arabia. The emir of Kuwait and the al Sabah family barely escaped with their lives. Iraqi armored units crossed the Kuwait-Saudi border to occupy the city of Khafji on the coast highway. If American and British intelligence had been half as good as it was thought to be, this disaster might never have happened.

The Iraqi invasion of tiny oil-rich Kuwait by an army that had been pummeled and punished for eight years in the Iran-Iraq War came as a complete surprise to everyone. A CIA officer I have known since my days on Ronald Reagan's NSC staff told me afterward that his warnings about an Iraqi buildup along the Kuwaiti frontier in July had been set aside because the administration of George H. W. Bush was preoccupied by the events surrounding the collapse of the Soviet Union. A military officer with whom I had served put it differently: "Given their losses in the war with Iran, who would have thought that the Iraqi military could recover in just two years?"

Whatever the reasons for underestimating and misunderstanding Iraqi capabilities and intentions, Saddam's attack, which he pretentiously called the "Revolution of August Second," shocked not only the United States but the rest of the world as well. The Saudis, who hadn't seen it coming either, immediately called for help.

The United States responded straight away, reinforcing Saudi defenses with U.S. Air Force fighter squadrons, a carrier battle group, and a Marine Expeditionary Unit. By the time Saddam proclaimed Kuwait to be the "nineteenth province of Iraq," an even bigger buildup—one that would not only defend Saudi Arabia but also evict the Iraqis from Kuwait—was also under way.

On August 6, 1990, the UN Security Council condemned the Iraqi seizure of Kuwait, and debate in the council began on a resolution authorizing the use of force to expel the invaders. The United States started building what would become a remarkable thirty-eight-nation coalition of more than 700,000 troops from NATO and Arab soldiers from Egypt, Saudi Arabia, the UAE, Bahrain, even Syria—under the command of an American general, H. Norman Schwarzkopf.

As the buildup in Saudi Arabia and the Persian Gulf got under way and Saddam threatened to use Western hostages in Iraq as "human shields," the finger pointing began. Congressional critics of the Bush administration wanted to know how the U.S. could have been so surprised. Blame initially focused on April Glaspie, the U.S. ambassador to Iraq, for delivering what some said was a mixed message to the Iraqi foreign ministry.

Administration spokesmen appearing on the Sunday talking-head TV shows tended to explain Saddam's motivations as an oil grab. College professors, "Arabologists", retired diplomats, and archaeologists sat for hours in front of the cameras pontificating on Iraq's age-old claims to Kuwaiti territory, the wrongs of British imperial rule, and the evils of America's support for Israel—as if all this somehow explained or justified the Iraqi invasion. Even the environmental lobby managed to get into the debate by insisting that the whole mess was the consequence of America's dependence on cheap foreign oil.

What all these accounts failed to grasp was what had been happening inside Iraq from the time the Iran-Iraq War ended on July 21, 1988. The badly battered Iraqi army—primarily Shi'ite and Kurdish conscripts led by Sunni officers—came back from the front to a country deeply in debt, with few jobs to offer and a homeland internally at war with itself. The Baath socialist health care, education, and public works programs that had been the regime's sole appeal for the affections of the average Iraqi had been terminated in the mid-1980s, when the costs of the war spiraled out of control. And now that the troops were home, they learned that rumors they had heard of horrific atrocities in Kurdish and Shi'ite enclaves of the country were actually true.

Shortly after the Iran-Iraq cease-fire, Saddam sought relief from the billions he owed to Saudi Arabia, Kuwait, and the Soviets for the arms he had used against the ayatollah. He tried borrowing more from the international banks, OPEC, the EU, even the Japanese. His diplomats made overtures to the UN and the United States, quietly reminding Washington of the intelligence support the CIA had provided to Iraq when an Iranian victory seemed possible.

Throughout the war, Saddam had held things together in Iraq by depicting himself as the savior of the nation. He had presented himself to his people and the world as the one person who could keep Iraq from being turned into another Shi'ite theocracy. He told anyone who would listen that he was fighting a regime that tortured Western hostages, hijacked airplanes, and blew up embassies. For eight years, it had worked. Arms and money had flowed into the country from every neighboring state and much of Europe, despite a UN arms embargo for both Iran and Iraq.

But with the war over, stories of the atrocities committed by the regime began appearing in the Western press. Suddenly, the gratitude was gone, as was Saddam's rationale for the hardship, rationing, and repression he had enforced. With mounting debt and a restive, potentially threatening army sitting in the barracks, Saddam looked for a way to keep the army busy and to pay some bills. He found a way to do both in Kuwait.

Lacking any real human intelligence (HUMINT) from inside Iraq, the U.S. administration knew little of this at the time. Defectors from the regime who made their way to Jordan or Turkey discovered that their accounts of what was going on were widely discounted. One such man who claimed to know that Saddam intended to "sack" Kuwait was dismissed because he was thought to have a "personal agenda."

✪ ✪ ✪

Actually, "sack" may understate what Saddam did to Kuwait. While the UN debated a series of resolutions insisting on Iraqi withdrawal, and as antiwar activists rallied in U.S. cities and European capitals trying to prevent a resort to arms, Saddam stripped Kuwait of everything that could be carried away. Looting of the Kuwaiti treasury, the national museum, mosques, churches, public buildings, businesses, and private homes was so pervasive that U.S. satellites were able to capture images of long truck convoys carrying the booty back to Baghdad.

Kuwaiti women and young girls were raped, many of them repeatedly—by Iraqi soldiers. At Ali Al Salem airbase, west of Kuwait City, Ali Hassan al-Majid—the head of the Amn Al Khass secret police and the man nicknamed "Chemical Ali" for using nerve gas against the Kurds—set up a torture chamber for any Kuwaiti military officers or government officials caught by the occupiers. Within a matter of three weeks, the only things the Iraqis hadn't wrecked in Kuwait were the water system, the sanitation system, and the oil-production infrastructure, which Saddam planned to use to help pay down his debt.

On January 15, 1991, as a third UN deadline for Iraq to withdraw from Kuwait was ignored, President George H. W. Bush set a deadline of his own: twenty-four hours. A last-minute appeal from the UN, Russia, and France for Saddam to withdraw passed without action from Baghdad, other than the quiet withdrawal of the last Republican Guard division from Kuwait—an action that went undetected by coalition forces arrayed in Saudi Arabia, Turkey, and the Persian Gulf.

Saddam may have thought President Bush was bluffing, but shortly after 0200 on January 17, when the dictator failed to respond to the ultimatum, the first cruise missiles and Stealth aircraft strikes of Operation Desert Storm began to rain down on Iraq and on Saddam's forces deployed in Kuwait. For the next thirty-eight days, military and government installations throughout Iraq and the 385,000 Iraqi army troops along the Kuwaiti-Saudi Arabian border were subjected to around-the-clock aerial bombardment. Saddam's response: anti-aircraft missiles that brought down thirteen allied aircraft and a promise that Iraq would achieve a "great victory in the mother of all battles."

Then, just before dawn on February 24, with the 1st Marine Division on the right and the U.S. Army's Big Red One (the 1st Infantry Division) leading the charge on the left, Schwarzkopf launched his ground attack. As U.S. and British armor rolled across the "line of death"—the artificial berm the occupiers had constructed along the border with stolen Kuwait equipment—Iraqi defenses collapsed. Sunni officers fled, leaving Shi'ite and Kurdish conscripts to either surrender or be buried in their trenches. Those who were able to escape wreaked their final wave of destruction, killing Kuwaiti civilians and blowing up or torching more than half of the country's oil wells. If Saddam couldn't have them, nobody would.

By the time the sun rose on February 28, coalition forces had liberated Kuwait, taken more than 150,000 Iraqi prisoners, and cut the

Baghdad-Basra highway and rail line. The "mother of all battles" had taken fewer than one hundred hours. The international media, having predicted a long and difficult campaign with "thousands of U.S. war dead," seemed chagrined to report that 148 American servicemen died during Desert Storm, and that total coalition forces losses were 358 killed and 1,235 wounded.

With more than a third of the Iraqi army destroyed or rendered ineffective, some advocated continuing the drive all the way to Baghdad to topple Saddam Hussein's regime. But in Washington, London, Cairo, and Riyadh, others argued that none of the twelve UN resolutions dealing with Iraq's invasion of Kuwait authorized the use of force to invade Iraq and bring down Saddam. The resolutions were limited in scope, permitting the coalition forces only to expel Iraqi forces from Kuwait. And so when General Schwarzkopf summoned Iraqi military commanders to talks at the crossroads town of Safwan on March 3, he was authorized to negotiate a "ceasefire" and nothing more. There was to be no demand for a general surrender and no insistence on a regime change. In Baghdad, Saddam quickly agreed to the terms:

- no-fly areas for fixed-wing aircraft in northern and southern Iraq
- a full accounting for Kuwaiti and allied MIAs and immediate repatriation of POWs
- the immediate return of all Kuwaiti property taken in the invasion
- an immediate end to the Iraqi WMD program and the destruction of all such weapons stockpiles
- an end to Iraqi support for international terrorism
- a promise to abide by all United Nations resolutions

Some in Washington and London wondered why Saddam so readily agreed to these onerous conditions. By the time combat operations ceased at 0800 on February 28, U.S. and British military officers were well aware that Saddam had succeeded in extricating his Republican

Guard divisions, virtually unscathed, from the coalition juggernaut. But lacking adequate intelligence about what was happening in Baghdad—or even a few miles from where the allied advance had stopped—they did not know that Saddam was already seeing the beginning of yet another internal rebellion.

Some of this revolt began even before the allied victory. In February, a Baath Party headquarters had been destroyed and its occupants burned alive during a Shi'ite food riot in the town of Diwaniyah, on the banks of the Euphrates. By the end of the month, when the allied advance halted, the Shi'ite towns in the south and Kurdish enclaves in the north had been showered with leaflets and broadcasts from U.S. psychological operations units urging the two communities to rise up and overthrow the "Butcher of Baghdad."

Given the situation, no one should have been particularly surprised that within hours of General Schwarzkopf sitting down with his defeated opponents at Safwan, those who had suffered most under Saddam's heel decided it was time to fight back. Shi'ite uprisings in Basra, Karbala, and Najaf, aided by Iraqi army deserters, were easily crushed by Republican Guard troops who were told that they were saving Iraq from Khomeini-inspired operatives intent on establishing an Iranian theocracy in the land between the rivers. With allied troops sometimes within earshot, Republican Guard tanks, supported by helicopter gunships, massacred the lightly armed mujahideen and their families. Artillery pounded mosques, homes, ancient shrines, and anyone who took refuge there. Once the Republican Guard had done the "heavy work," the dreaded Amn Al Khass arrived, usually in the dead of night, to hunt down survivors. In entire towns throughout the southern part of Iraq, every male between the ages of fifteen and thirty simply disappeared. All through the month of March, bulldozers worked through the night. It would take more than a decade to confirm that what they were digging were mass graves.

In the Kurdish areas of the north the outcome was much the same, though because of the terrain—and because Saddam perceived the Shi'ite intifada to be the most immediate threat—it took a little longer.

At the end of March, Saddam shifted three Republican Guard divisions from the killing fields of southern Iraq to the mountainous north. Kurdish pesh merga fighters, who had taken control of Zakho, Sulaimaniyah, and Kirkuk, and threatened Mosul, were no match for armor, massed artillery, and helicopter gunships. These were people with firsthand knowledge of what Saddam's chemical weapons could do. Though resistance was futile and the carnage horrifying, they valiantly fought on, hoping for the coalition allies, with half a million troops still in the region, to come to their rescue.

Washington and London met Kurdish appeals for help with paralysis. Initial hopes that the Iraqi military would stage a coup in the aftermath of the Kuwaiti debacle were unrealized. Uncertain about who might take over if the Shi'ites and Kurds succeeded, sympathetic to Saudi concerns about Iranian intentions, and warned by NATO ally Turkey that an independent Kurdistan would not be tolerated, the U.S. and Britain opted to do nothing.

By the end of April it was all over. Though the final toll will probably never be known, perhaps as many as 250,000 Shi'ites were killed, and almost as many Kurds. More than two million refugees had been created. Scores of villages in the north and south of the country had been emptied of every living soul. The Kurds and the Shi'ites had failed to unite in common cause against their common enemy, and Saddam had utterly destroyed any hopes they had for freedom or independence. In the end, the only help that America delivered was the massive airlift of food, medicine, tents, and blankets to nearly one million displaced Kurds in Operation Provide Comfort.

Saddam had survived once again.

✪ ✪ ✪

By May 1991, the land between the rivers was a terrible place. Baghdad, heavily bombed throughout the war, was a shambles. Every bridge across the Tigris was damaged or destroyed. Electrical power, water, sewer systems, telephone service, even mail delivery were sporadic at best in the capital and almost nonexistent throughout the rest of the country. The treasures looted from Kuwait were being pawned to buy food.

Realizing that perception is reality in Iraq, Saddam set out to convince the Iraqi people, if not the rest of the world, that he had won the "mother of all battles." He purged the military and the Baath Party in order to put a new face on the regime and to eliminate internal dissent. Despite rampant debt and inflation, Saddam embarked on a massive rebuilding campaign.

Within months of the Safwan Cease Fire Agreement, despite economic sanctions imposed by UN Resolution 687, critical infrastructure was being rebuilt, new presidential palaces were under construction, and new weapons were being purchased on the black market. And though dozens of UN inspectors were now wandering through his arsenals, Saddam continued to acquire and build more weapons of mass destruction—chemical, biological, and nuclear.

In August 1991, UN Resolutions 706 and 707 established what came to be known as the Oil-for-Food Program, allowing Iraq to sell fixed amounts of crude oil in exchange for food and medicines, ostensibly for consumption by the starving Iraqi people. This noble idea was doomed from the start.

First, the program had to rely on Iraqi administrators—who just happened to be members of the Baath Party. The result was that desperately needed food and medicines were dispersed through the Baath Party apparatus based on loyalty to Saddam. The people quickly learned the new rules: Turn in your neighbor as an opponent of the regime and you eat. Speak out against the rampant inflation or the building of a new palace and your children starve. Second, the amount of oil that the UN resolutions permitted to be sold, though adjusted several times over the years, was never close to Iraq's maximum production output. The Western world was willfully blind when it came to Iraq's excess oil capacity. With oil prices above $20 a barrel, a lucrative black market soon developed via a pipeline through Syria and overland by truck through friendly Jordan and the territory of two enemies, Turkey and Iran.

The new source of "secret" revenue emboldened the Iraqi dictator. When President George H. W. Bush was defeated in his bid for reelection, Saddam claimed it was because Iraq had beaten the Americans in the "mother of all battles." He then ratcheted up the obstacles in his game of cat and mouse with the UN weapons inspectors. The black market black gold also gave him the cash to line his own pockets and start financing new adventures.

In late April 1993, an assassination plot was discovered—a plan to kill former president George H. W. Bush while he visited Kuwait. Explosives hidden in a Toyota Land Cruiser were to be detonated when the former president's motorcade passed by. The Kuwaiti Security Service intercepted the vehicle and arrested seventeen people in connection with the scheme. Confessions by the perpetrators and FBI forensic work traced the conspiracy to Saddam's intelligence service, the Mukhabarat.

In retaliation, President Clinton ordered an air strike on Baghdad—not aimed at Saddam Hussein but at the Mukhabarat's headquarters. Twenty-three cruise missiles later, six low-level Iraqi government employees were dead and Saddam was thumbing his nose at "American impotence," and continuing his game of hide-and-seek with the UNSCOM (UN Special Commission) inspectors.

Then, in August 1995, Saddam's son-in-law, Hussein Kamil, the head of Iraq's Ministry of Defense Industries and the man responsible for all of Iraq's banned weapons, defected to Amman, Jordan. Before Kamil had a change of heart and returned to Iraq to be murdered by Saddam, he told British intelligence all he knew about Baghdad's weapons of mass destruction. Using information supplied by Kamil, the UNSCOM inspectors found a treasure trove of information about Iraq's nuclear, chemical, and biological weapons programs.

In October 1997, Saddam accused the U.S. personnel in UNSCOM of being spies and ordered them out of the country. Richard Butler, the tough Australian heading the UN mission, withdrew the rest of his investigators. But when the Clinton administration dispatched a carrier battle group to the Persian Gulf, Saddam said it was all just a misunderstanding, and the inspectors returned only to find that most of the monitoring equipment they had left behind had been destroyed by Baghdad's "concealment team."

✪ ✪ ✪

For the next year, the on-again, off-again inspections continued. The Clinton administration threatened the use of force again in early 1998 but backed down when polls showed public opinion overwhelmingly opposed fighting another war in Iraq.

By the summer of 1998, the Clinton administration was deeply embroiled in scandal, and Saddam was able to play the White House like a harp. On August 5, he threw all the UNSCOM inspectors out of Iraq and announced that they would not be allowed back into the country. A few days after this announcement, an Iraqi defector, Dr. Khidir Hamza, formerly the head of Saddam's nuclear weapons program, appeared on my radio show. In response to a listener's call, he said, "Saddam will do anything necessary to keep his 'special' weapons. It's all he has to keep him in power. It's too bad this White House doesn't know what needs to be done."

Once again the UN dithered over what to do, and the Clinton administration, by now enmeshed in the Monica Lewinsky affair, deployed U.S. forces to the region—an action that some say was only intended to divert attention from his impeachment proceedings. On December 16, as the U.S. House of Representatives prepared to vote to impeach him, President Clinton launched Operation Desert Fox— a twenty-four-hour-long aerial assault with guided bombs and cruise missiles—aimed at Republican Guard garrisons throughout Iraq. It didn't change a thing. At the end of the day Bill Clinton was impeached, Saddam Hussein was still in power, and the UNSCOM inspectors never returned to Iraq.

After Operation Desert Fox, in December 1998, the Clinton administration did its best to simply ignore Saddam Hussein. Smarting under criticism from its liberal allies about the cruelty of sanctions, the administration sought to describe the "new" U.S. policy toward Iraq as "containment." It involved little more than U.S. and British aircraft based in Kuwait and Turkey, and on carriers in the Persian Gulf, making daily flights over Iraq to enforce expanded no-fly zones. Little or nothing was said or done about Iraq's illicit oil sales, which financed Saddam's WMD programs and personal enrichment. One U.S. Navy pilot described it to me this way: "Saddam ships oil to Bahrain in the UN Oil-for-Food Program. We buy the oil from the UN and refine it into jet fuel. We put the jet fuel in my F-18 and I go bomb Iraq for violations of UN resolutions. It's nuts."

It might have stayed that way had George W. Bush not been declared the victor in the much-contested 2000 presidential election. Less than a month after he took office, Iraqi anti-aircraft missiles fired on a routine U.S. aerial patrol. The next day, after a hasty conference call between President Bush and Prime Minister Tony Blair of Britain, a twenty-five-plane U.S.-British air strike took out five Iraqi air defense sites. In the aftermath, the new president ordered an immediate review of U.S. policy toward Iraq. And in another dramatic shift from the prior administration, the Pentagon, not the State Department, was assigned the role of "lead agency."

By the summer of 2001 the debate was fully engaged in Washington, with the State Department doves pitted against the Pentagon hawks. When stories in the press described George Bush as leaning toward action to get rid of Saddam once and for all, congressional critics of the new president sought to depict him as a reckless cowboy. Then a series of leaked intelligence reports indicated that Saddam had reinstituted his nuclear weapons program while other reports accused Saddam of harboring terrorists, such as the assassins Abu Nidal and Abu Abbas, the mastermind of the *Achille Lauro* hijacking. Ahmed Chalabi, the head of the Iraqi National Congress who had been exiled to London by the Clinton administration, was invited back to Washington. After learning that the CIA and the State Department had only dispensed $5 million of the $97 million that Congress had appropriated in 1998 for the Iraqi Liberation Act, the Pentagon was put in charge of the funding for Iraqi resistance activities. All of this might have remained a war of words but for an event that would change America forever: September 11, 2001.

✪ ✪ ✪

When nineteen Islamic terrorists seized four U.S. airliners and killed at least 2,731 people on American soil that terrible Tuesday, I was on Northwest Airlines flight 238 headed into Reagan National. While we were en route to Washington's closest airport, American Airlines Flight 77, which had been hijacked as it departed Dulles Airport a few minutes earlier, slammed into the west wall of the Pentagon at 0937. My flight was immediately diverted to Dulles, and I eventually arrived at the FOX

News studios in Washington hours later. By the time we finally finished broadcasting that night around midnight, questions were already being raised about what role Saddam might have played in the attack.

A month later, I was aboard the USS *Bataan* with the Marines who were preparing to make a heloborne assault into Kandahar, Afghanistan, to take on the Taliban and Osama bin Laden's Al Qaeda, and those questions were still being asked. A short while after I returned home, other U.S. forces found evidence that bin Laden had been trying to acquire nuclear material. Could he have gotten some from Iraq?

And in February 2003, seventeen months after the Twin Towers in New York were brought down into two terrible piles of rubble and bodies, as U.S. and British forces prepared in Kuwait to attack Iraq, the answer still is not known.

What is known is that Saddam Hussein had once again defied the United Nations weapons inspectors. The hapless Hans Blix finally gave up even the pretense of being able to conduct a realistic investigation into what Saddam may or may not have done with his tons of poison gas, chemical warheads, anthrax, and nuclear materials. Without credible human sources inside Iraq, no U.S. or British intelligence agency knows for certain either. But in the aftermath of September 11, the fear of Saddam using any of these—or giving them to others to use in a terrorist attack—was palpable in the governments of the United States and Great Britain. Not so elsewhere.

In his 2002 State of the Union address, President Bush described Iran, Iraq, and North Korea as "an axis of evil." He was derided for that depiction.

In his September 12, 2002, address to the United Nations, President Bush chronicled all of Saddam's past abuses and asked for a resolution with a clear deadline for compliance. France and Russia refused to pass the resolution.

In Congress it was different. On October 10, a bill authorizing the president to use military force against Saddam passed the House by a vote of 296 to 133, and in the Senate by 77 to 23.

Shortly before Christmas, the first U.S. Marine contingent arrived in Kuwait prepared to go to war in the land between the two rivers.

PREFACE

★ HQ, 3RD BATTALION, 66TH ARMORED REGIMENT
4TH INFANTRY DIVISION
West of Tikrit, Iraq
Saturday, 26 April 2003
0100 Hours Local

The satellite telephone vibrating against my chest awakens me with a start after less than half an hour of sleep. Many years ago, as a Marine officer, I learned to nap with a radio handset tucked into my helmet, up against my ear, so that an urgent call on the command net would rouse me. Since being in Iraq, I've done a similar thing, catching snatches of sleep with an Iridium satellite phone placed inside my flak jacket, up against my chest, so that I won't miss a message from the FOX News Channel foreign desk. These calls have been coming nearly nightly for two months, alerting us to prepare for a live "hit" with a FOX News Channel host or correspondent in New York or Washington.

But tonight's communication is different, the message is both welcome and bittersweet. "Come on home," says Brian Knoblock, the head of FOX News Channel foreign operations.

I awaken Griff Jenkins, my very brave and resourceful field producer and cameraman. He arises, smiling, and starts packing our camera equipment and satellite broadcast gear in the dark. We are the last FOX News Channel field team still embedded in Operation Iraqi Freedom. Our cameras are full of sand. The portable generator has been gone for days—left for dead beside an Iraqi airstrip. Our manpack satellite broadcast gear has been cooked by the sun, soaked in the Tigris, and bathed in dirt. The rest of our equipment is just about shot. And so are we.

Yet leaving these soldiers, sailors, airmen, and Marines we've been covering since before the start of this "Second Iraq War" isn't easy. We have been eating the same meals, breathing the same dust, sharing their fears, frustrations, and euphoria—and enjoying their protection—for too long not to feel awkward at leaving them. We're going home. They are not.

Well before dawn breaks across the Tigris, while Griff sorts through our gear, I go into the Battalion Tactical Operations Center (TOC) to plug in my laptop computer and enter these final notes—a last Sit Rep (situation report) from the war we have been covering since before it started on March 20. At a computer and radio console inside the TOC, a watch officer—called a "battle captain" in this U.S. Army armor unit—hands me a clipboard holding a printout of the daily Air Tasking Order. "Pick your flight and make your reservation early to avoid the rush," he says with a smile. He points to a flight scheduled for shortly after first light—an H-60 Black Hawk—with space for two passengers headed for Baghdad. He puts Griff and me on the flight manifest and says, "We'll miss you guys. The Colonel [Lt. Col. Larry Jackson] believes the toughest part of this war is still ahead of us." Unfortunately, he's right.

✪ ✪ ✪

The 4th Infantry Division—the 4th ID in military shorthand—is also known as the "Digital Division" because of all its high-tech equipment. These seventeen thousand highly trained and motivated soldiers were supposed to have entered the fight through Turkey, charging south toward Baghdad from bases that had been carefully negotiated by Pentagon planners months before the shooting began. But in the convoluted course between NATO headquarters outside Brussels, the UN in New York, and the State Department in Washington, the Turks said no and the plan fell off track.

Instead of fighting their way into Iraq, the 4th ID had to come in weeks later, through Kuwait, and then travel by convoy to Saddam's hometown over ground seized by other soldiers and Marines who had come before them. Many of the troopers in this prized unit regard their belated arrival as a terrible insult foisted upon them by the State Department. "They held a war and Colin Powell—the SOB—made us late," volunteered one 4th ID officer.

Other officers and senior non-commissioned officers are much less concerned about the action they have missed and more anxious about what lies ahead. They have seen low-intensity combat before and know it can be just as deadly and demanding as any other form of armed conflict. "This is just another phase in what's going to be a long war," says Lt. Col. Larry "Pepper" Jackson, commanding officer of 3rd Battalion, 66th Armored Regiment. "My mission is to hunt down HVTs [high-value targets—the U.S. military's euphemism for terrorist chieftains and enemy leaders], find any evidence of weapons of mass destruction, protect the oil refinery down the road, restore essential infrastructure [electricity, water, sanitation, and medical services], provide security for the local population, and protect my own force from attack by terrorists, Baathists, and criminals. I've got plenty to do, but I've got great troops to get the job done."

"Great troops." I've been hearing those words for most of my adult life. I used to say that—and mean it—about the Marines I led in war and in peace. I have also heard those words a lot since arriving in Kuwait, before the start of the war. Now, having lived with the troops and seen them fight, it's apparent that they really are just that: great troops.

I have a standard of comparison. I first saw the carnage of combat as a rifle platoon commander in Vietnam. And I've been an eyewitness to the valor and horror of war in Lebanon, Central America, Afghanistan, and Israel. In my experience, there have never been brighter, better-trained, better-equipped soldiers, sailors, airmen, Guardsmen, and Marines than those now serving in Iraq. And the credit for this goes to the staff non-commissioned officers, chiefs, and junior officers who held the military together during the budget cuts, social engineering, fruitless deployments, and lack of training in the 1990s.

In the combat arms—infantry, artillery, armor, airborne, reconnaissance, and special operations—they are all male, since current law forbids putting women into combat units. That doesn't mean young American women aren't in harm's way. Women serve in combat support assignments in every branch of our Armed Forces. That means young American women like Army PFC Jessica Lynch, arguably the most famous female in recent U.S. military history, can easily find themselves under fire. Cpl. Amanda Hoenes of HMM-268 qualified as combat aircrew in Iraq, and during one terrible night over Baghdad in a CH-46, I watched her skillfully employ a .50-caliber machine gun to dispatch the enemy troops who were firing on us. Given our current force structure—with women constituting almost 14 percent of the Army and 6 percent of the Marine Corps—it's fair to say that this war could not have been fought without the fairer sex.

Without taking anything away from women like the Army's Jessica Lynch or the Marines' Amanda Hoenes and the role they play in our military, it's still important to recognize that nearly all those on the ground who took the fight to Saddam are males. And while there is no typical soldier or Marine, it is possible to describe the average young American who carries a weapon into battle.

He's a volunteer, 19.6 years old, making him about six months older than his grandfather was when drafted to serve in World War II and Korea or his father was when conscripted for Vietnam. He isn't old enough to buy a beer, and if he were back home in the United States we'd call him a boy. But because he's in uniform and fighting a war, we call him a soldier, sailor, airman, or Marine.

This young man in uniform was probably a team sports athlete in high school and graduated somewhere in the middle of the pack, making him better educated than any prior generation in our military. Unlike many of his peers, he's never drawn an unemployment check and he doesn't ever want to.

He had a job in high school in order to buy a car that was already about ten years old. He bought the car to take his high school sweetheart out on dates, and when he left for a war halfway around the world, she promised to wait for him.

Unfortunately, unless they were married before his departure—about 15–25 percent of those who live near their military bases are—she is likely to be dating another guy by the time this Iraqi war veteran returns home. When our trooper does get back, he'll call her new beau a "wimp." And she'll know he's right.

About three times a week, he grabs a few minutes to write home. When the mailbag arrives by helicopter, he's hoping to get a letter from his girl and his mom, though he'll never admit to the latter. If his girl or his mom sends him a care package with disposable razors, shaving cream, toothpaste, M&Ms, beef jerky, toilet paper, and baby wipes, he'll share them with his whole squad and be a hero for a day.

He has a short haircut and tight muscles, and wears a four-pound Kevlar helmet and an eighteen-pound flak jacket to work. He can march all day in one-hundred degree heat with a sixty-pound pack on his back. This young man in uniform knows how to use every weapon in his unit and can fieldstrip and reassemble his own weapon in less than a minute—in the dark.

Over here he's gone weeks without bathing but cleans his weapon every day.

His rifle company gunny (gunnery sergeant in the Marines or sergeant first class in the Army) has been in combat before. Yet this is the first time he and his lieutenant have been shot at. Under fire he obeys orders instantly. But if asked, he'll always have an opinion on how to do something better. Often he'll be right.

He's been taught chemistry, physics, and ballistics, and can navigate with a map and compass but prefers the GPS he bought at the base exchange. When he catches a break, which isn't often, he reads paperback books; he loves thrillers.

Before joining the military he couldn't be bludgeoned into picking up his room, doing his laundry, or washing the dishes, but now he's remarkably self-sufficient. He prepares his own meals, washes and mends his own clothes, digs his own foxhole and latrine, and keeps his feet dry and his canteens full.

The kid who once wouldn't share a candy bar with his little brother will now offer his last drop of water to a wounded comrade, give his only ration to a hungry Iraqi child, and split his ammo with a mate in a firefight. He's been trained to use his body like a weapon and his weapon as if it were part of his body—and uses either to take a life or save one, because that is his job. But he's patient and compassionate too. He will offer his own food and water to enemy prisoners of war, and go out of his way to make certain that captured enemy wounded get medical help.

The youngster who used to stay in the sack until noon now exists on just three or four hours of sleep a day. When he comes home to the United States, he'll be, on average, twelve pounds lighter than when he left.

By now he's already had more responsibility and seen more suffering and death than most of his civilian contemporaries will see in their entire lifetimes.

He's learned a whole new vernacular of foreign-sounding words. It's not Iraqi Arabic, but military shorthand. He uses words like "CONUS," "h-hour," "zulu time," "incoming," "snafu," and "fubar" that mean nothing to most civilians.

He's been told that grown men don't cry, but he has wept unashamedly in public over a fallen friend, because he knows heroes aren't defined by the way they die but how they live. And though he can now take profanity to the level of an art form, it's also likely that he has a Bible in his rucksack and isn't afraid to be seen reading it.

He's proud to be serving his country, reveres his commander in chief, and knows that he is respected in return. While he is modest about his own courage and military prowess, he's absolutely certain that his is the toughest unit in the U.S. Armed Forces.

When he gets home, he won't talk much about the horror of war and probably won't have post-traumatic stress disorder, but he will want more fresh milk, salads, and homemade cookies than anyone ever thought possible. And when he goes to a ball game or some formal event, he'll resent those who carelessly ignore the national anthem when it's played or don't join in when the pledge of allegiance is recited. He'll put his hand over his heart, gaze at the American flag, and sing or recite proudly and loudly.

✪ ✪ ✪

These are the young Americans who beat the Butcher of Baghdad. Their skill and daring, discipline and endurance are without parallel in the world today.

"Good troops" indeed. They are a credit to their parents and to this nation. This book is for and about them.

INTRODUCTION
REALITY TELEVISION

⭐ AFTER ACTION REPORT
   USS *Abraham Lincoln*
   Pacific Ocean Vic 131°W, 30°N
   Thursday, 1 May 2003
   0900 Hours Local

Shortly after my return to the United States from Iraq, President George W. Bush, a former F-102 pilot, wearing a military flight suit, roared onto the flight deck of the U.S. aircraft carrier USS *Abraham Lincoln* in a U.S. Navy W-3B Viking. Shortly after landing, he welcomed the crew home and congratulated them for serving with distinction in the war against terrorism and during Operation Iraqi Freedom. Later, wearing a business suit, he addressed the nation from the flight deck.

The president's remarks had barely been transcribed before the criticism began. Some in the media described the trip to the carrier as a publicity stunt, and castigated the White House for an extravagant waste of tax dollars. White House spokesman Ari Fleischer tried to defend the trip by pointing out that the cost of the flight in the

Viking would have been nearly the same as the president taking a helicopter, but that a helicopter would have taken longer and would have been more hazardous and, according to the Secret Service, less secure. Fleischer's defense was ignored.

Then Senator Robert Byrd of West Virginia, the so-called Dean of the Senate, rose to berate the commander in chief, saying, "To me, it is an affront to the Americans killed or injured in Iraq for the president to exploit the trappings of war for the momentary spectacle of a speech."

The controversy—and particularly Senator Byrd's divisive statements—sparked a flood of e-mails from those I had come to know in Iraq and scores of other men and women of the military. Many soldiers, sailors, airmen, and Marines felt that the criticism of President Bush was an effort to divide them from their commander in chief, a man they may or may not have voted for but whom, in the aftermath of September 11, they widely admired.

Though West Virginia has more citizens serving in the Armed Forces, per capita, than any other state, Senator Byrd persisted in his attack, prompting a deluge of mail into my office—much of it highly derogatory to Senator Byrd—some of it intended to remind Americans that the good senator had once been a member of the Ku Klux Klan. One such missive began with, "Senator Byrd, who in his salad days spent more time in white sheets than in camouflage uniforms, just doesn't get it." Another characterized the senator's rant as "Byrd Droppings."

Yet the media lapped up Byrd's remarks and raced around Washington seeking more outrageous partisanship to feed the hungry maw of the nonstop news cycle. Forgotten in all of this were the 5,500 officers and sailors of the USS *Abraham Lincoln*. In late December 2002, they had been headed home to San Diego through the Indian Ocean after a six-month deployment in support of Operation Enduring

Freedom in Afghanistan. The crew was looking forward to seeing their wives and children, who were eagerly awaiting their arrival in southern California. Then came their new orders: turn around and head north, back up the Persian Gulf, and prepare for war.

For the next four months, the crew of the *Abraham Lincoln* served without leave, carrying out their orders. They had already launched almost six hundred combat sorties in support of Operation Enduring Freedom in Afghanistan and nearly a thousand more in support of Operation Southern Watch, enforcing the no-fly zones over Iraq. Then they handled 1,558 combat sorties supporting the Marines, soldiers, and special operations teams of Operation Iraqi Freedom. And they did it all—more than three thousand sorties—without casualties. When their mission was completed, they had been deployed for 290 consecutive days and had traveled more than 100,000 miles—the equivalent of circling the globe four times.

None of this mattered to the president's ardent critics, who also chose to ignore the extraordinary compliment President Bush had paid to the crew of "Honest Abe." By landing on a moving aircraft carrier at sea—an extraordinarily difficult feat—the commander in chief was offering the crew of the *Abraham Lincoln* the ultimate accolade. He put his life in the hands of a Navy pilot and the crew of the carrier—never doubting that they would bring him in safely.

✪ ✪ ✪

All of this was a rude awakening to those of us who had just returned from the harsh realities of Iraq. There, brave men and women were serving in harm's way, in great personal danger. Even when there was little danger, the requirements of duty and the conditions under which they served were difficult at best and downright horrible at worst.

But being back home, hearing the commander in chief of the Armed Forces of the United States being described as a "deskbound president who assumes the garb of a warrior for the purposes of a speech," and accused of "flamboyant showmanship" and "self-congratulatory gestures" by a U.S. senator, made many of the troops ask "What am I doing here?"

Before the story waned, Congressman Henry Waxman, citing "clear political overtones," was calling for a congressional investigation of the president's flight. But most of the sailors and Marines aboard the USS *Abraham Lincoln* wondered about the political motivations of the president's detractors. Meanwhile, others in Congress began calling for a "regime change" at the White House.

Among the troops who communicated with me in the weeks right after I returned home, the strident partisanship of the attacks on President Bush was topic number one. What we didn't know then was that this was just the opening volley. It was about to get a whole lot worse.

✪ AFTER ACTION REPORT
Washington, DC
Friday, 12 May 2003
0900 Hours Local

After the vicious assault on the president, it should probably have been expected that those who were embedded with the troops—and who reported good things about them—would be the next targets. It seems that almost all of us who lived with the troops came away favorably impressed.

I've spent much of my life in the military and have concluded, based on how these warriors performed under combat, that the soldiers, sailors, airmen, Guardsmen, and Marines serving in Iraq are without parallel. There has never been a brighter, better-trained, better-equipped group of people under arms than those who responded to our country's call in this war. No military force in history has ever gone so far, so fast, with so few casualties as this group of young Americans.

I said that repeatedly during my time with the troops and I know no other way to put it. It seemed fairly self-evident to nearly every embedded correspondent, and certainly was to me—and I don't pretend to be nearly as observant as a "professional journalist." I didn't learn journalism at the Naval Academy. But I did learn to recognize courage, competence, commitment, and compassion—all qualities that these youngsters have in abundance.

I did not expect the ire of the fourth estate for what their colleagues had said—that these young American men and women of the Armed Forces really are remarkable troops. But that's exactly what happened. Apparently, I and some others who were embedded "lived with the troops too long, got too close to them." We lost "objectivity," and became "flag-waving advocates," as was reported in one weekly newsmagazine.

Time magazine's James Poniewozik, among others, scolded us for covering the war from the American perspective, branding us as "biased" for the way we reported the swift victory over the vaunted Republican Guard troops and Saddam's fedayeen. *Harper's Magazine* publisher John MacArthur, citing the way embedded reporters covered Marine Cpl. Edward Chin scaling the statue of Saddam and momentarily draping the huge black metal sculpture with Old Glory, accused not only the embedded media, but also the U.S. military, of being "propagandistic" for "the Bush reelection campaign."

The reality is considerably different. Most of us who were embedded with the troops simply allowed the young Americans doing the fighting to tell their story. They said how proud they were to help liberate a repressed people. They spoke openly about being honored to be in the service of their country. And they showed modesty and restraint in talking about their own courage and military prowess. We didn't make this stuff up. The troops said it in their own words.

These words from our troops may have shocked and surprised the editors of the *New York Times*, the *Washington Post, Harper's*, and *Time*. Just because a young American goes live on FOX News Channel and tells America that he believes his country is doing something right doesn't mean those of us who held the microphones and cameras have lost our objectivity. The media elites may not like hearing young Americans raised on a steady diet of political correctness, inane sitcoms, and video games talk about virtue, values, and valor— but that's the way they are. That's reality television.

Here is an eyewitness account of the war in Iraq, not as the negative mainstream media and defamatory politicians would like you to see it, but as it actually happened, and often from the perspective of those who should know, because they were there—the men and women of the 1st Marine Expeditionary Force and the U.S. Army's 4th Infantry Division.

CHAPTER ONE
THE ROAD TO HELL

✪ OPERATION IRAQI FREEDOM SIT REP #1
Kuwait International Airport, Kuwait
Thursday, 6 March 2003
2330 Hours Local

"Are you here as a member of the Armed Forces or as a member of the media?" asks the neatly uniformed but unsmiling Kuwaiti immigration official.

"I'm here to cover the war for FOX News Channel," I reply. "Does it matter?"

"Oh yes," he says, trying to be both firm and polite at the same time. "If you are here with the media, you are limited to a sixty-day stay and you must be escorted by the Ministry of Information. If you are here with the American military, there is no time limit and your visa will be stamped by the Ministry of Defense."

"Well, this time it's the media," I respond, hoping that my honesty won't precipitate an inordinate delay in passing through the immigration and customs bureaucracy.

It's my first mistake on this trip and entitles me to a two-hour wait for an absent civil servant from the Ministry of Information.

I had been through this same airport in November 2001, traveling back to Bahrain after covering the U.S. Air Force pilots flying over Afghanistan from Kuwaiti bases during Operation Enduring Freedom. Then, I had been asked only for my passport and U.S. military identity card, and had been amused when a Kuwaiti customs official dryly observed, "It's nice to see that you are traveling on your own passport these days, Colonel North."

Back in the 1980s, when I served as the United States government's counter-terrorism coordinator, I had been issued a U.S. passport with the name William P. Goode next to my picture and an Irish passport under the name of John Clancy. Whether the Kuwaiti official had remembered or a computer warning entry had alerted him to the fact, I had been reassured that by 2001, my prior use of "alias" travel documents wasn't reason enough to have me miss my flight.

Tonight it's a different problem. Without the appropriate Ministry of Information official on hand, no American media representatives are being allowed to enter Kuwait. The people of the tiny, oil-rich emirate may be grateful to us for liberating their country in 1991, but that gratitude doesn't extend to members of America's fourth estate.

The Kuwaitis aren't alone in their distrust of the American media. Most of our own military have a justifiable concern that the decision to embed reporters with U.S. units preparing for combat is unwise at best and a formula for disaster at worst. Many senior NCOs (non-commissioned officers) and officers can still vividly recall how the media turned on them in Vietnam, and since then, the less they have to do with the press, the better off they feel.

"Think about it," a Marine colonel challenged me before I left the States. "If you were a battalion commander in combat, would you want a guy with a TV camera and a live mike walking around talking to privates and PFCs?" I had to admit to him that I wouldn't.

"Do you remember the bogus CNN 'Tailwind' story?" an Army brigadier had responded when I asked him about his attitude toward having print and broadcast journalists traveling with front-line units and filing uncensored reports. "They [CNN and *Time* magazine] created that story out of whole cloth," he said of the discredited and now admittedly false account that U.S. forces had used sarin, a nerve agent, in Vietnam in an attempt to gas American deserters. CNN first broadcast the story on June 7, 1998, only to retract it a month later, but I could sense that the wound was still raw. The brigadier shook his head and muttered, "There wasn't a shred of truth to 'Tailwind,' but we're still answering the mail on that one. Just imagine the stories of atrocities, needless casualties, and bungled ops your pals in the media will spin from Iraq."

These thoughts are much on my mind when the appropriate Kuwaiti official finally arrives and carefully peruses a long printout of "approved" media representatives. He finds my name on the list and, with a flourish, slams a hand stamp with purple ink on my passport, my visa, and a "special media" pass.

As I walk out of the airport's customs-and-immigration restricted area, my field producer, Griff Jenkins, who flew to Kuwait several days earlier, greets me. I'm introduced to another Ministry of Information official, who hands me a sheaf of papers explaining, in several languages, the rules of behavior for "guest journalists," along with suggestions for a "historical perspective" on the region. As he drops us at the Marriott Hotel in downtown Kuwait City, he politely says, "Welcome back to Kuwait, Colonel North." Then, almost as an afterthought, he adds with a smile, "Please remember, correspondents aren't allowed to be armed."

As we enter the hotel, dawn is just beginning to insinuate itself over the Persian Gulf. In a matter of minutes, the sun will be casting long shadows over the confluence of the Tigris and Euphrates rivers, 120 miles to the northwest—in Iraq.

✪ OPERATION IRAQI FREEDOM SIT REP #2
   Ad Dawhah Port Facility, Kuwait
   Saturday, 8 March 2003
   1300 Hours Local

It is clear that the people here are worried. Ali, our driver, lent to FOX News Channel by the Ministry of Information to "facilitate" getting around the emirate, talks about little other than the imminent onset of hostilities. "It has to start soon," he opines. "There is no more space in the hotels here for reporters."

He's right about that. In the Marriott, where the FOX News Channel bureau has been set up, every room is occupied. It's the same in every other hotel in Kuwait. The Sheraton and the Inter-Continental—just down the street from where FOX has its head-quarters—have now taken on the appearance of network affiliates. Commercial Humvees, brand new 4x4 Ford Excursions, and GMC Suburbans with satellite dishes secured to their roof racks line every hotel parking lot. Many of them have "TV" emblazoned on their sides with duct tape. Some are even painted to match the military's flat desert tan. There are so many U.S. and European reporters, producers, writers, and technicians here that the streets outside every hostelry look like those of a major American city.

As we approach the port area, Ali has to negotiate a series of military checkpoints. At each, Kuwaiti soldiers and interior ministry police inspect the inside and outside of the vehicle, using a mirror on

a long wand to peer beneath the van. Ali produces his license and a
yellow travel pass for the vehicle, and Griff and I hand over our passports, visas, press credentials, and a sheet of paper signed by the
Ministry of Information official at our hotel, giving us permission to
visit the port area.

Ali endures this ritual three times without complaint before we
actually arrive at our destination. "Yesterday they caught an Iraqi spy
trying to get into the port," he says. Then he adds with a sigh, "It's
going to be this way until you finish Saddam. I hope you go all the
way and do it right this time."

I ignore Ali's iteration of the frequently repeated Kuwaiti gibe at
the United States for leaving Saddam in power at the end of the
1990–1991 Gulf War. Instead I press him on the apprehension of this
Iraqi spy. I had not heard about the arrest, and it's precisely the kind
of story we want FOX to break—if we can confirm it. But Ali claims
he doesn't know any more about the spy and changes the subject.

"Were you afraid during the missile attack last night?" he asks,
referring to the sirens that had gone off all over Kuwait City at about
one in the morning.

"Not especially," I answer, instantly concerned that my reply
sounded foolhardy. The fact is, I had grabbed my network-issued gas
mask and lightweight chemical suit and raced for the FOX rooftop
"studio," not out of bravado but because I knew that it was a safer
place to be than the hotel basement bomb shelter if the Iraqis were
firing chemical-laden Scud missiles at the city.

"I understand that one of your new Patriot missiles shot it down
before it hit. Is that true?" Ali asks.

"That's the way it sounded to me," I reply, recalling the deep boom
off to the north of the city. "According to the news this morning, it
dropped into Khalj al Kuwayt," I add, referring to the bay just north

of the capital—and falling into the trap of providing a recycled story I'd heard on the radio earlier in the day.

"But is that what really happened?" Ali presses, once again reflecting the uncertainty he and his countrymen are feeling as the allied buildup in Kuwait enters its fourth month.

"I don't know what really happened, Ali," I say, as sympathetically as possible. He had told me the day before how he and his family had to flee when the Iraqis invaded in 1990 and how anxious his little girl was over what might happen to them.

In fact, I looked for a report from Central Command that morning—something that would explain the sirens and the loud explosion. There was nothing.

As we arrive at the main gate of the port, an enormous military convoy is departing through the exit, about fifty yards away. There are at least fifty HETs—forty-wheeled, heavy equipment transporters, loaded with desert-painted M-1 Abrams tanks and Bradley fighting vehicles—forming up on the highway. Military police in Humvees with .50-caliber machine guns mounted on top scurry in and among the HETs like gnats swarming around a herd of cattle.

As I reach for my camera to shoot some footage of the convoy forming up, Ali holds up his hand and says politely but firmly, "Don't do that here, Oliver. If you get caught we will not only not make it inside, we probably won't make it back to Kuwait City tonight either." I put the camera back in its bag and nod to Ali. He works for the Kuwaiti government and doesn't want to lose his job.

Griff Jenkins and I have coerced Ali into driving us to Kuwait's commercial port, at the mouth of the Persian Gulf, so that we can shop for some necessities at the allied forces military exchange aboard the base. I'm the only one with a U.S. military identity card, and we have a long shopping list from the other two FOX teams that will be going into Iraq with U.S. units. Ali waits in the van while Griff and I head into the enormous air-conditioned warehouse that serves as the exchange.

Inside the cavernous building is a well-ordered mob scene. At least a thousand American and allied soldiers, sailors, airmen, and Marines are queued up at more than a dozen checkout lines. Nearly all of them are garbed in desert camouflage, though the varying patterns adopted by the different American, British, and Australian service branches lend a distinctively international air to the scene.

Nation of origin or branch of service doesn't seem to matter when it comes to what they are buying. Each shopping basket seems identical, and nearly every one contains packages of disposable razors, shaving cream, scores of socks, bungee cords, CDs, cameras, film, videotape, batteries of every size and description, flashlights, sunscreen, insect repellent, sunglasses, foot powder, large packages of toilet paper, containers of baby wipes, and candies—particularly M&Ms and Skittles, which supposedly won't melt in the oppressive heat—and brown, green, and tan T-shirts. Many shoppers also have GPS receivers, purchased in the electronics department of the exchange—an area that appears to be stocked with as many choices as any warehouse discount store back in the States.

Griff and I pick up the items on our list and join one of the slow-moving checkout lines. It's not long before I am recognized and there is a rush to take photos and get autographs. I'm soon out of the signature cards that FOX gives me for this purpose and I end up using a laundry marker to sign desert camouflage hats, helmets, and flak jackets. I begin to hope that I never meet the supply sergeants in these units for fear they will bill me for all the headgear that never gets turned in.

"What unit are you going to be with when the shooting starts, sir?" asks a U.S. Army sergeant first class as we creep toward the line of cash registers. He's a sharp-looking, well-built soldier with a close haircut and a 3rd Infantry Division patch on one shoulder and a small American flag on the other. His hands and neck are deeply tanned, as is his face—except where his sunglasses have stopped the UV radiation, leaving him with the reverse-raccoon look so common among real desert fighters. It's one of the ways you can tell the genuine warriors from the BS artists who talk about war and get their tans at swimming pools or the beach.

"We don't know for sure yet," I reply. "But I'm told that my cameraman and I are going to be assigned to the Marine air wing."

"Humph . . . the air wing," he chides me with a smile. "I thought you used to be an infantryman."

"I was, but we all go where we're sent," I answer, feeling a bit defensive about my assignment.

"Well," he says, "I understand we're going to have a FOX correspondent with my battalion. I sure hope he knows what he's doing. I don't want to have to nursemaid some prima donna who can't find his way to the latrine." Then he adds, almost prophetically, "Once the shooting starts, I think we're going to be pretty busy."

✪ OPERATION IRAQI FREEDOM SIT REP #3
Coalition Press Information Center
Hilton Hotel, Kuwait City, Kuwait
10 March 2003
0900 Hours Local

"It figures that the military would take the nicest hotel in the city," says a producer from NBC as we walk out of the ninety-plus-degree heat into the air-conditioned comfort of the Hilton. U.S. Central Command, known as CENTCOM, has taken over this spacious facility to use as a press center. It's also the place where we get our embedding assignments, countless hours of briefings, immunization shots, gas masks, and chemical protective suits.

There is a general "mill drill" in front of the reception desk, where members of the media are clamoring for any information that's being offered by the four public affairs officers behind the desk—two Army and two Air Force—who are being barraged with questions. Finally, a diminutive Navy lieutenant, dressed in desert camouflage, comes out of a room behind the desk. She looks at the chaos, steps up on a chair behind the counter, and shouts, "If you already have your press credentials, back away from the desk and line up!" The milling stops.

She continues, "If you are here for your shots, line up over there!" Some of the crowd starts to move that way. "If you are here to draw your chemical protective equipment, move over here!" More of the crowd heads in that direction. "If you don't know why you are here or if you've come here to hassle us about your assignment—tough. Go away and come back tomorrow."

As she steps down off the chair, she looks at one of her Air Force colleagues and says, for the benefit of all, "Don't take this crap. Tell 'em what you want 'em to do and repeat it as often as necessary. These are reporters, not sheep. Sheep you can herd. Reporters are like cats. Ever tried herding cats?"

The crowd in front of the desk melts away as the reporters, commentators, cameramen, producers, field techs, and assorted media types from half a dozen countries assemble, some grumbling, in their respective lines. Now that there is some order, it appears that there are about 200 to 250 of us. Since I need both to draw my chemical protective equipment and get my shots, I go to the shortest line—the one for the shots.

We've all been told that getting the shots for anthrax and smallpox is optional, but the briefing is mandatory. A colonel in the U.S. Army Medical Corps, wearing eagles on the collar of his desert camouflage uniform, is waiting on the small stage as we file into the room. He introduces himself as Col. Larry Godfrey and he begins by reminding us once again that being inoculated against the diseases Saddam Hussein is thought to have in his arsenal is purely voluntary. A very detailed exposition on each disease follows. It goes on for fifteen or twenty minutes and contains all kinds of dry data on mortality rates—from the diseases as well as the drugs created to prevent them.

I look around the room and notice that two or three of my colleagues are taking notes, and I assume that they must be correspondents for *Scientific American* or the AMA journal. Most of us are simply sitting mutely, barely paying attention as the colonel wraps up his presentation with, "So if you have decided to receive the shots, you must write a check to 'Treasurer of the United States' for $109 and complete the 'Release of Liability' form."

Col. Godfrey concludes his presentation by asking if there are any questions. Of course there are; no room full of reporters can resist an invitation like that. They pepper him with queries about "Gulf War syndrome," how many members of the Armed Forces have been court-martialed for refusing to get the shots, and what makes him think Saddam has these kinds of "bugs" in his arsenal. When the Q&A is over, an Army medic appears with a pile of forms and says, "Everybody who's getting the shots, please raise your hand." Nobody moves.

Instead there is a lot of head shaking and quiet grumbling. Comments like, "I'm not crazy," and "If it's safe, why do we have to sign a release form?" can be heard as the masters of the media start gathering their belongings, preparing to move outside for the lecture on chemical protective equipment. As they shuffle toward the door, Col. Godfrey says from the stage, "Thank you for your attention. On your way out, you may want to look at this."

A sequence of horrific photographs appears on the screen: people in the final stages of death from smallpox and anthrax. As the terrible images flash there is a sudden stillness in the room. A voice says, "Oh my God!"

Suddenly, there is a rush to get the "Release of Liability" forms. I already have mine, so I'm the first in line—anthrax in one arm, smallpox in the other. As it turns out, the reporters create a very long line after all.

After getting through the shot line we are escorted outside, where we form a line beside several long tables, behind which are seated a half dozen Army NCOs. One of the potentates of the press gripes, "I feel like I'm in kindergarten again." Without missing a beat, an Army noncom replies, "In kindergarten, the children do what they're told."

We're all measured and fitted for chemical protective suits and gas masks. After the equipment is issued, everyone is taken to the tennis courts, where Army and Marine chemical and biological warfare specialists demonstrate how the equipment is worn and then drill everyone on how to put it all on in less than ten seconds. In the aftermath of the anthrax and smallpox photos, no one is laughing.

CHAPTER TWO
SITZKRIEG!

★ OPERATION IRAQI FREEDOM SIT REP #4
Tactical Assembly Area (TAA) Ripper, Kuwait
Tuesday, 11 March 2003
1300 Hours Local

TAA Ripper is a dusty, dun-colored, tent camp parked on a barren, flat, windblown desert plain, lacking both vegetation and recognizable terrain features. It is scorching hot and the heat rises in waves off the desert floor. Behind every moving tank, armored vehicle, or truck, a plume of talcum-like dust rises and hangs in the air. Without a GPS receiver, it's impossible to know where you are or where you are going.

Canvas cities like this one are spread over the desert in northern Kuwait—"up close and personal to the Iraqi border," as a Marine gunny puts it. Each one of these Tactical Assembly Areas is "home away from home" for a U.S. or British ground combat unit. From the air they all look about the same: row upon row of large tents, surrounded by a ten-foot-high wall of earth topped with razor wire. This one is the temporary home of the fabled 7th Marine Regiment—one of three Regimental Combat Teams in the 1st Marine Division, the major ground component of the 1st Marine Expeditionary Force (known simply as I-MEF).

The entrance to TAA Ripper reminds me of the cavalry outposts in the Old West. Only instead of a log-walled fort, it's a sandbagged watchtower with a Marine manning an FN M-240G light machine gun who yells, "Halt."

Griff Jenkins, Adam Housley from the FOX News Channel bureau in Kuwait City, and I disembark from the air-conditioned comfort of our GMC Suburban to stand in the blazing sun while a team of Marine MPs examines the big SUV, inside and out. Since the beginning of the year, Marines have been killed over here by terrorists, so these guys aren't taking any chances.

With the inspection of the vehicle complete, we're waved inside the compound and directed to the Regimental Command Post. As we disembark again, a rifle company of Marines shuffles past, weapons slung over their shoulders, the sweat showing on the sleeves and trousers of their desert camouflage uniforms. They all have gas masks on their hips and bulky chemical protective suits in rucksacks. Web belts and carrying harnesses are crammed with canteens and canvas pouches for transporting the tools of war: magazines, grenades, ammunition, first aid kits, and radios. Their flak jackets and helmets are covered with grime, and dust swirls in the dead air as they pass. It occurs to me that the antiwar activists in Hollywood and the striped-pants bureaucrats at the United Nations who have succeeded in delaying the inevitable ought to see them.

Most of the Marines at TAA Ripper have been here for two months or more, having left California—either Camp Pendleton or the Marines' sprawling desert training base in Twentynine Palms—back in January. They are blissfully unaware of the political machinations at the United Nations that have held them in this dusty desert limbo for more than a month, poised like a diver prepared for a plunge at the end of the board. Few seem to be aware of the protests by the "Blame America First" crowd in San Francisco and on the streets of many European cities.

They do know that the French have "wimped out once again." And they are quick to remind any journalist who will listen that it's okay because, as one Marine put it, "the French have always been there when they needed us."

In front of a nearby tent is a small crimson banner on a silver-tipped staff. Gold letters stitched onto the fabric read, "Co. L, 3rd Bn, 7th Marines." I enter the relative darkness of the tent and it's like a furnace. As my eyes adjust to the gloom I spot, a few feet inside the entrance, a Marine, head down on a field desk, clearly asleep. Behind him on a plywood shelf are two radio sets, the coiled handset cords looping down into the sand. Beside the sleeping Marine, open on the field desk, is a yellow, dog-eared edition of the *Atlanta Journal-Constitution* dated February 6, 2003. Mail from home takes almost three weeks to get here, and any newspapers enclosed in a care package circulate through a thirteen-man squad, then around the rest of a forty-five-man platoon, until the paper is worn thin and the print is barely legible.

This newspaper has clearly made the circuit. The lead story is all about the dramatic speech Secretary of State Colin Powell had made the day before at the United Nations, laying out the case for going after Saddam Hussein. The story is complete with satellite photos, diagrams of chemical weapons facilities, and transcribed intercepts of Iraqi communications. Next to one such translated conversation between two Iraqi officers, some Marine wag had written in ball-point pen, "These guys talk too much."

I decide not to awaken the sleeping Marine and proceed back outside, to be accosted by a crowd of Marines who had been on the way back to their billets from the mess tent when they spotted our civilian vehicle. They have surrounded Jenkins and Housley and are peppering the pair with questions such as "what's happening back in the States."

This goes on for several minutes until a gunnery sergeant comes along and shoos the Marines off with a growled "Go clean your weapons" type of command. The Marines scatter, and as soon as they are out of earshot, he tells the three of us that Col. Steve Hummer, the regimental commander, is "down at Commando"—the 1st Marine Division CP (command post)—"for a briefing." The gunnery sergeant adds, "He won't be back before nightfall." Since we have to be back in Kuwait City before dark, in lieu of an interview with the regimental commander we accept his offer of some chow and walk to the mess tent. On the way he answers our questions and describes their situation, though he is careful to say nothing about their mission.

Most of the troops are billeted in frame tents holding twenty to twenty-five Marines, roughly half a platoon. The plywood floors, 2x4 support frames, and canvas have been erected by a U.S. military contractor. Contractors have also poured concrete pads for generators, maintenance space, communications equipment, and other heavy equipment, and installed some utilities.

"The rest of what you see here," the gunny continues, "we brought in with us when we came from the States, or we offloaded it from the MPS."

"MPS" is Marine vernacular for the Maritime Prepositioning Ships—the large "roll-on roll-off" vessels full of military equipment, weapons, and ammunition that are strategically placed to expedite the deployment of U.S. military units. Five such ships were dispatched from their Indian Ocean base at Diego Garcia to Kuwait back in January.

"This MPS offload was a lot easier than during the first Gulf War, because of all the contract stuff," says the gunnery sergeant, pointing around the area—and he looks at me, knowing he's baited the hook.

"Okay, I'll bite. What 'contract stuff'?" I reply.

"The construction and logistics contractors, Colonel," the gunny answers. "The civilian outfits that put all this stuff up. They have been working on these base camps out here in the desert for more than a year. This stuff didn't just all happen overnight. Some very smart people started planning for this gunfight in the desert a long time before we got our predeployment orders back in December."

As we approach the mess tent, an enormous green scoop loader with a Seabee logo grinds past us and dumps a bucket load of sand atop a prefabricated concrete shelter. Navy Construction Battalion and Marine Engineer personnel wearing hard hats instead of helmets are constructing these bunkers throughout the camp. The gunny gestures toward the structure being buried beneath the sand and says, "This camp is closest to the border, so we're adding a few more bunkers just in case Saddam hits us before we hit him."

We enter the mess tent and join a long line of Marines. The food service is also a contract operation, run by a Kuwaiti contractor. The Marines are being served by locals from a steam line on plastic trays rather than the old metal mess kits that had been in use when I retired. The food isn't great, but it's palatable, and there is salad, fresh fruit, and ice to put in the drinks—all things that can't be found in an MRE, the "Meal, Ready-to-Eat" combat rations.

"Any concerns about 'locals' preparing and serving the food—and coming and going around this base?" I ask the gunny.

He pauses to reflect a moment, then says, "Some, I suppose. But the contractor has been vetted, all the workers are too, by the Kuwaiti security service. They are escorted on and off the base and closely supervised while they are here. Most of them are from Bangladesh or the Philippines. I guess the risk is worth it, because for every one of them back here fixing food, it releases one of our own. That means we have another shooter in a combat unit."

We finish our meal and go back outside. A "show and tell" has been arranged for fifteen to twenty foreign journalists. The goal, I'm told, is to familiarize these overseas reporters with Marine Corps weapons, equipment, and organization. Because FOX News Channel isn't part of the contingent, we're not allowed to bring any cameras. Apparently the press corps covering the war doesn't want to be covered itself, so I just tag along.

It's quickly evident that these masters of the overseas media are less interested in the weapons on display than they are in what the Marines who use them have to say. They swirl around the young troopers like sharks looking for prey. Questions fly about everything from the weather to opinions on the UN, antiwar protests, and their commander in chief, and how long they have been here waiting for the war to start.

In response, the Marines, most of them corporals and sergeants, are brutally frank. Despite the delay in getting done what they came here to do, these young warriors revere their commander in chief. And whether the nice folks at the UN or the critics in Europe and antiwar activists in the United States like it or not, these Marines have a refreshing certainty about their mission, Saddam Hussein, and the need to evict him from Iraq. This isn't because they are naïve or "poor, uneducated minorities," as some liberal politicians have alleged in advocating a reinstitution of conscription. Supporters of a draft say that it's necessary to equalize the pool of conscripts, so that white upper- and middle-class Americans are made to serve as well as those from lower economic groups, and minority groups. Yet these all-volunteer troops are already predominantly white, middle-income Americans and they are all high school graduates. Minorities are, if anything, underrepresented in these units.

The "mission focus" of these young Americans in uniform doesn't stem from being "brainwashed" by their superiors. And not because these Marines are "bloodthirsty," as some of these foreign journalists seem to believe. In fact, *none* of the soldiers, sailors, airmen, or

Marines with whom I have spoken over the last several days has told me that they are over here "itching for a fight."

What has apparently been missed by many of the media elites who are here covering the preparations for a fight in the Iraqi desert is the fact that no one who has ever really been to a war ever really wants to go to another one. And a remarkable percentage of these young men already have combat experience. One commander I spoke with estimated that nearly half his officers and senior non-commissioned officers have served under fire before—in the first Gulf War, the Balkans, or Afghanistan, and in some cases, all three. They know better than any correspondent, reporter, or politician the true nature of war: that it is the most terrible of human endeavors.

Yet precisely because so many of them have combat experience, they are anxious to get on with the task at hand. They know that the sooner it gets started, the sooner it will be over. Many of them express frustration that what was supposed to be a blitzkrieg has become a "sitzkrieg." One young NCO says, "We're the best there is, but this is going to be the most 'telegraphed punch' in military history."

And that's not the only problem with further delay. A "recon Marine"—one of those whose job it is to penetrate deep inside enemy territory to scout out routes, objectives, and enemy targets to be hit— says, "We do our best work under conditions of marginal visibility. We don't like to operate when the moon is like a big light bulb in the night sky."

I watch as the foreign reporters scribble furiously while talking to an NBC NCO—one of those responsible for ensuring that the Marines survive an attack by weapons of mass destruction. The "NBC" isn't the network—it stands for "nuclear, biological, and chemical." His comment gets their attention: "The longer we wait, the more time Saddam has to plot and carry out a chemical, biological, or nuclear attack—and the hotter it's going to be wearing those protective suits and masks."

As the reporters head back to their vans, I ask a Marine staff sergeant how he thinks it went. He shrugs and replies, "They will probably say we were whining and complaining, but what the troops were saying is all just common sense. What I don't get is why we're letting these foreign reporters hang around with us. They are more hostile than the Iraqis."

I walk over to eavesdrop on the departing correspondents, who are now hammering away at their escorts. One female correspondent, with what sounds to me like a French accent, is asking—or is it *telling?*—one of the Marine minders that she has "never seen so much bravado, machismo, or arrogance" in her life. The young NCO listens to her complaint, appears to mull over her grievance, and then replies, "Yes, ma'am, that's why they call themselves United States Marines."

✪ OPERATION IRAQI FREEDOM SIT REP #5
HMM-268 Forward Operating Base
Ali Al Salem Air Base, Kuwait
Wednesday, 12 March 2003
1445 Hours Local

We're finally embedded in our assigned unit: Marine Medium Helicopter Squadron (HMM) 268. From now until the end of the war, we'll be living with and flying with the Red Dragons. Their twelve CH-46 helicopters are parked on the flight line about 150 meters from the squadron ready room—a frame tent with a plywood floor erected next to a steel maintenance building that serves as the headquarters for Marine Air Group (MAG) 39. I note that there are several large sandbagged bunkers within a few feet of the building.

My FOX News Channel colleagues received my assignment to this squadron with some amusement. Since I had served as an infantry officer for twenty-two years, everyone—myself included—assumed that the Pentagon public affairs officers who are running the embedding process would send me to a Marine ground combat unit. And since FOX News Channel's Greg Kelly is a Marine AV-8 Harrier pilot, we all expected that he would be posted to a Marine aviation component. So much for assumptions.

As it turns out, Rick Leventhal and Christian Galdabini are heading off in a FOX Humvee to cover the Marines' 3rd Light Armored Reconnaissance Battalion. Greg Kelly and Mal James have been assigned to cover the Army's 3rd Infantry Division, so they are taking the other FOX vehicle. Both the Kelly and Leventhal teams have what seems to be several tons of equipment. But since Griff Jenkins and I are covering—and therefore flying in—Marine helicopters, we must carry all of our equipment on our backs or manhandle it on and off the birds.

To accommodate the weight and space restrictions on the helicopters, Griff and I spent countless hours in Kuwait City reconfiguring our loads and repacking our gear until we were down to an absolute minimum. We finally managed to squeeze all our electronic equipment, satellite gear, cameras, miles of videotape, batteries, electrical leads, transmission cables, and computers into two rugged Pelican cases. We also have a small diesel generator for emergency electrical power. All of our personal equipment, clothing, chemical protective suits, shaving kits, canteens, extra boots, ponchos, gloves, dust goggles, flashlights, and assorted "comfort items," like toilet paper and baby wipes, get jammed into our Osprey backpacks.

When we're "saddled up" with our body armor, gas masks, and backpacks, carrying the Pelican cases and generator, we look like a couple of pack mules, but we can quickly move all our equipment on or off a CH-46 helicopter in just two trips up and down the ramp.

Lt. Col. Jerry Driscoll, the squadron commander, seems genuinely glad to see us. He introduces us to the pilots and aircrews and takes us around the Ali Al Salem Air Base so that we can get our bearings. One of the squadron pilots, 1st Lt. Ken Williamson, is assigned to serve as our liaison and run interference for us with the air group. He introduces himself as "the oldest flying first lieutenant in the Marine Corps," and delivers us to our new home, the "field grade tent" in the squadron area, with the admonition, "You guys should have stayed with the lieutenants and captains. We live closer to the bunker."

The officers and Marines of the squadron are all billeted in frame tents identical to those of the 7th Marines. But here, even though this entire canvas city was erected in January, when the squadron first arrived in Kuwait, the Seabees are just now in the process of installing modular showers and replacing the portable heads with "toilet trailers." It's the first time in my Marine Corps experience that I've seen the "air wing" living rougher than the "grunts."

Lt. Williamson points out the U.S. Army Patriot PAC-3 missile battery and an anti-aircraft missile battery providing protection from incoming Iraqi Scud missiles and any other threat from the air. Before leaving us in our new abode, he points to a telephone pole with a large loudspeaker on top. "That's what we call the 'Great Giant Voice.' If you hear them announce a missile attack or a chemical alarm, grab your gas mask, flak jacket, and chemical suit and head for the nearest bunker and stay there until the 'all clear' is sounded." Griff immediately looks around for his gas mask and realizes he's left it in the ready room.

✪ OPERATION IRAQI FREEDOM SIT REP #6
HMM-268 Forward Operating Base
Ali Al Salem Air Base, Kuwait
Thursday, 13 March 2003
0900 Hours Local

"Dust storm!" Maj. John Graham, the squadron XO (executive offi-cer), muttered late last night as he stumbled into our tent in the dark-ness, trying to find his folding cot. I rolled over and went back to sleep. Now it's three hours after sunrise but it's impossible to see more than a few feet outside our tent. Inside, the air is full of fine dust that settles on everything. Gusts of wind whip the sides and roof of our shelter with a racket that sounds as if it could rip the canvas apart. The 2x4 frame holding the tent up groans as though the beams might snap at any moment. Without the sun to warm the desert floor, it's actually cold, and I pull on a sweater beneath my field jacket.

Griff and I were supposed to fly with the squadron this morning out to one of the ranges so that the gunners could "zero" their weapons. But the training missions and all other nonessential flights have been canceled for the duration of the storm. Instead, we've been summoned to a briefing for all the correspondents assigned to MAG-39 squadrons.

First Lt. John Neiman is the air group's public affairs officer (PAO), and even though there are no official "censors" to review what we print or broadcast, the PAO has been ordered to give all of us the parameters concerning what we may report.

As in all past wars, someone "up the chain of command" has decided what the media can and cannot say, print, or show on the air. Those of us in the fourth estate who are accompanying the com-bat units being assembled on the Iraqi periphery have also been admonished not to report exact unit troop strength figures. We've already been directed that we may not state exactly where we are. Instead, we are told to euphemistically describe this remote and very austere air base as "in the vicinity of the Iraqi border."

Quite understandably, we're also not permitted to report where we are going—or when. Some of the other correspondents covering other squadrons in MAG-39 chafe at what they perceive to be restrictions on the "freedom of the press." Most, however, seem to understand the rationale for the limitations. Those who find the burden of "self-censorship" too onerous can always "unvolunteer" and simply go home.

That option, of course, doesn't apply to the rest of the volunteers over here—the soldiers, sailors, airmen, and Marines, more than 200,000 of them, who are now deployed in the trackless desert along the Iraqi border. On days like this, with a vicious sandstorm blowing across the dry, flat "moonscape," going home sounds even more attractive than usual. Life in this extreme climate and terrain prompts a longing not just for the companionship of loved ones but also for the simple pleasure of living without sand. One Marine said today, "I don't think I'll ever go to the beach again for the rest of my life."

Two months ago, HMM-268 was at Camp Pendleton, California, without any particular plans to travel—although like all Marines in this post–September 11 environment, they were prepared for various contingencies. Then, on January 10, the word came down: "Prepare your aircraft for immediate embarkation."

Four days later the squadron's twelve CH-46 helicopters, their blades removed, were all packed and sealed, and on January 15, the aging aircraft were lifted aboard a commercial ship in San Diego. Accompanying the birds was a detachment of a dozen Marines, led by a sergeant. "Now think of this," said 1st Lt. Williamson. "Here's a shipment worth more than sixty million dollars being signed for by a twenty-two-year-old Marine sergeant. Where else would you get that kind of responsibility at that age?" Where else indeed?

The rest of the Red Dragons departed from California at midnight on February 9 (for reasons still inexplicable to this old leatherneck, the U.S. Marines never go anywhere in daylight). When they arrived "in country" on February 11, the unit, officers and enlisted alike, pitched in to build tents and fill sandbags—more than twenty thousand that first week alone, according to Chief Warrant Officer Sean Wennes.

"Why so many sandbags?" asked one of the horde of media that have descended on this remote desert air base. "Because these tents don't even stop a sandstorm. They sure wouldn't stop a Scud," replied Cpl. Phillip Sapio. "Sometimes a sandbag is all you have between us and them." By "them," of course, the Marine means the Iraqis—who deny even having any of the long-range weapons capable of carrying chemical or biological warheads into the heart of this desert base.

"Six hours after the helicopters arrived in port, they had been stripped of the weatherproof covers, had their rotor blades replaced, and were ready for flight," explained Lt. Col. Driscoll. "Some people think that's extraordinary. And maybe for some organizations it would be—but for these Marines, this is what we do for a living," he added.

Picking up and moving isn't the only thing that these Marines do for a living: they must also be prepared to fight when they *get* to where they are going. The Red Dragon helicopters have to be ready at a moment's notice to carry Marine infantrymen in a heloborne assault, resupply the units in contact, insert reconnaissance patrols deep into enemy territory, and evacuate casualties. That means their "Frogs," or "Phrogs"—the nickname Marines gave to the twin-rotor CH-46 Sea Knight helicopters nearly forty years ago—must be constantly maintained. Right now, in the middle of a sandstorm, that's difficult at best.

After the PAO security briefing, Griff and I walk over to the flight line and find Marine maintenance technicians wearing gas masks so that they can work on aircraft in conditions that can only be described as "extreme." It's now nearly noon, but conditions have not improved. The wind, blowing steadily at twenty-five to thirty knots, howls like a banshee through antenna guy wires. The storm has the strange effect of turning daylight into dusk, blotting out the sun, and giving an orange hue to every structure, man, and machine. Visibility is still less than twenty yards. The air appears to be foggy, the way it does along the Atlantic or Pacific Coast when there is a large storm offshore. But the "fog" in the air isn't water vapor, it's dirt—tiny particles of sand that the Marines inhale with every breath and swallow with every mouthful of food. It whips through the air, jamming weapons, seeping into every crevice, and clogging the intakes of jet engines and the filters of the gas masks we all carry everywhere, all the time. Griff asks one of the maintenance technicians who has just climbed down from one of the birds if the dust and dirt will affect the performance of his aircraft. The Marine veteran, tongue planted firmly in his cheek, replies, "Dust storms aren't allowed to affect us. It's contrary to Marine Corps policy."

As we're walking back to the squadron area, my Iridium satellite pager goes off, informing me to call the foreign desk at FOX News Channel in New York. Brian Knoblock, head of our overseas operations, asks if we can bring up our satellite videophone and do a live report for *FOX & Friends* on how the storm is affecting war preparations. We are in the process of setting up our equipment when the "Great Giant Voice" blares that the base is under attack by incoming missiles and to take shelter immediately. As bad as it seems, apparently the sandstorm isn't affecting Saddam's rocket forces. We grab our flak jackets and helmets and run for the nearest bunker. This time, Griff has his gas mask.

CHAPTER THREE
GOOD TO GO

★ OPERATION IRAQI FREEDOM SIT REP #7
HMM-268 Forward Operating Base
Ali Al Salem Air Base, Kuwait
Sunday, 16 March 2003
2330 Hours Local

It's been an exhausting but productive couple of days. As soon as the sandstorm passed, Gunnery Sgt. Dennis Pennington, a weapons and tactics instructor, arranged to fly all the helicopter gunners—the Marines who man the .50-caliber machine guns mounted on the left and right sides of the CH-46 helicopters—out to the Udari range so that they could test-fire every weapon in the squadron armory. Griff and I videotaped the entire exercise as Gunny Pennington, a very experienced combat veteran, coached young Marines who had never fired a shot in anger on rules of engagement, how to lead a target, and the best way to protect a helo that has to land in a "hot" landing zone (LZ). They came back sweaty, dirty, and tired—but confident that they were ready if and when the shooting starts. Gunny Pennington's encouraging assessment: "They know what to do and they know how to do it."

Everyone here believes that war with Iraq is imminent. President Bush met in the Azores today with Prime Minister Tony Blair of the UK, President José Maria Aznar of Spain, and Prime Minister José Manuel Durao Barroso of Portugal. Marines here repeatedly asked Griff what news was coming from the conference. When the four heads of state issued their communiqué, declaring that efforts to reach a diplomatic solution would end in twenty-four hours, dozens of Marines were huddled around our tiny video receiver, linked by satellite with FOX News Channel in New York.

Back on March 5, France, Germany, and Russia joined forces and declared that they would "not allow" a resolution authorizing the use of force against Iraq to pass in the UN Security Council. Despite this, everyone here expects that when President Bush addresses the nation tomorrow night, Saddam's refusal to come clean on his weapons of mass destruction will mean war. They aren't jumping up and down, talking tough, or swaggering with bravado, but there is a palpable sense of resolve—an aura of quiet competence in these Marines. Though no one has said that they are itching for a fight, it's pretty clear that they are tired of waiting. Every one of them seems to know that they have done everything they can to prepare for what lies ahead.

Even though today is Sunday, except for a very brief pause early this morning for chapel services, it's been a full day of training, and has been that way since the sandstorm finally passed. Starting Friday, all the MAG-39 pilots and aircrews that will be flying into Iraq have been coming in groups of fifteen to twenty to the MAG-39 Air Operations Center—a partitioned area inside the steel building next to the squadron ready room tents. There, intelligence officers brief them on the enemy situation. The Air Group S-3 then issues a detailed Operations Order and the Survival, Escape, Resistance, and Evasion (SERE) plan in the event they go down behind enemy lines. After all this, the Air Group S-1 has them all update their next-of-kin (NOK) information.

As the pilots and aircrews depart the Ops Center, there is no back-slapping or joking around as there was when they arrived. Nothing focuses the mind of a Marine like an NOK form. It contains the details of who is to be informed, and how, when a Marine is killed, wounded, or missing in action.

While none of this is a laughing matter, Griff and I have managed, quite unintentionally, to provide just a bit of comic relief. Late Friday night we went out near the Iraqi border with a couple of CH-46s so that the pilots could practice landings, takeoffs, and low-level flying while wearing night-vision goggles (NVGs). After two or three practice landings, we had them put us down in an LZ a few kilometers south of the border so that we could check out how well our night lens could videotape the birds as they came back in. Almost immediately after the two helicopters took off, leaving us alone in the desert, three jeeps came racing across the open terrain and surrounded us, their headlights blinding our NVGs.

The two CH-46s waved off their landing and pulled away as five or six men carrying submachine guns poured out from the jeeps. "Oh great," said Griff as the armed men encircled us, their weapons at the ready. "How's your Arabic?" he asked me as one of the men who had jumped from the jeeps yelled something unintelligible through a bull-horn. Now we could make out their uniforms—Kuwaiti Border Patrol.

Relieved that it wasn't an Iraqi patrol, we quickly produced our Kuwaiti Ministry of Information–issued media credentials—to no effect. We might well have spent the night in a lockup if I hadn't been able to explain that we were videotaping U.S. Marine helicopters and pointed at the orbiting CH-46s. Suddenly, our inquisitor smiled and said in broken English, "Ahh...U.S. Marines. Good, good." The weapons were quickly slung over shoulders and the patrolmen came up to us, shook hands, and returned to their vehicles waving, and repeating over and over, "Marines good...Marines okay!"

As soon as their jeeps departed the landing zone, the two birds came back in and we quickly loaded our gear, took off, and headed back to Ali Al Salem Air Base. After we landed, I asked Maj. John Graham, the squadron XO, what he would have done if the armed men in the jeeps had taken us away. Without hesitating he deadpanned, "I wasn't worried about you guys, I figured you'd had it anyway. I was trying to figure out how to explain to the skipper that our two embedded correspondents had gone AWOL."

An even more comical incident occurred earlier today while we were doing a live feed to FOX News Channel in New York City from beside the HMM-268 ready room tent. In the midst of my report with Col. Dave Hunt, one of the FOX military analysts in New York, the "Great Giant Voice" sounded another alert. Since the sandstorm, these alerts have been coming several times a day. But this time the chemical attack alarm was sounded as well. Marines came running from the squadron ready room tents and the MAG-39 Ops Center, hastily putting on their flak jackets, gas masks, helmets, and chemical protective suits.

As I wrapped up my report, Lt. Col. Hudson, the air group XO— a generally calm and unexcitable officer—came running out of the MAG-39 CP and yelled, "Everyone into the bunker, full MOPP. *Now!* This is not a drill!"

I looked into the camera, and said to Dave Hunt, "Well, I guess that's it from here for now. We are apparently under chemical attack, so we'll have to get back to you later." I assumed that New York would cut away at that point. I shouted to Griff to head for the bunker and I put on my gas mask, ripped open the sealed plastic bags containing my two-piece, military-issue chemical protective suit, and proceeded to start putting it on.

Unfortunately, try as I might, I could not pull the chemical protective trousers up over my waist or put on the suspenders. For more than a minute I fumbled with the trousers and suspenders—all of it on live TV—at one point observing out loud, "Man, these things shouldn't be this tight in the crotch." Meanwhile, unbeknownst to me, Dave Hunt was carrying on a running commentary about the courage of our FOX News Channel embedded correspondents, "willing to brave enemy incoming to make sure that the story gets out."

Finally, just as the Patriot PAC 3 battery across the airfield opened up on the inbound enemy missile, I noticed through the lenses of my gas mask why I couldn't get the trousers up—they were tangled in the microphone and IFB cords between my legs. By the time I unsnarled the mess, the Iraqi missile had been knocked down, and a few minutes later the "All clear" was sounded. By the time the Marines who had dutifully sought shelter exited the bunkers, I was in "full MOPP," had the microphone up to the speaking port on the gas mask, and was describing the attack. Many of the younger Marines were amazed that I had enough confidence in the Patriot ABMs (anti-ballistic missiles) to stay outside during an attack. But of course, they knew nothing of my chemical suit–mike cord fiasco. And I was blissfully unaware that the whole thing had been carried live on FOX News Channel. Unfortunately, a good number of my former Marine colleagues watching the news saw it, and were happy to enlighten me. For days afterward, I was subjected to ribald, chiding e-mails from old friends about how to put on a chemical protective suit in less than five minutes.

✪ THE WHITE HOUSE
Washington, DC
Monday, 17 March 2003
2000 Hours Local

It is three in the morning here in Iraq, and as President George Bush appears on the tiny screen, dozens of Marines are gathered around our satellite audio-video transceiver to hear their commander in chief address the American people. When he says that the time has come for Saddam Hussein and his sons to leave Iraq and gives them a deadline of forty-eight hours to do so, a few heads nod in agreement, but nobody says a word. There is a similar reaction when he says, "Their refusal to do so will result in military conflict, commenced at a time of our choosing." And again when he adds, "The tyrant will soon be gone."

Without naming them, President Bush castigates the leaders of France, Germany, Russia, and China for their stubborn opposition to his new resolution for UN authorization to use force to disarm and topple Hussein and accomplish a regime change for Iraq. The United States, Britain, and Spain withdrew the proposal before it came to a vote, since France had said it would veto the resolution even if all other voting nations approved it.

When the president says, "These governments share our assessment of the danger but not our resolve to meet it," and "The United Nations has not lived up to its responsibilities, so we will rise to ours," there are more nods from the hushed crowd. No one in this little gathering objects to his claim that "the Iraqi regime has used diplomacy to gain time and advantage" and that "diplomacy can't go on forever in the face of a global threat."

When President Bush encourages the Iraqi people with the promise "The day of your liberation is near," I watch as several of those who will have to make good on this commitment simply pat the back of the Marine nearest them.

As he closes with his customary "May God continue to bless America," he looks grim. So do the Marines who have just heard him speak. Without so much as a word, the crowd breaks up and the Marines go back to their duties or to sleep.

The sword has been readied. The steel has been honed. The blade is drawn.

✪ OPERATION IRAQI FREEDOM SIT REP #8
HMM-268 Forward Operating Base
Ali Al Salem Air Base, Kuwait
Tuesday, 18 March 2003
0930 Hours Local

Today, more than 200,000 U.S. soldiers, sailors, airmen, and Marines, joined by a coalition of international partners, are poised to begin what they believe is the next campaign in the war on terrorism. Some here have taken to calling it the Baghdad Urban Renewal Project.

According to what we have heard on our satellite videophone, at this very minute the Iraqi Parliament, in an emergency meeting, is considering the ultimatum given them last night by President Bush. Everyone here expects the Iraqis to reject it.

Many of these young Americans are taking time today to write home. They understand that their spouses, family members, and friends are concerned for their safety. They know, because of our satellite feed, that back in the United States there are unfounded reports that the troops here are unprepared and ill equipped for the mission that lies ahead. A bevy of "experts," including former generals and admirals, have been adding fuel to this fire by saying that our chemical protective suits don't work, and that there are not enough troops, the right weapons, or enough equipment to take on Saddam's 480,000-man military.

At 0800 this morning Lt. Col. Jerry Driscoll summoned all the pilots in the squadron to a meeting in the ready room and assigned missions for the opening of hostilities. Most here believe that the order could come down at any moment after the president's forty-eight-hour deadline for Saddam's departure expires. On "Go-Day" or "Game Day," as it is variously called here, HMM-268 will be the lead air element carrying British Royal Marine Commandos into the attack on Al Faw Peninsula. The squadron will also be conducting inserts and extracts of reconnaissance units well inside Iraq and cas-evac missions—the evacuation of casualties from fire-swept "hot" landing zones.

Driscoll tells his pilots to check over their survival gear and get some rest in the hours ahead. And then he adds that there will be fewer than the usual number of flights today so that the maintenance crews can check the birds over for any last-minute mechanical, hydraulic, electronic, or ordnance problems. The Red Dragon "wrench turners" and crew chiefs have been working around the clock, in fair weather and foul, looking after these aging birds. Today they will at least have sunshine, though it is likely to get very hot. The desert sun can make bubbles on the flight line tarmac and turn the skin of an aircraft into a griddle that will sear exposed flesh that touches it.

None of the combat-experienced Marines from Gulf War I, the Balkans, or Afghanistan have told me they wanted another war. But now that we've got one, these are the people we want to fight in it. Most of the Marines I am with have been here for two months or more. They have participated almost daily and nightly using some of the most sophisticated equipment and weaponry the world has ever seen. They are smart, fit, and ready.

These Marines are well trained; they know their jobs, and are prepared to do them—even when the worst begins to happen around them. That can-do attitude prevails with the pilots who are flying the planes and the troops who are getting on and off them. It's evident in every crew chief, every .50-caliber gunner, and each of the mechanics and technicians who keep these airplanes flying. It is an extraordinary sense of teamwork that has gotten them this far and for which the Marine Corps is famous. There is no airplane that launches without a complete check from the mechanics who maintain them day and night.

To ensure that a wounded soldier, sailor, airman, or Marine gets the fastest and finest medical attention necessary, all four services are participating in a remarkable experiment that is the brainchild of a Navy chief. When a trooper is wounded badly enough to require evacuation, he will be picked up by a Marine CH-46 specially configured with nine or more litters. The twin .50-caliber machine guns mounted port and starboard and the stand-up headroom inside the "fighting frogs" make them ideal for this purpose. Every cas-evac bird has aboard two medical corpsmen. Thirty-six of the best corpsmen have been pulled from throughout the U.S. Navy and assigned to what's called the "I-MEF Cas-Evac Unit." They are all emergency medical specialists and experts on treating shock and trauma. Their motto: "We Bring You Home." One volunteer for this special unit had to be flown to Kuwait from Antarctica!

As soon as the wounded are aboard a CH-46, they will be treated for shock and blood loss by the two Navy corpsmen, while the bird sprints to a U.S. Army shock-trauma hospital. Instead of being twenty to thirty miles from the battle area, these small field hospital tents—staffed by Army doctors, nurses, and medics ready for immediate, life-saving surgery—will be positioned just five or six miles from the front lines. Once the wounded are stabilized, they will be flown back to Kuwait on an Army H-60 Black Hawk or aboard a Marine C-130. The plan is to have these large four-engined C-130s land on captured airfields, highways, or even the desert floor.

When they arrive in Kuwait, the wounded will be rushed into a U.S. Air Force expeditionary hospital for further treatment. If advanced surgery is needed, the casualty will be loaded on an Air Force C-9 Nightingale for transport to one of several large hospitals in Germany.

At the conclusion of Lt. Col. Driscoll's briefing, the Squadron S-2 informed the pilots that yesterday U.S. Central Command had dropped nearly two million leaflets over military and civilian sites in nearly twenty locations across Iraq. That brings the total number of leaflets dropped to more than twelve million so far this year. The goal of these leaflet drops is to protect civilian lives and deter the Iraqi military from fighting back once hostilities begin. Yesterday's leaflet drop stressed that coalition forces do not wish to harm innocent Iraqis. One message informed Iraqi citizens that they could be the victims if Saddam Hussein uses chemical weapons. Another message encouraged the Iraqi military officers to refrain from using weapons of mass destruction, and others told Iraqi troops how to surrender safely.

One of the Cobra pilots from Marine Light Attack Helicopter Squadron (HMLA) 267 who will be accompanying the CH-46s made the observation that surrender would be the best way for an Iraqi soldier to save his life because "if he points a gun at me, he's dead."

✪ OPERATION IRAQI FREEDOM SIT REP #9
HMM-268 Forward Operating Base
Ali Al Salem Air Base, Kuwait
Wednesday, 19 March 2003
2300 Hours Local

The president's deadline for Saddam and his sons to depart Iraq expires in five hours. Apparently, from what little news we are receiving, the Iraqi Parliament never bothered to seriously debate the U.S. ultimatum. They probably knew that their dictator and commander in chief wanted them to reject it. So they did.

A few hours ago, the Parliament of the United Kingdom, by a vote of 412 to 149, approved the use of military force to disarm Iraq and oust its leader. An antiwar amendment said to reflect British public sentiment against hostilities in Iraq was defeated.

Saddam Hussein had been given ten days to comply and to turn over his weapons of mass destruction, but he hasn't. Coalition aircraft continue dropping information leaflets into Iraq stating that war could start at any time.

UN Secretary-General Kofi Annan, French President Jacques Chirac, and German Chancellor Gerhard Schroeder are now claiming that an invasion of Iraq will sabotage any future UN efforts at disarmament, and that there is "no justification for war, and no reason to end the weapons inspections." In Paris and New York, French diplomats have announced that President Bush's ultimatum was "contrary to the will of the United Nations Security Council."

French foreign minister Dominique de Villepin urged the UN, "Let us triple the number of inspectors. Let us open more regional offices [in Iraq]…set up a specialized body to keep under surveillance the sites that have already been inspected." Chirac, unalterably opposed to a U.S.-led coalition removing Saddam from power, sought to protect French commercial interests in Baghdad by pleading "We want Iraq to disarm, but we believe this disarmament must happen peacefully."

One Marine watching these developments on our little satellite transceiver threw up his hands and said, "These guys need a reality check. When was the last time an aggressive dictator like Saddam Hussein 'peacefully' disarmed? Iraq doesn't play by Swiss diplomatic rules and the path to peace doesn't meander through the United Nations."

Here in the desert, France and Chirac are despised as much as Iraq and Saddam. Never one to miss the opportunity to prove that accountability is always the enemy of empty promises, Chirac also suggested that Iraq should be given a minimum of four or five more months to come clean. But then he clarified his position, lest it be taken too seriously: "There is no deadline," he added. "Only the inspectors themselves can say when such a deadline is set and how."

Chirac finally admitted that his goal was to oppose "American plans for dominance." Others with a more cynical view of the situation have said that Chirac's remarks about "American dominance" are nothing but a smoke screen for French venality since they have much to hide.

Everyone here knows that the French helped Iraq build its nuclear reactor—the Osarik facility that Israel destroyed in 1981. But there is also widespread belief here in Kuwait that the French are afraid that when U.S. forces get to Baghdad, intelligence officers and FBI agents will find evidence of French arms sales and involvement in providing the Iraqis with the means of producing chemical and biological weapons and delivery systems—nearly all of which Paris provided to the Iraqis on credit. If Saddam goes down, the French won't get paid.

The Marines, who are taught history in boot camp, know that in spite of heavy Marine losses at Belleau Wood in World War I, the French shot at and killed U.S. troops during the landings in North Africa in 1942. All this has prompted a lively exchange of jokes about France and criticism that "the UN is dancing to the tune of a French horn."

Though the news here is thin, we've learned, as the deadline nears in just a few hours, that Egyptian president Hosni Mubarak now believes that Iraq has brought the entire Gulf region to the edge of war. And we've heard that France and Germany want yet another opportunity to bring their objections formally before the UN Security Council. Antiwar protesters are being given prominent coverage, even on FOX, which is now the only news source that we're getting. Meanwhile, this morning seventeen Iraqi soldiers couldn't wait—they surrendered to American forces on the Kuwaiti border to Iraq.

★ DORA COMMAND COMPLEX
Downtown Baghdad
Thursday, 20 March 2003
0530 Hours Local

The war is now on. It began with a cruise missile attack followed by an air strike about an hour and a half after the expiration of President Bush's deadline for Saddam Hussein and his sons to leave Iraq. The target: an Iraqi command, control, and communications center in downtown Baghdad.

We had originally been told that there would be no action until tomorrow—just in case someone in Saddam's inner circle was planning to take him out and save us the trouble. According to one of my old Navy SEAL pals, the decision to launch tonight's strike was made in Washington after someone claimed to know that Saddam Hussein, several of his top military aides, and at least one of his sons had been seen entering the Dora command-and-control complex to spend the night.

The SEALs, Delta Force operators, and CIA paramilitary officers—some of them pulled out of Afghanistan—have been in and out of Iraq for months now trying to make contact with dissidents. According to those I talked to, they were generally unsuccessful, because Saddam's internal security apparatus, the *Amn Al Khass*, headed by his son Qusay, had all but eliminated internal opposition except among the Kurds in the far north.

Until now, the only indigenous intelligence sources available anywhere near Baghdad have been individuals loyal to Ahmad Chalabi, head of the Iraqi National Congress. And since Chalabi is a pariah at the State Department and the CIA, my SEAL and Delta contacts regarded it unlikely that the CIA would have been able to provide the Pentagon with the intelligence of Saddam's location for this first strike.

In the days leading up to the start of hostilities, Chalabi had arrived in the Kurdish mountain bastion of As Sulaymaniyah, Iraq, via Iran. From there, with protection provided by his own followers and a small handful of armed "civilians" on contract to the Pentagon, Chalabi has been granting interviews, making broadcasts into Baghdad, and generally planning to become Iraq's next leader. In my many meetings with him, he often told me that he intended to become the first democratically elected president of Iraq. If he does, it will be in spite of our State Department and CIA, not because of them.

The special operators who *would* talk about it believe that Chalabi, or one of his people, was the source of the Dora targeting information and that it was passed not to the CIA but directly to the Pentagon. When it got there, the CIA couldn't confirm or deny the information, but President Bush gave the go-ahead for the strike, since the command center was a legitimate military target.

In Qatar, U.S. Central Command quickly set aside plans to start the war twenty-four hours later and came up with a "double tap" plan, using a first wave of sea-launched Tomahawk cruise missiles, followed by USAF F-117A Nighthawk stealth aircraft armed with two-thousand-pound bunker buster EGBU-27 guided bombs steered to the precise location by GPS technology.

The Tomahawks launched by the USS *Milius*, USS *Donald Cook*, USS *Bunker Hill*, USS *Cowpens*, USS *Montpelier*, and USS *Cheyenne* hit first, knocking down aboveground structures. Then, the bunker buster bombs with delayed fuses designed to penetrate reinforced concrete rained down on the target.

Al Jazeera, the Arabic-language satellite television network that has been so supportive of Osama bin Laden, was on the air almost immediately showing ambulances and first aid workers removing dead and injured, and accusing the United States of killing innocent Iraqi civilians.

In the HMM-268 ready room, squadron pilots took time from laminating their flight charts and maps of Al Faw Peninsula to watch. They were staring at the Al Jazeera coverage when President Bush came on the air to address the nation.

✪ THE WHITE HOUSE
Washington, DC
Wednesday, 19 March 2003
2215 Hours Local

For the second time in as many days, Marines of all ranks are watching their commander in chief address their countrymen about war. They surround our tiny TV monitor and stare intently at the screen. But unlike the last time, they are no longer silent. When President Bush says that the "opening stages of what will be a broad and concerted campaign" to liberate Iraq has begun, someone in the group says, emphatically, "Finally!"

Shortly after the president concludes his remarks, the Iraqis issue a brief statement that "the enemies of God committed the stupidity of aggression against our homeland and our people," and call upon the Saddam *fedayeen* paramilitary volunteers to defend Iraq. Their commander, Uday Hussein, urges them to be ready to die as martyrs in destroying the American and British "invaders."

✪ TAA GIBRALTAR
Northern Kuwaiti Desert
Thursday, 20 March 2003
2000 Hours Local

The sun was just setting as the eight CH-46s from HMM-268 landed an hour ago at this remote British base just a few kilometers from the Iraqi border. Shortly after we touched down, dozens of other helicopters landed around us, until all that could be seen were helicopters—U.S. Marine CH-46s, CH-53s, UH1Ns, and Cobras, and a handful of British Pumas and CH-47s, all dispersed on the desert floor.

As we flew here, at twenty-five feet off the ground and 120 knots, from Ali Al Salem Air Base, the highways below us were crowded with convoys of military equipment, tanks, armored vehicles, artillery pieces, trucks, and Humvees all racing north toward the border with Iraq. Approaching our landing point, I could see up north of us batteries of 155mm howitzers deploying in firing order. The war has been "on" for fourteen hours, and yet for us it has been a strangely surreal day.

This morning, at about 0930 local, the "Great Giant Voice" announced that a missile raid was inbound and we once more raced for the shelters with our gas masks. Once again, Griff couldn't find his. About the time that the Patriot batteries opened fire on the incoming Iraqi missiles, he found it and came dashing into the bunker.

Deadly as it could be in a chemical weapons attack without it, Griff constantly losing his gas mask has become something of a joke within the squadron. So is a photo of Griff curled up asleep on a bench in the ready room, stuffed in a large yellow mailbag. One of the lieutenants took the picture early one freezing cold morning after we had decided that we were too tired to walk back down to the squadron billeting area. I had my poncho liner, but Griff had left his down at our tent. Thus the "U.S. Postal Service Issue sleeping bag."

We're not lacking any gear tonight. Right after the morning missile attack, we loaded all our cameras, satellite broadcast equipment, and personal paraphernalia aboard two of the CH-46s in preparation for tonight's mission—carrying the Royal Marines of Four Two Commando in a heloborne assault on Al Faw Peninsula. HMM-268 will be the first birds in the assault, with the squadron commander, Lt. Col. Jerry Driscoll, flying lead for two four-plane divisions full of troops.

While we wait for the signal to lift from Ali Al Salem, we all gather once again around our little TV and learn that the United States and Great Britain had increased their security alert status in anticipation of terrorist attacks, and that in the U.S., the Department of Homeland Security had increased its terrorism alert level to orange, the second-highest level. Americans overseas were warned of possible terror attacks in retaliation for the start of war against Iraq.

While British Tornado jets roared past us loaded with bombs to soften up Iraqi defenses in our landing zones, the news from the United States was all about the Department of the Treasury freezing all nondiplomatic Iraqi government funds that were on deposit in the United States and urging all other governments to do the same with Iraqi funds deposited in their countries' banks.

After hearing this piece of news, one of the pilots sitting on the ground beside me commented, "Gee, I'm sure glad we didn't forget that item on the checklist. I wouldn't want to get shot at by some Iraqi anti-aircraft gunner who hadn't had his assets frozen."

✪ ✪ ✪

It is now dark—except for some oil well fires burning to our north. Through my NVGs I can see the British Royal Marines who will be riding into combat with us within a few hours. Our "stick" of eight men is sitting on the ground just aft of the lowered helicopter ramp, resting on their rucksacks talking quietly. I crawl up on one of the stub wings to eat an MRE, drink some water, say a quiet prayer for safety, and catch a little nap before the final briefing and the assault. I've learned in five prior gunfights—Vietnam, Central America, Beirut, Tehran, and Afghanistan—that you had better eat, drink, sleep, and pray when you can, because once the shooting starts, you may not have time to do any of them.

But unusual for me, sleep won't come. Instead, the words of President Bush to those gathered here on the desert floor keep going through my mind: "The peace of a troubled world and the hopes of an oppressed people now depend on you." The words themselves did not convey a particular sense of foreboding, yet something keeps me awake. I climb back off the bird and go inside the aircraft to get the Bible I carry in my pack—not knowing that within hours, twelve of the men around me will be dead—the first American and British casualties of Operation Iraqi Freedom.

CHAPTER FOUR
HELICOPTER DOWN!

★ OPERATION IRAQI FREEDOM SIT REP #10
TAA Gibraltar, Vic Iraqi-Kuwaiti Border
Friday, 21 March 2003
0300 Hours Local

The silence immediately around us is almost eerie. But now that the last of more than fifty helicopters has landed and shut down, the sound of 155mm artillery and multiple rocket launchers can be heard firing off in the distance. With darkness settled in around us, the flash of the guns and occasionally the arc of rocket-assisted projectiles (RAP rounds) can be seen on the horizon. Lying or sitting on the ground, one can feel the concussions, which prompts one of the British Royal Marines to comment, "Pity the poor bloke who's on the receiving end of that."

One of his less experienced mates asks no one in particular, "Is that ours or theirs?"

When no one responds I reply, "It's ours. That's the 11th Marines, firing a Regimental TOT [time on target] on Safwan Hill, clearing the way for the 5th and 7th Marines to cross the berm into Iraq."

Safwan Hill is a pile of sandstone that dominates the terrain just north of the Iraqi-Kuwaiti border. It appears on the aviation chart I'm carrying simply as "466" but it is believed to be an Iraqi observation post. From the hill, just west of the Iraqi border town of Safwan, the Iraqi army can undoubtedly observe and bring fire to bear on any of the 1st Marine Division's 22,000 troops and several thousand combat vehicles as they break through the berm along the demilitarized zone on the attack north.

According to the scuttlebutt among the troops, Maj. Gen. James Mattis, the division commander, has ordered that the hill be "a foot shorter" before the first Marine crosses into Iraq. The 11th Marines' artillery and strike aircraft from Navy carriers in the Persian Gulf and Ahmed Al Jaber Air Base in Kuwait are trying to comply by dumping tons of high explosives on the target.

Before combat operations commenced, Mattis; his boss, Lt. Gen. James Conway, the commander of I-MEF; and Maj. Gen. Jim Amos, commanding the 3rd Marine Aircraft Wing (Reinforced) all issued guidance to those they were leading into battle. Copies of the 1st Marine Division commander's eloquent message were widely distributed to all hands:

· · ·

For decades, Saddam Hussein has tortured, imprisoned, raped, and murdered the Iraqi people; invaded neighboring countries without provocation; and threatened the world with weapons of mass destruction. The time has come to end his reign of terror. On your young shoulders rests the hope of mankind.

When I give you the word, together we will cross the Line of Departure, close with those forces that choose to fight, and destroy them. Our fight is not with the Iraqi people, nor is it with members of the Iraqi army who choose to surrender. While we will move swiftly and aggressively against those who resist, we will treat all others with decency, demonstrating chivalry and soldierly compassion for people who have endured a lifetime under Saddam's oppression.

Chemical attack, treachery, and use of the innocent as human shields can be expected, as can other unethical tactics . . . Be the hunter—not the hunted. Never be caught with your guard down. Use good judgment and act in the best interest of our nation.

You are part of the world's most feared and trusted fighting force. Engage your brain before you engage your weapon. Share your courage with each other as we enter Iraq. Keep faith in your comrades to your left and right and in the Marine Air overhead.

For the mission's sake, for our country's sake, and the sake of the men who carried the Division's colors in past battles—"who fought for life and never lost their nerve"—carry out your mission and keep your honor clean. Demonstrate to the world there is "No Better Friend—No Worse Enemy" than a U.S. Marine.

· · ·

At the MAG-39 Forward Ops Center, set up beside a UH1N about 150 yards behind our helicopter, one of the communicators confirms that all is going according to the modified plan, even though the H-hour for the ground attack had to be advanced twelve hours because of the unscheduled "decapitation" strike on the Dora Command Center. Until March 19, Gen. Franks's plan of attack had called for a simultaneous air and ground strike, designed to deceive the Iraqis who were anticipating another prolonged air assault like the thirty-eight-day bombardment that had preceded the ground attack during Operation Desert Storm in 1991. Officers at CENTCOM had taken to talking openly about the "shock and awe" of an air campaign as though it would go on for days before any ground troops crossed the border.

Instead, Franks had agreed that coincident air and ground attacks would take place just before dawn on March 21. But once Baghdad had been hit, waiting longer for the ground attack seemed to the Marines like an invitation for Saddam loyalists to start destroying the country's oil infrastructure. So at 2030 hours local, on March 20, RCT-5 (Regimental Combat Team) was given the order to blast through the berm west of Safwan and head north, making it the first ground combat unit to put "boots on the ground" inside Iraq.

It wasn't, however, the first contact with the enemy. Earlier in the afternoon, at about 1600 hours local, elements of the 3rd Light Armored Reconnaissance (3rd LAR) Battalion, serving as a screening force for RCT-7, had engaged several Iraqi APCs south of the Iraqi-Kuwaiti border. FOX News Channel correspondent Rick Leventhal, embedded with the 3rd LAR, reported that the Marine LAV 25s had promptly dispatched the enemy vehicles using TOW anti-tank missiles and the 25mm chain guns mounted on the LAVs.

Now the big guns have fallen silent. In the darkness, all but invisible from less than three kilometers away, there is the sound of hundreds of armored vehicles and trucks, moving without lights, echoing across the desert as RCT-7 moves up for the attack. The first mission for RCT-5 and RCT-7 is to drive straight past Safwan, and north to seize the vital Rumaylah oil fields, gas-oil separation plants (GOSPs), and pumping stations near Az Zubayr before the Iraqis can destroy them.

A slight wind has come up, blowing a light cloud of dust and smoke our way as the word comes down to "saddle up" and launch. While the Royal Marines gather their gear and start boarding their assigned helicopters, Griff and I shake hands and we each head to our respective aircraft to grab our cameras so that we can start recording this first assault deep into Iraq.

After discussing the matter with Lt. Col. Driscoll and Maj. Chris Charleville, the HMM-268 Operations Officer, we have agreed that Griff and I will fly on different birds. By doing so, we'll minimize interference with ground combat element load plans, and spread out the weight/space requirements for our satellite equipment and camera gear. But there is another reason for splitting up our two-man team that no one mentions: if a bird goes down, we can be reasonably sure that half of our videotape and one of us will survive to tell the story.

Ten commandos, including the Royal Marine Battalion commander, all carrying heavy packs and weapons, cram themselves into my aircraft. Many of these Brits have seen action before—some of them in the Falklands back in 1981, others in Northern Ireland, Gulf War I, Bosnia, and Kosovo—and some of the oldest have served in all of these difficult and dangerous places. But tonight's mission may well be their toughest. If all goes as planned, this lightly armed infantry battalion will disembark north of Basra, Iraq's second largest city, and establish a blocking position. Their goal: to keep enemy reinforcements from reaching the Basra garrison—believed to be elements of the Iraqi 51st Mechanized Division and a Republican Guard regiment.

Other elements of the British 3rd Commando Brigade and the American 15th Marine Expeditionary Unit (MEU) are to capture the oil port at Umm Qasr, just across the Kuwaiti border about thirty miles south of Basra, while Navy SEALs, Royal Marines, and British Special Ops units coming in from the Persian Gulf seize the oil terminals at Ma'amir and Al Faw. This complicated, high-speed endeavor is aimed at preventing the destruction of Iraq's wells and infrastructure and the kind of catastrophe Saddam wreaked on Kuwait and the waters of the Persian Gulf back in 1991.

As Gunnery Sgt. Pennington checks the troops to make sure that they are all strapped in, I climb through the forward personnel door, grab my tiny Sony Digital Pro camera with its night-vision lens, and fasten a gunner's belt around my flak jacket, high on my chest. With the gunner's belt tethered to a tie down on the deck of the helicopter, I can move about inside the troop compartment and still step forward into the cockpit between the pilot and copilot or even lean out the right side personnel door hatch, just forward of the .50-caliber mount. To ensure that I can hear and record radio and intercom communications, Pennington has rigged up a "cranial" helmet for me and hooked it into the aircraft communications system.

Lt. Col. Jerry Driscoll is in the cockpit with Capt. Aaron Eckerberg, his copilot, running down the preflight checklist just as though we were about to take a training flight at Camp Pendleton. I hear the electronic ping of the Singars encryption system as each of the other birds in our flight "checks in" with Driscoll, confirming that they are "ready to turn"—that is, prepared to start their engines and lift off for Iraq. I hear a bird in our flight—I don't catch which one—call in to inform that Griff, using his newly acquired nickname, "Mailbag," is aboard with his gear. All is ready.

Then, before the engines are started, another call over the radio: Navy SEALs and British Special Boat Service operators in the vicinity of our insert LZ are in contact with enemy troops. An AC-130 gunship and USAF A-10s are being called in to "soften up" the zone and take out enemy anti-aircraft batteries nearby. And so we wait. After about thirty minutes I notice that despite the tension, Pennington is following North's Rule of "sleep when you can." Sitting on the floor, leaning back against a case of .50-caliber ammo, he's the picture of absolute confidence—and fast asleep.

Finally, shortly after 0200, the terse message comes over the radio from Col. Rich Spencer, the MAG-39 CO, "We're good to go. Godspeed, gentlemen." The largest night heloborne assault in history is now underway.

The whine of the APUs (auxiliary power unit) on the rear of the birds is soon overwhelmed by the sound of more than one hundred engines and rotors turning. In front of us, total darkness. As we lift off, out the side of the bird my camera catches the plume of dust as we rise into the darkness. Inside, the Royal Marines insert magazines in their weapons and chamber a round. Pennington and Cpl. Nathan Kendall, the left-side .50-caliber gunner, lock and load their machine guns with belts of ammo as we head for the border at more than one hundred knots (about 115 mph) and less than fifty feet above ground.

My videotape of the assault lift shows that initially visibility is fairly clear as we proceed north toward Iraq, though there are increasing amounts of dust in the air, and occasionally I have to flip my NVGs up because the fires from several burning oil wells cause them to "flare" and temporarily blind me. I can clearly see the other three birds, flying close behind us, no more than five or ten rotor widths away, carrying elements of the Battalion Command Group. All four helicopters are supposed to land in the same zone to disgorge their passengers. The next four birds, trailing a mile or so behind us, will land in the assault LZ after we take off. As I aim the camera back into our troop compartment, only the eyes of the Royal Marines' camouflage-painted faces show clearly through my night-vision lens.

Seconds later, when I turn to "shoot" again out the open hatch, the sky has suddenly turned hazy. The ground below, whipping by at more than one hundred knots, is still visible through my NVGs, but out in front of us a local sandstorm—a miniature *sharqi*—has reduced forward visibility to just a few yards. The windblown dust, perhaps created by the firing on Safwan Hill, or the movement of thousands of our armored vehicles off to our west, has mixed with the smoke from a handful of burning oil wells, obliterating the sky. Through my NVGs, the air around us appears to be filled with "pixie dust"—as though looking through the frosted glass inside a light bulb. As we approach the border, the highway that was built in more peaceful times to connect Basra with Kuwait City is just visible below us. I'm musing about seeing a car drive beneath us when I hear Driscoll say over the intercom, "Power lines ahead. We're pulling up to go over. Gunny, give me a 'clear' when we're past."

I step back inside as we pull up so that Pennington can stick his head out the open hatch. When we pass over the lines, I hear him yell "Clear!" over the noise. And then, as the bird starts to descend again, there is an urgent call over the secure radio: "Dash Three, Dash Four, pull up! Pull up!"

Suddenly, there is a blinding flash on the left side and slightly below our helicopter. Though our bird never wavers on its course, up in the cockpit, Lt. Col. Driscoll is instantly on the intercom and the radio: "What was that?"

Pennington responds first, his voice flat, coming through the lip mike: "Dash Three has gone down, sir."

There is a moment of silence while the magnitude of what's just happened sinks in. My camera, pointed over the port side .50-caliber machine gun, captures the terrible fireball. I know the answer even before Driscoll comes up on the radio and asks the question "Any survivors?"

"Dash One, this is Dash Four. Negative. No way."

Driscoll calls out on the secure Search and Rescue net anyway: "Helicopter down..." and then the grid coordinates from his GPS. "Request you launch the TRAP [Tactical Recovery of Aircraft and Pilot] mission to that location."

Within seconds of the crash, everyone on our helo has figured out what happened, though no one knows what brought Dash Three down. I can sense the stunned reaction, even though it is impossible to hear anything over the roar of the engines and rotors other than what comes through my earphones.

The Royal Marine Battalion commander unfastens his seat belt, comes forward, and sticks his head into the cockpit. He and Driscoll confer for a few moments and then he backs out and stands upright, a tiny flashlight in his hand. Standing right next to me, he flips through the pages of a small notebook until he finds the list of those who were manifested on Dash Three. He shakes his head and says, just loud enough for me to hear, "War's bloody awful. Those poor lads." And then, looking back toward his Marines, he shouts, "We're pressing on!"

But we can't. In just a matter of a few miles and a few minutes, the weather and visibility detiorate considerably. The AC-130 working over our insert LZ reports heavy anti-aircraft fire and that the approach to our zone is obscured by ground fog, dust, and smoke from the oil fires. All this is being monitored by I-MEF HQ and the MAG-39 Air Ops Center. After several minutes of radio chatter, the command "Abort the mission," is broadcast to all the aircraft. The decision has been made well up the chain of command to wait until after first light and to try again when the weather and visibility are better.

Now, with more than fifty helicopters in the air, the challenge becomes getting them all safely back to where we started without bumping into one another in the haze.

Driscoll calls the battalion commander back up into the cockpit to inform him of the decision that has just come down. As the Royal Marine lieutenant colonel backs out and heads back to his troop seat, he is clearly agitated.

Our route back to the pickup zone in Kuwait takes us back over the still-burning wreckage of Dash Three. As all aboard crane their necks to see what they can through the portholes, a thought suddenly comes to me: *Was Griff on Dash Two or Dash Three?*

By the time we make it back to our landing point, it's nearly 0400 and I have all but convinced myself that Griff had boarded Dash

Two—the helicopter that had been parked about twenty meters to our right side when we took off for the assault. As soon as the commandos have disembarked and our bird shuts down, I run over to the helo parked to our right and ask the crew chief if Griff is aboard.

When he replies, "No, sir," adrenaline surges through my gut, and I have immediate remorse. *How am I going tell his lovely wife, Kathleen, and daughter, Madeline, that Griff has been killed?*

Overwhelmed with dread, I run over to several other birds as they land, but there is still no sign of Griff. He's been my producer for more than eight years and I'm sick at the thought that he is lying dead in the wreckage of Dash Three. Wearing my NVGs, I make my way back to my helicopter, but the pilots are gone, summoned to a briefing with the MAG-39 CO. Pennington is on top of our bird, checking things out with a small flashlight held in his teeth. When he climbs down and puts his NVGs back down, I ask him, "Do we know yet who was aboard the bird that went down?"

"Yes, but you can't report it until we notify next of kin," he replies. And then he continues, "Major Aubin and I came to 268 from MAWTS [Marine Aviation Weapons and Tactics Squadron]. He and Captain Beaupre were two of the best pilots I know. And Staff Sergeant Waters-Bey and Corporal Kennedy both really knew their stuff. They were all really good men. You know that, you've flown with all of 'em."

"What about the PAX?" I ask, not wanting to say Griff's name.

"There seems to be some kind of mix-up on the manifest," he responds. "Apparently the troop list only shows seven PAX, but before takeoff, Major Aubin reported 'twelve souls on board.' That means there were eight in back, in addition to the crew. The Brits are checking."

This confirms my worst suspicions and I say, "Oh Lord, then Griff must have been the eighth person aboard. How can I get out to where the bird went down?"

"I'll check" he replies and then adds, "I'm sorry, Colonel."

As I'm boarding our bird to await word on how I can get to the wreckage, and silently praying, *Dear Lord, please let Griff be alive*, my satellite pager goes off. It's the FOX News Channel foreign desk in New York. I dial the number in Manhattan on my Iridium sat-phone, identify myself, and am informed that CBS has just run a story that there has been a helicopter crash with sixteen American and British casualties—and do I know anything about it.

I reply, "Yes. I saw it happen and I have it on tape, but there is uncertainty about how many were aboard, and my field producer Griff Jenkins may be among them. Please don't make any announcements about this until I can get confirmation. I'll call you as soon as I have more."

As I put the phone back in my flak jacket pocket, a civilian pickup truck, driven by Capt. Frank Laemmle, one of the HMM-268 squadron pilots, pulls up next to our bird. He's been here since yesterday, helping to run the pickup zone and serving as a liaison with the British. He asks if the MAG-39 Operations officers can look at my videotape to see if it might help them figure out what happened to Dash Three.

We ride together in the cab of the truck to where the pilots have gathered next to Col. Spencer's UH1N and I play the tape for them to see. One of the assistant operations officers asks if they can have a copy of the tape to take back to Ali Al Salem Air Base for use in the investigation of what brought Dash Three down. Since I have no way of transmitting what's on the cassette to New York from out here anyway, and because what's in my camera can't air until the next of kin of the casualties are notified, I agree.

As I turn to reboard the truck for a ride back to my bird, I see, through my NVGs, Gunny Pennington walking up. He says, "Look who I found!" and steps aside to reveal Griff.

To the surprise of everyone except Pennington, I yell, "Thank God!" and grab Jenkins around the neck, giving him a big hug.

Clearly confused by my embrace, he gives me one in return and then explains, "When we came back after turning around, there was too much dust, so Dash Two had to land way on the other side of the zone rather than next to you, where we belonged."

Instead of riding in the truck, we walk back to the helicopter where my gear is stowed. I'm immensely glad to see him and tell him about my up-and-down emotional uncertainty about whether he had been aboard Dash Three.

When we arrive back at the bird, I call New York and tell the FOX News Channel foreign desk duty officer with great relief that I've found Griff alive and well, and that I've been asked to make a copy of our tape and not to air what's on it until the NOK notification is complete. I then tell him that four U.S. Marines are confirmed dead and eight British commandos are believed to have been killed when Dash Three went down.

It is nearly dawn. Without sleep for more than twenty-four hours, I'm consumed with several overwhelming emotions: great joy that Griff is safe, but also a feeling of sadness and guilt that I was grateful that he had survived while others did not, and the sense of profound sorrow I've had every time I see Marines lose their lives. War truly is the most horrible of human endeavors.

✪ OPERATION IRAQI FREEDOM SIT REP #11
HMM-268 Forward Operating Base
Ali Al Salem Air Base, Kuwait
Friday, 21 March 2003
2000 Hours Local

With first light, the weather over the Basra LZs improves considerably, allowing the helicopter assault, aborted the night before, to be carried out. But by then the seven remaining HMM-268 helicopters have returned to base, replaced by British Pumas and CH-47s. The MAG-39 S-1 has already prepared the usual terse official casualty report for release after the Marines Corps had personally notified the families of those killed:

> On 21 March at approximately 0200 local, Major Jay Thomas Aubin, 36, of Waterville, Maine; Captain Ryan Anthony Beaupre, 30, from St. Anne, Illinois; Staff Sergeant Kendall Damon Waters-Bey, 29, of Baltimore, Maryland; and Corporal Brian Matthew Kennedy, 25, from Houston, Texas, were killed when their CH-46 helicopter crashed in Kuwait while carrying out combat operations in Operation Iraqi Freedom.

The British Marines, already heavily engaged north of Basra, are unable to confirm who was aboard the ill-fated helicopter for more than forty-eight hours, and when they do, CENTCOM adds the names of the British commandos killed in the crash:

> Major Jason Ward, Captain Philip Stuart Guy, Warrant Officer Mark Stratford, Color Sergeant John Cecil, Operations Mechanic Second Class Ian Seymour, Lance Bombardier Llewelyn Karl Evans, and Marine Sholto Hedenskog.

By 1000 an investigation into the cause of the crash is already under way. After a few hours of rest, Lt. Col. Driscoll summons his pilots and then his aircrews to brief them on the crash—and rally them for the day's missions: four aircraft assigned as cas-evac, for 5th Marines, four more birds on ready alert for other emergency missions, and the remaining three into maintenance.

A few minutes before 1100, the "Great Giant Voice" sounds the alarm and everyone heads for the bunkers. For the Marines, donning a gas mask, pulling on the chemical protective suit, and finding a seat inside the sandbag-covered concrete is now getting to be old hat.

When the Patriot battery to our west opens fire with two loud concussions, nobody even flinches. Near the entrance, two Marine NCOs are playing cards. Several others are reading paperback books through the "bug-eye" lenses of their gas masks. Even Griff is getting the hang of this now. He's not only better about keeping his gas mask with him, but I notice that when the "All clear" is finally sounded, he's fast asleep.

While I'm on the air a few minutes past noon—it's 0505 in the eastern U.S.—the squadron receives a "tasking" from the Direct Air Support Center (DASC) to position two helicopters forward, because both 5th and 7th Marines are in heavy contact with elements of the Iraqi 51st Mechanized Division, where casualties are expected.

Griff and I break down our gear and head up to the flight line with Maj. John Graham, the squadron XO. Lt. Col. Driscoll had intended to fly the mission, but his MAG-39 and 3rd MAW (Marine Aircraft Wing) superiors wanted him to remain in Kuwait to be available for next-of-kin notifications and the investigation into last night's crash.

Just before Griff and I depart for the flight line, I find Jerry Driscoll alone in the rear of the ready room tent, drafting the most difficult correspondence anyone ever has to write: letters from a commander to the relatives of his dead Marines. Having had to write such missives myself, I know exactly how he feels. The burden of command is never heavier than at a time such as this.

The flight north to where the 5th Marines are engaged is unremarkable. Flying a CH-46 at thirty to fifty feet over the desert at better than one hundred knots is certainly challenging to the pilot and copilot. At that altitude and speed, the ground—and therefore death—is less than a second away. That reminder comes, no doubt, on the heels of the Dash Three crash. But for those in the back of the aircraft, it is tedium—reminding me of the old adage that "war is 95 percent boredom and 5 percent stark terror."

As we whip over the trackless desert that is southern Iraq, we can see large herds of camels, an occasional dried-up irrigation ditch, the heat rising in ripples out in front of us, and little else. There is not a tree or an oasis of any kind in sight. I'm glad I packed my GPS and topped off my water before we left.

After a half an hour or so, off to our right—east of our flight path—the smoke and flame from three of the seven oil well heads that Saddam loyalists succeeded in blowing up become visible. And then the call from the 5th Marines air officer—call sign "Fingers." They have two emergency and one priority cas-evacs. He transmits the grid coordinates over the secure radio, and after Maj. Graham enters them into the helicopter's GPS navigation system, we alter our course to make the pickup.

As we make our approach, I can see up ahead what appears to be several small dwellings and, inside a chain-link fence, an oil installation. It's one of the GOSPs that were the initial D-day objectives for the 5th and 7th Marines.

A radio call to the unit on the ground confirms that we're at the right place, but the voice on the ground informs that "the zone isn't hot, but it isn't cold either." Leaning out the hatch with my camera running, I see a green smoke grenade go off marking the landing point and showing the wind direction. The officer or NCO running this zone knows what he's doing.

The LZ is surrounded by several LVTs and armed Humvees. When we get closer, I notice that there is no one up and walking around. The Marines are all prone or crouched while manning the .50-caliber, 240-Golf machine guns, or TOWs on the Humvees. The "up guns"—coaxial-mounted 40mm grenade launchers atop the LVT turrets—are all aimed outside the little perimeter.

As the two birds touch down on the dirt roadway, Marines rush toward us carrying three litters. Two are loaded aboard our helicopter;

one is placed aboard Griff's bird behind us. Following instructions not to broadcast the identity of wounded or dead combatants from either side, I allow my camera lens to catch only the faces of the litter bearers as they run on and off the bird.

They are nearly all very young. Wearing their chemical protective suits, flak jackets, and Kevlar helmets, they are sweating profusely. As the litters holding the casualties are strapped in, Maj. Graham tells Cpl. Mireles, our crew chief, to give the litter bearers several boxes of our bottled water to take back with them.

Our two shock-trauma medical corpsmen start treating the wounded even before we take off, and it's only then that one of the docs notices that one of the two casualties, wrapped in a foil-lined shock blanket, isn't a Marine—it's a severely burned eleven- or twelve-year-old Iraqi girl, and her devastating injuries appear to be several days old.

A radio call to the unit on the ground confirms that the child was brought to the Marines by a relative and that she had been burned in a cooking fuel accident before the war even started. The girl's parents begged the Marine unit that captured the GOSP for help and they decided to load her on our bird with their wounded because there was nothing more that could be done for her in the field.

Unfortunately, there is very little that the docs aboard our helo can do for her either. Kuwait refuses to allow any Iraqi prisoners or wounded—civilian or military—into their territory. Maj. Graham makes a command decision to take the burned girl out to the hospital ship USS *Saipan* in the Persian Gulf and he files a flight plan to do so.

But as we head southeast for the Gulf, DASC calls up on the radio and asks if the two helicopters have life rafts aboard. They don't. Everything that's not essential to our mission has been stripped from the ancient birds to remove weight. We weren't supposed to be operating anywhere near water so we don't even have life vests aboard.

Maj. Graham is now faced with a terrible dilemma: return the child to where we picked her up or take her and the other casualties out to sea in hopes that she can be saved. He asks over the intercom how we in the back feel about flying over water without flotation gear. We all agree—"Go for it."

Half an hour later we're aboard the USS *Saipan*, an amphibious assault ship that I have been on many times before. She has a full hospital aboard and all that's needed to treat the severest of wounds.

While the birds refuel, Griff is given a tour of the ship, and the crew gives us as much cold water and freshly baked cookies as we can carry. Just before dark we return to the flight line at Ali Al Salem Air Base.

✪ HMM-268 READY ROOM, MAG-39
   Ali Al Salem Air Base, Kuwait
   Friday, 21 March 2003
   2300 Hours Local

Griff and I are preparing for a live feed for the 5 p.m. (EST) FOX News Channel broadcast and have our satellite transceiver set up outside the squadron ready room tent. And finally, as the first full day of war comes to an end, we have a chance to get a clear picture of what's been happening.

CENTCOM headquarters in Qatar reports that the Iraqi 51st Mechanized Division has collapsed, yielding more than eight thousand enemy prisoners of war, and for the first time an Iraqi division commander and his deputy have personally surrendered. On the far right, the British 7th Armoured Division is on the outskirts of Basra. The U.S. Marines' RCT-7 has captured all of the crucial oil infrastructure targets in the vicinity of Az Zubayr, and 3rd Battalion, 7th Marines along with a company from 1st Tank Battalion have subdued Safwan. Farther west, RCT-5 has seized all of their objectives intact, including the six major GOSPs and the Ar Rumaylah oil fields. And on the far-left flank of the I-MEF advance, RCT-1 has raced more than fifty kilometers across the desert and is already just south of Jalibah.

As before, dozens of Marines of all ranks are gathered around us to watch huge explosions rock the enemy capital on our TV. When FOX newsman David Asman, whose son is serving with Task Force (TF) Tarawa, informs us that the Army's 3rd Infantry Division has advanced sixty miles into Iraq, there are cheers. The only bad news: Two more U.S. Marines—a second lieutenant with the 1st Battalion, 5th Marines and a corporal from 2nd Battalion, 1st Marines—have been killed in action. And there is one other unpleasant item: The missiles missed. Saddam is still alive.

CHAPTER FIVE

RUNNING THE GAUNTLET ON BLOODY SUNDAY

✪ OPERATION IRAQI FREEDOM SIT REP #12
RCT-5 Command Post
10 km north of Ur, Iraq, south of the Euphrates River
Saturday, 22 March 2003
2300 Hours Local

It's been a very long day for the pilots, aircrews, and medical corpsmen of HMM-268. Our two birds have now been "on station" for more than twenty-four hours, and these guys have been flying for most of it. The pilots have taken to napping in the cockpits while the rest of us—crew chiefs, gunners, corpsmen, and the two-man FOX News Channel team—doze on the troop seats and litters in the back of the helicopters, catching sleep in brief snatches.

Our two haze-gray CH-46 helicopters are parked directly behind the 5th Marines Regimental Command Post, a hastily erected tent and camouflage net thrown up over two back-to-back LVTC-7s (Landing Vehicle, Tracked, Command). This is Col. Joe Dunford's "Alpha" Command Group. A mirror-image "Bravo" Command Group is leapfrogging ahead of us with the lead battalions of RCT-5. Once

"Bravo" finds a good site, Col. Dunford will displace forward. He has moved his CP five times in the last twenty-four hours as the 5th Marines roared up Route 8 and then up Route 1, past the recently discovered ancient ruins of Ur—the birthplace of Abraham. But we didn't take the time to visit.

Throughout the last twenty-four hours, contact with the enemy has been remarkably light, as have the friendly casualties. It's pretty clear that the speed at which the 1st Marine Expeditionary Force is moving has taken the Iraqis very much by surprise. Though we've had a lot of cas-evac missions, they have all been routine, many for wounded Iraqi EPWs (enemy prisoners of war). Best of all, none of the zones have been "hot."

Alongside the highway, there are scores of oil-filled ditches, called "flame trenches." Apparently the Iraqis abandoned their positions before these could be set afire, since only a few have been blazing, spewing black smoke into the sky as we fly over or drive by in the Marine convoys. There are also hundreds of revetments for armored vehicles that the Iraqis had dug with bulldozers—nearly all of which are empty. In places where they did succeed in placing a tank or armored vehicle in a revetment, the enemy equipment is now a smoldering wreck, hit by F-18s, AV-8s, Cobra Gunships, or in some cases by fire from Marine M-1 Abrams tanks or the 25mm Bushmasters on their LAVs.

It's now becoming a ritual: Every time we land, even if for a few minutes, day or night, Griff and I rush out the back of our respective helicopters to find a Humvee, truck, tank, or armored vehicle to set up and plug in our equipment. With the help of a crusty Marine master sergeant, "Comms Chief," we have jury-rigged a power inverter—that converts 24 volt DC to 110 volt, 60 cycle, AC—through a "pigtail" plug so that we can connect to almost any Marine vehicle and power our broadcast equipment.

While one of us sets up the satellite antenna and hooks up the power, the other positions the camera and connects it to the audio-video link on the satellite transceiver. And instantly we're surrounded by Marines of every rank who are hungry for news of what's happening elsewhere in the war—waiting to catch a glimpse of our FOX News Channel satellite feed on the small monitor.

They aren't alone. A correspondent embedded with a combat unit has anything but the "big picture" of what's going on in the war. That perspective may be possible for reporters at a major headquarters facility like CENTCOM, I-MEF, or the U.S. Army's V Corps, but in a ground combat unit or a front-line helicopter squadron, one sees only a very narrow slice of the war. What's happening just a few miles away might as well be in another solar system. Other than occasional opportunities to stick my head inside the CP tent and look at the operations map or sit in on a commander's briefing, my best sources of information on how the war is going elsewhere are the live reports from other embedded correspondents. While we wait to go on the air, Griff and I watch, just like the Marines, as FOX News Channel correspondents Greg Kelly, with the 3rd Infantry Division, and Rick Leventhal, embedded with the 3rd Light Armored Reconnaissance Battalion, describe what's happening with their units.

That's how we learn that the 3rd Infantry Division has been racing through the desert—well off to our west—spearheading the main attack for the U.S. Army's V Corps. Supported from the air by USAF B-2s, B-52s, F-117s, A-10s, F-15s, F-16s, and their own Apache attack helicopters, the 3rd Infantry Division is aiming straight for the southern approaches to Baghdad and pressing hard against Saddam's Republican Guard Medina division.

But earlier this evening, a raid by thirty-two Apaches of the 11th Attack Helicopter Regiment went seriously awry. Dispatched after dark to attack elements of the Medina division, the Apaches ran into a terrible barrage of anti-aircraft and small-arms fire that damaged nearly every aircraft participating in the attack. Worst of all, the Iraqis managed to capture one of the downed aircrews.

While Greg Kelly's reports give us an idea of how things are going with the U.S. Army drive off to the west, Rick Leventhal, our FOX News Channel correspondent with the Marines' 3rd Light Armored Reconnaissance Battalion, has been filling in the gaps on what we know about the rest of I-MEF Supporting Attack. Once Iraq's southern oil fields, GOSPs, and distribution facilities were secured, the primary mission for 1st, 5th, and 7th Regimental Combat Teams and Task Force Tarawa was to threaten Baghdad from the southeast. Thus far there has been far less opposition than expected.

Before dawn, the sixty-thousand-strong Marine Air-Ground Task Force completes its first task of the war—securing Iraq's crucial oil infrastructure in the south. The British 3rd Commando Brigade is now in control of the waterborne approaches to Basra, and the British 7th Armored Division and 16th Air Assault Brigade have successfully isolated Basra from the north.

By first light this morning, all three of the 1st Marine Division's Regimental Combat Teams—the 1st, 5th, and 7th—have reoriented themselves and are on the move to accomplish their second objective: closing as fast as possible on Baghdad's eastern approaches. Moving with them is Task Force Tarawa, a Marine Expeditionary Brigade built around the 2nd Marine Regiment from Camp Lejeune, North Carolina. As soon as the Iraqi oil infrastructure is secured, TF Tarawa charges across the desert to seize the Iraqi air force base at Jalibah.

By the time darkness obscures the dust raised by thousands of constantly moving Marine vehicles, TF Tarawa is just outside the Shi'ite holy city of An Nasiriyah—a critical road junction and crossing point on the Euphrates. Further to the west, RCT-1 had driven hard across the desert and closed up on RCT-5 and RCT-7, which are spread out along Route 1 and farther south on Route 8.

As soon as the air base at Jalibah is in U.S. hands, the 3rd Marine Air Wing establishes a Forward Arming and Refueling Point (FARP) on the roadside, turning highways into runways, and begins cycling in C-130s loaded with fuel, ordnance, and equipment. Nearby, an Army shock-trauma hospital has been erected in a matter of hours to provide immediate lifesaving surgery for the severely wounded. FARPs are being built all along the route to Baghdad, and the Marines are naming them after America's Major League Baseball parks.

Just before nightfall this evening I fly on an "armed recon" back down Route 1 aboard a UH1N from HMLA-267. The pilots have been told to reconnoiter out along the flanks of the two I-MEF columns and look for signs of enemy activity. As my camera rolls on the Cobra gunships escorting our flight back to the RCT-5 CP, I can see below us an awesome sight: tens of thousands of I-MEF troops, weapons, and vehicles poised for a two-pronged attack to the northwest.

Columns of RCT-1 and TF Tarawa armor stretch north from the intersection of Routes 1, 7, and 8 to nearly the outskirts of An Nasiriyah. Farther east, RCT-5 and RCT-7 are lined up prepared for their push up Route 1.

As far as we can see, the desert floor is covered with U.S. and British troops and military equipment. The breathtaking array of tanks, light armored vehicles, trucks, amphibious assault vehicles, Humvees, artillery pieces, rocket launchers, portable bridging, and engineer equipment goes on as far as the eye can see. But other than a handful of wrecked Iraqi tanks and armored vehicles and a few flaming oil trenches with plumes of black smoke belching into the sky, there is no sign of the enemy—as we will duly report on our return.

Shortly after dark we get the word that the general commanding the Iraqi 51st Mechanized Division and his deputy walked up to some Marines in an AAV (Amphibious Assault Vehicle) and surrendered. Their division of Iraqi Shi'ite and Kurdish conscripts had vanished and the division simply ceased to exist—thus explaining the absence of enemy activity in the immediate area.

Hopeful that we won't have to move again before dawn, Griff and I wolf down an MRE and set up our equipment in the dark, preparing for our nightly "hit" on *Hannity & Colmes*. As usual, once the tiny video transceiver locks into New York's signal, those who want to catch up on the war news surround us.

For those of us watching from Iraq, there is a telling difference between the reports coming from embedded journalists over here and the armchair admirals, barroom brigadiers, and sound-bite "special forces" pontificating about the war from New York, Atlanta, Washington, and London. The journalists traveling with the coalition forces seem to be presenting a straightforward account of what's been happening—though many seem honestly amazed at how good the American soldiers, sailors, and Marines are at the work of war.

Thus far, the embedded reporters I've seen have been emphasizing the military prowess of the coalition forces, the pinpoint accuracy of the precision-guided bombs and missiles, and the minimal casualties and collateral damage inflicted upon Iraqi civilians. Several of the embedded journalists seem genuinely surprised at the humanity and compassion of coalition troops who go out of their way—often at great personal risk—to care for Iraqi civilians, enemy prisoners, and wounded combatants.

That's apparently not the case for some correspondents who are covering the war from Baghdad. For the troops who gather around our miniature TV screen, the best entertainment in Iraq has become the regular press briefings proffered by the Iraqi information minister, Saeed al-Sahhaf. Nicknamed Baghdad Bob, Saddam's official spokesman is ridiculed for his outrageous take on the "news." His claims that Iraqi forces have "destroyed" the Army's 3rd Infantry Division and "halted" the Marine advance are greeted here with derision, even if they are taken seriously by some who are reporting from the Iraqi capital.

This morning Baghdad Bob reported that 207 civilians were killed in allied raids on the city during the previous night. He also says that Iraqi soldiers have driven American and British troops back from Basra after killing hundreds, perhaps thousands of them. The Marines find all this to be highly amusing.

But as funny as Baghdad Bob has become to the troops fighting here in Iraq, there's a serious criticism about the reporting on this war that is, for them, anything but a laughing matter.

Their complaint about the media is how U.S. television outlets regularly broadcast footage fed from Al Jazeera, referred to in the ranks as "Jihad TV." Most of the troops recall that Al Jazeera was a "cheering section" for Osama bin Laden in Afghanistan after September 11, and they widely believe that the network is little more than an anti-American propaganda tool in the Arab world. Al Jazeera's broadcasts of Iraqi claims about civilian casualties inflicted by coalition forces and their apparent willingness to accept as fact any story provided by the regime are infuriating to those who believe that they are liberating the Iraqi people from a deadly despot.

By the end of the weekend they have even more reason to despise the Al Jazeera network.

✪ OPERATION IRAQI FREEDOM SIT REP #13
   With HMM-268
   Vic RCT-5 Command Post
   20 km north of Ur, Iraq, on the Euphrates River
   Sunday, 23 March 2003
   2300 Hours Local

This day does not begin well. Shortly after midnight we move yet again—leapfrogging forward to stay with Col. Dunford as he displaces his command group once more farther north, up Route 1. As soon as we arrive at the new CP site, Griff and I once again fumble in the dark to set up our satellite gear so that we can go live for the 6:00 p.m. (EST) evening news broadcast. It took us almost a full hour to get up on the air, because in the new location, in the dark, and without lights, Griff and I can't find a Humvee to plug in our satellite equipment. Finally, shortly after 0100 hours local, about thirty seconds before we're due to go on the air, Griff gets our system up and we are able to go live with Washington.

Tony Snow asks me about the CH-46 crash on the night the war started, and I tell him what I know—with the exception of the names of the twelve Americans and Brits killed in the crash. The snafu over identifying the British dead has postponed their notifying next of kin, and MAG-39 has begged us to delay broadcasting our videotape of the crash. The U.S. Marines want to make sure that all of the families of the dead Royal Marine commandos receive their sad news before our exclusive video of the crash airs worldwide.

Worse yet, since our D-day crash, there has been another accident—this time two Royal Navy helicopters collided in the dark over the Persian Gulf. Seven helicopter crewmen were first declared to be missing in the water. Later, all seven were confirmed as killed. For the pilots and aircrews of HMM-268 who lost four of their own on the first night of the war, this is like rubbing salt into a raw wound. But it is just a foretaste of what is to come.

Shortly after we finish our 0100 broadcast, as we're preparing to get some much needed sleep, a runner from the 5th Marines CP races up to our helicopter with information that a U.S. Army convoy is fighting for its life south of us inside the city of An Nasiriyah. Our four pilots climb out of their cockpits and follow the messenger up to the CP. There they're told that their Marine CH-46s need to be prepared to launch on short notice for possible emergency cas-evac missions in the area of An Nasiriyah.

Inside the 5th Marines CP, officers and communicators are closely monitoring radio nets that are reporting on the battle to our south. The known locations of friendly and enemy units are being plotted on a large battle map with grease pencil. Over in the corner, Col. Joe Dunford, the RCT-5 commander, is huddled with his S-3.

The map shows that the Iraqi 11th Infantry Division is garrisoned in and around An Nasiriyah, a predominantly Shi'ite city of more than 400,000, bounded on the north by the Saddam Canal and to the south by the Euphrates. In 1991, Saddam had brutally repressed an uprising in An Nasiriyah and the occupants were generally thought to be hostile to the regime. Marine engineers and U.S. Naval Construction Battalion "Seabee" specialists judged that the city's four bridges—two to the south over the river, and the pair to the north over the canal—were capable of holding the seventy-two-ton weight of an M-1 Abrams tank if the spans could be captured before Saddam's troops seriously damaged or destroyed them.

Because rapid movement over the Euphrates and the Saddam Canal was crucial to the 1st Marine Division's scheme of maneuver, Task Force Tarawa and RCT-1 had been given the mission of seizing the four bridges just after first light on March 23. TF Tarawa's armored columns were poised about thirteen kilometers south of the Euphrates, ready to strike at the appointed time. The plan called for TF Tarawa to seize the southern spans and open the route through An Nasiriyah so that RCT-1 could race through the city and grab the northern bridges before the Iraqis knew what hit them.

But now, just hours before the attack to seize the bridges was scheduled to commence, an Army convoy of the 507th Maintenance Company, trying to close up on the 3rd Infantry Division, had taken a wrong turn and been ambushed near the easternmost of An Nasiriyah's southern bridges. It is apparently in imminent danger of being wiped out. Marine TF Tarawa, the closest U.S. military unit, is given the mission of mounting a rescue operation.

At about 0300, TF Tarawa moves out, heading up Route 7 toward the ambush site, with a company of tanks in the lead, followed by 1st Battalion, 2nd Marines mounted in AAVs and trucks. Shortly after dawn, Iraqis along the railway bridge south of An Nasiriyah ambushed the lead elements of this heavily armed column. But unlike the soft-skinned Army trucks driven by mechanics, cooks, supply clerks, and other logistics personnel that had been so easy to pick off earlier in the night, the already combat-tested Marines, supported by AH1W Cobra gunships, replied with an overwhelming, disciplined firepower, destroying ten Iraqi tanks.

By noon, most of 2nd Marine Regiment is engaged in and around An Nasiriyah and anyone not otherwise occupied is seeking to learn how it is proceeding. The Cobras and armed UH1Ns that have been supporting 5th Marines are pulled off and sent to support TF Tarawa's fight. Hoping to get some footage of the action, I jump on a UH1N and fly to the FARP that has been established at the captured Tallil Air Base, southwest of An Nasiriyah. The Army shock-trauma hospital set up there to process casualties is already struggling to keep up. As the day wears on, the number of killed and wounded mounts rapidly.

Cobra pilots returning to rearm and refuel describe Marines fighting from their vehicles as regular Iraqi army units and civilian-clad fedayeen pummeled them with small-arms fire and RPGs (rocket-propelled grenade) from one- and two-story buildings lining "the gauntlet." The foreign fighters are said to be from Syria, Saudi Arabia, Jordan, Lebanon, and Egypt. One of the pilots says that these so-called fedayeen are entering the city from the north riding in buses, private autos, even motorcycles—all spoiling for a fight.

Despite the mounting Marine casualties, there is some good news: 1st Battalion, 2nd Marines have rescued a half dozen or more wounded soldiers of the 507th who had been hiding out in the outskirts of An Nasiriyah since the ambush of their ill-fated convoy.

There are few "walking wounded" to interview. The most grievously injured are quickly stabilized by Army doctors and nurses and dispatched back to Kuwait on U.S. Army Black Hawks and Marine C-130s. There, in an Air Force expeditionary hospital, they are either given further treatment or evacuated all the way to Germany aboard a USAF C-9 Nightingale.

Finally, mid-afternoon, I am able to cajole the crew of one of the CH-46s to take me aboard on a cas-evac mission. As we approach the pickup zone north of An Nasiriyah it is obvious that this has been the scene of a terrible fight. Blasted and smoldering American vehicles are intermingled with wrecked Iraqi tanks and civilian vehicles. Just north of the bridge, a Marine LVT apparently torn apart by an RPG or an anti-tank rocket still has the bodies of dead Marines inside.

As the wounded are loaded, I can see RPGs and gunfire raining down from the buildings a few hundred meters away. Cobra gunships are raking the rooftops and alleys of nearby buildings with 2.75-inch and 5-inch rockets, TOW and Hellfire missiles, and bursts of fire from their 20mm Gatling guns. Farther to the south, 155mm artillery rounds are obliterating structures and city streets. The din of rifle and machine gun fire from the Marines on the LVTs deployed around the zone—and from other dismounted infantrymen in ditches beside the road—can be heard even over the decibels of the helicopter engines and rotors. Every time an Iraqi or fedayeen fighter shows himself, the Marines respond with a fusillade of fire from their 240-Golf machine guns, rifles, and grenade launchers. As the up-guns of the LVTs accurately lobbed rounds with good effect into second-story windows, litter bearers, hunched down to reduce their target profile, race for the helicopters, carrying their dead and wounded comrades.

Several of the killed and injured have terrible wounds inflicted by a USAF A-10 that has swept over the gunfight strafing the 2nd Marines' column. Despite extraordinary efforts to prevent such friendly-fire incidents, the pilot somehow mistook the Marine AAVs for Iraqis, and the carnage caused by the "Warthog's" 25mm armor-piercing rounds is horrific.

By the time we arrive back at the FARP it is beginning to get dark and I hitch a ride back up Route 1 with a 5th Marines resupply convoy that is just forming up. Unlike the long, slow-moving 507th Maintenance Company convoy that was ambushed the night before, these Marine vehicles are loaded for bear. There are fewer than fifty vehicles in the procession, and interspersed among the supply trucks and tankers, every third or fourth vehicle is either an M-1 Abrams tank, an AAV, a LAV, or a "hardened" Humvee with a machine gun, TOW, or grenade launcher in its turret. Nearly all the seven-ton trucks has a manned .50-caliber machine gun over their cabs, and the Marine riflemen standing in the AAVs have the muzzles of their rifles and 240-Golf machine guns pointing outboard as though daring a suicidal fedayeen fighter to fire at them.

I ride in a Humvee with the convoy commander, a Marine reserve MP lieutenant. He would ordinarily have been going to work in a pin-striped suit if he were back home in the States, but today he's wearing a flak jacket and helmet, briefing drivers and troop commanders on an "Ambush SOP" and their "immediate action drill" in the gathering dusk at a captured Iraqi air base. His Frag Order is as well thought through and professionally delivered as any issued by a career officer.

After a brief description of the friendly and enemy situation, he tells them that their mission is to safely deliver critically needed ammo, food, water, and fuel to RCT-5, approximately twenty-five kilometers up Highway 1. Emphasizing that they are to avoid rather than engage the enemy, he continues, "Minimum speed—thirty kilometers per hour. No lights. All drivers and gunners use NVGs. Stay closed up. Keep track of where you are on your GPS. If we're hit, open fire to the flanks and keep moving. If a vehicle is disabled, the next two follow-on vehicles will pull alongside to provide suppression fire and pick up passengers and wounded. If possible, the M-88 tank retriever at the back of the column will take the damaged vehicle under tow. If the damaged vehicle can't be moved, the last tank in line will destroy the vehicle and its contents with its main gun. Leave no one behind." After giving everyone the radio frequencies for the convoy and the Cobra gunship escorts, and then ensuring that every vehicle has an infrared strobe mounted on its antenna for IFF (Identification Friend or Foe), the lieutenant asks, "Any questions?" There are none.

We literally roar up the road and arrive without incident at the 5th Marines CP shortly after 2130—perhaps the fastest overland trip I've ever made in a Marine vehicle. I immediately go to find Griff and our helicopters and learn that during the few hours I have been gone, four new CH-46s have arrived—and that Jerry Driscoll, the squadron commander, has returned with them. When I find them they are clustered around our little satellite transceiver watching FOX News Channel—and they are very angry at what they are seeing.

Throughout the Task Force Tarawa firefight in An Nasiriyah, Iraqi state television and Al Jazeera have been broadcasting gory videotape and pictures of dead American soldiers killed in the 507th Maintenance Company ambush. Even worse than the gruesome sight of American dead are shots of five American soldiers from the 507th—now prisoners—whom the Iraqis captured last night.

At a news conference Iraqi Defense Minister Sultan Hashim Ahmed claimed, "Baghdad will respect the Geneva Convention and will not harm captured American soldiers." Yet, the very Geneva Conventions on the treatment of prisoners that the Iraqis are citing forbids photographing or parading captives before TV cameras. Those watching on our little TV monitor are outraged.

In the dark, one of the Marines says, "This reminds me of Somalia." He was no doubt thinking of the notorious 1993 incident in Mogadishu when an Army Delta Force and Ranger unit suffered eighteen killed and more than seventy wounded in an event made famous in the book and movie *Black Hawk Down*.

But from what little I have been able to see of the gunfight in An Nasiriyah, it was nothing like what had happened in "Mog." Back in 1993, the Rangers and Delta Force operators had no armor, artillery, or fixed-wing air support. A Pakistani general under UN control commanded the Quick Reaction Force (QRF) that came to their rescue more than twelve hours later. Last night's ambush of the thin-skinned army vehicles of disoriented logistics and support troops—including female soldiers—of the 507th has been a disaster, no doubt. But TF Tarawa is anything but a UN QRF. The Marines in TF Tarawa are a well-trained, heavily armed, air-ground combat team that had already seen action by the night of March 23. And though the Marines had already begun referring to the highway through An Nasiriyah as "the gauntlet" or "Ambush Alley," they responded in less than three hours, in darkness, when the 507th needed help. Unlike the situation in Somalia, TF Tarawa was able to bring to bear enormous coordinated, disciplined firepower against the regular Iraqi army and irregular forces arrayed against them inside the city. And while the aging LVT7s proved vulnerable to RPGs, French-made anti-armor rockets, and 25mm armor-piercing projectiles fired from an errant A-10 Warthog, TF Tarawa's M-1 Abrams, with their thermal sights made short work of enemy troops holed up in buildings.

Shortly after the horrific images of dead and captured Americans appeared on American television, President Bush came on TV to say, "Saddam Hussein is losing control of his country." He also points out that the U.S.-led coalition forces are achieving their objectives, and he warns the Iraqis, "The people who mistreat U.S. prisoners of war will be treated as war criminals."

A short while later, in Great Britain, Prime Minister Tony Blair expresses his anger and displeasure at the Iraqis for televising the

American prisoners of war. He calls it a "flagrant violation of the Geneva Convention."

Then, from CENTCOM headquarters in Qatar, Lt. Gen. John Abazid, Gen. Franks's deputy, offers a more comprehensive explanation of the engagement at a press briefing. He says that a U.S. Army supply convoy has been ambushed by Iraqi troops near An Nasiriyah, that in the encounter, several American soldiers have been hurt, and that a dozen more are missing. The CENTCOM update also notes that "Marines of the 1st Marine Expeditionary Force are heavily engaged in An Nasiriyah" and that "there have been casualties." While no numbers of killed and wounded are provided, the Marines now know that the toll to take the bridges and secure the route through An Nasiriyah has been high. And though Lt. Gen. Abazid hasn't said so, the Marines also know that one of the missing from the deadly Army convoy is a young female soldier. What we don't know until later is her name: PFC Jessica Lynch, a twenty-year-old supply clerk from the 507th Maintenance Company.

✪ OPERATION IRAQI FREEDOM SIT REP #14
  With HMM-268
  Camden Yards FARP, Vic RCT-5 Command Post
  On Route 1, 40 km north of the Euphrates River
  Monday, 24 March 2003
  1800 Hours Local

We've been on the move again since dawn, leaving the cleanup of An Nasiriyah to Task Force Tarawa and RCT-1. Despite continued resistance from bands of Baathists and fedayeen inside the city, Gen. James Mattis, the 1st Marine Division commander, has decided to proceed with his original plan for a two-pronged attack north toward Baghdad. RCT-5, with RCT-7, will continue the attack up Route 1 to Ad

Diwaniyah. To our east, TF Tarawa has been given the mission of securing An Nasiriyah and its bridges so that RCT-1 can pass through and attack two hundred kilometers north, up Route 7, to seize the city of Al Kut and its airfield on the north bank of the Tigris—scene of the great British defeat at the hands of the Turks in 1916.

By dawn this morning, Marine engineers and Seabees, working through the night without lights, put down a pontoon span over the Euphrates next to the Route 1 highway bridge in an effort to ease the congestion for units crossing the river and heading north toward Ad Diwaniyah. Even though the 5th Marines seized the concrete-and-steel highway bridge intact before the Iraqis could destroy it, only one M-1 tank at a time is being allowed to cross over the Euphrates.

The "backup" engineer span works as intended to ease the bottleneck at the Euphrates and by 1000 hours, RCT-5 is driving north—followed by RCT-7—up an unfinished four-lane highway designated as Route 1. Cobra gunships scouting ahead of the lead tanks in our column report only sporadic contact with Iraqi units deployed in our path as the long column of tanks and armored vehicles races north past desolate marshlands on both sides of the highway.

As Col. Joe Dunford's RCT-5 Command Group leapfrogs forward, Lt. Col. Jerry Driscoll's four HMM-268 CH-46s do so as well—even though it means moving the birds every few hours. Each time we land, Griff and I race out of our respective helicopters to set up our broadcast equipment. By noon we've done this three times since dawn. It would seem futile since we have little to report, except that the satellite connection with FOX News Channel in New York is now our best source of information on what's happening to Brig. Gen. Rick Natonski's Task Force Tarawa in An Nasiriyah and the latest on the American MIAs and POWs from the 507th Maintenance Company.

It's midday in Iraq and we're parked at the "Pac Bell" FARP on Route 1 when we tune in for the early Monday morning news in the United States. The news is not good.

Marine casualties in An Nasiriyah have continued to mount, and the RCT-1/TF Tarawa advance toward Al Kut is stalled. And now embedded correspondents are reporting that fedayeen irregulars wearing civilian clothes are approaching coalition forces waving white flags as if to surrender, but just as they are about to be taken into custody, they pull out weapons and begin shooting. There are other reports of foreign fighters using human shields and ambulances full of explosives driven by suicidal terrorists.

In Baghdad, Saddam is apparently unfazed by continuous precision air strikes—now more than one thousand per day—against his command-and-control nodes, government buildings in Baghdad, and military headquarters facilities throughout the country. Al Jazeera broadcasts continue to parrot Iraqi regime claims of massive civilian casualties inflicted by coalition forces—and the Arabic-language satellite network persists in repeatedly airing images of the Americans captured in the 507th Maintenance Company ambush, along with new shots of two U.S. Army Apache pilots being paraded before the cameras after they were captured when their helicopter was shot down.

All this is apparently enough to drive most of the chattering class of retired generals and admirals who appear regularly on U.S. television into deep depression. Retired generals Wesley Clark, Barry McCafferey, and others are prognosticating that the war will go on for months and that horrendous U.S. casualties should be expected, because Gen. Franks had made the monumental military blunder of attacking Saddam with too small a force and inadequate "softening up" by air power before the ground offensive began. With the notable exceptions of retired Army Maj. Gen. Paul Vallely and retired Air Force Lt. Gen. Tom MacInerney of FOX News Channel, nearly all of the other TV networks' "senior military analysts" are predicting a long and very bloody campaign.

Perhaps encouraged by the blathering from Washington and New York, or by Saddam's financial enticements for "fellow Arabs" to join the fight against the American and British "invaders," or simply motivated by the desire to become martyrs in the "Islamic jihad," a number of Arab foreigners are responding. In any event, the gory gunfight at An Nasiriyah has precipitated a wave of new volunteers for the fedayeen. They are coming by the hundreds in buses, cars, pickup trucks, and even motorcycles from Syria, Lebanon, Saudi Arabia, and Jordan. And because U.S. casualties from the engagement are so high—twenty killed in action and more than ninety wounded in action—many of the troops who fought to open the route through "the gauntlet" at An Nasiriyah are now referring to March 23 as "Bloody Sunday."

CHAPTER SIX
MOASS

✪ OPERATION IRAQI FREEDOM SIT REP #15
With HMM-268 Detachment
Somewhere on Route 1, north of the Euphrates River
Wednesday, 26 March 2003
1030 Hours Local

"It was MOASS—the Mother of All Sand Storms! If you were a tank commander, you couldn't see your front slope. If you were a driver, you couldn't see your ground guide."

—Gunnery Sergeant Erik Benitez, USMC

We can finally see more than a few meters around our helicopter. The worst sandstorm any of us has ever seen is finally blowing itself out.

It began after dark on Monday, March 24, with a low-pitched moaning wind that lashed into the helicopter, whipping dirt around inside the bird. The temperature dropped as the wind rose, and even though we were all wearing our chemical protective suits, I had to wrap up in my poncho liner to stay warm enough to sleep.

When Griff and I arose at 0330 hours to set up our gear for a 0400 "hit" on *Hannity & Colmes*, the wind was blowing so hard that we had to use a sandbag to anchor our satellite antenna to keep it from blowing over. And when we went on the air, the image, green-tinged by our night lens, sparkled as though sprinkled with pixie dust—an effect caused by ionized particles of sand suspended in the air.

Unfortunately, the blowing sand has the same effect on the night-vision goggles used by the Marines, considerably reducing the effectiveness of their NVGs. Some of the pilots suspect that this condition was a factor in the terrible crash of one of the squadron's CH-46s on the first night of the war. Whether or not it was a problem then, it is certainly one tonight. On the roadway fifty meters to our west, the never-ceasing stream of armored vehicles, trucks, artillery pieces, and tanks moving past us to the north has slowed to a crawl because the drivers can't see the rear of the vehicle in front of them. I'm glad that our birds haven't been called out for a cas-evac. The idea of flying at night through this pea soup at 120 knots (about 138 mph) only fifty feet above the ground is not appealing.

Dawn was late this morning—made so by the unearthly haze of wind-whipped sand. Although the sun came up, it didn't change things much. Only the color of the haze shifted. During the day the powdery dust turns everything—earth, sky, vehicles, even the haze-gray helicopters—the color of rust. It coats our clothing, lines our nostrils, cakes our skin, and stings our eyes if we venture outside the helicopter without dust goggles. Worse yet, it makes it almost impossible for the young Marines looking for the enemy to see anything much beyond a few meters—day or night.

Because the storm has already slowed the pace of operations, many of those in the RCT command group who have been very busy for five days and nights suddenly find themselves with little to do. Some catch up on much-needed sleep. Others engage in "bull sessions"—a long-standing military tradition, but one seemingly little enjoyed so far in this operation. Over a generously offered cup of hot coffee, prepared on the hood of a Humvee, I eavesdrop on a long discourse by two CIA paramilitary officers who are debating whether the storm that has descended on us is properly described as a *sharqi* or a *shamal*. They decide to resolve the issue by consulting the two Kuwaiti officers who are accompanying RCT-5 as interpreters. Unfortunately, the Kuwaitis are brothers and they disagree as well, prompting one of the Americans to observe with a shrug, "And it's been that way over here for thousands of years—the people in this part of the world can't even agree about the weather. Let's just say that this is a sandstorm of biblical proportions."

Climbing to the top of a one-story building that had once been a schoolhouse—turned into a small arsenal by Saddam's Baath Party cadre and now a CP for RCT-5—I find a four-man Marine fire team on lookout. Each member of the team has staked out a corner of the rooftop. They're wearing their helmets, body armor, and chemical suits, and in addition to their dust goggles, they've wrapped their faces Bedouin-style with the dark green slings from their first aid kits. The wind is fierce. It's actually cold. I ask the fire team leader, a corporal, what he sees.

The young Marine NCO looks at me somewhat skeptically and replies, "The entire Iraqi army could be out there and we wouldn't know it until they were knocking on the front door."

That may be true for this fire team, and perhaps for every other infantryman on the ground beneath this dust storm. But if the Iraqis thought that the sand blinding us had made them invisible, they were dead wrong.

Even as we stand on that windswept roof, unable to see anything more than a few yards away, we can hear the sound of the 11th Marines' 155mm howitzers firing RAP rounds over our heads. They aren't shooting in the blind. Although the dust storm prevents forward observers from spotting or adjusting fires, the batteries of big guns, multiple-launch rocket systems and the big-payload, high-altitude strike aircraft like the B-1s, B-2s, and B-52s still have plenty of good targets.

Iraqi artillery, rocket, and mortar men, normally wary of firing for fear of being hit almost immediately by an air strike, have been emboldened by the sandstorm's concealment. Last night, as the dust cloud enveloped, they started peppering the Marines' front-line units with 122mm Katyusha rockets, 152mm heavy artillery, and 82mm mortars.

But even before the Iraqi rounds hit the ground, American counter-battery radars linked to fire-control computers are plotting the location of the enemy launchers. And literally within seconds, whole battalions of American 155mm artillery pieces fire back at those who had just fired at us. These highly sophisticated measures can't prevent the Iraqis from firing at us through the rust-colored sky. But the quick response almost guarantees that those enemy gunners who do so will never fire again.

The sandstorm's restricted visibility means that low-level fixed-wing and rotary-wing close air support are out of action—and the Iraqis know it. But what they don't know is that high above them—aboard U-2, JSTARS, and EP-3 aircraft—automated target plotters are observing Iraqi troop movements and communications. The sensors aboard these platforms are generally unaffected by the reduced visibility on the ground, and within minutes of the detection of an Iraqi convoy or radio emission, one or more of a wide variety of GPS-guided munitions is very likely to come streaking out of the sky to obliterate the target.

While standing on the roof of the school–turned Baath ordnance depot–turned U.S. Marine CP, we can hear over the wind the sound of aircraft at high altitude. And minutes later we feel, as much as hear the rumble of a large warhead detonating well off to the north. Whether it was a two-thousand pound AGM-130 or JDAM or the explosion of a five-thousand pound GBU-37, we can't tell. All we know is that some unsuspecting Iraqi who thought he couldn't be seen has just been hit—prompting a predictable response from the Marines: "Yeah, man! Get some!"

A few minutes after this invisible demonstration of American military prowess, Griff appears out of the orange mist at the base of the building and shouts up to me, "We have a cas-evac. Let's go."

As I climb down to the ground and head inside for the mission briefing, my first thought is that the artillery barrage or the high-altitude strikes we've just heard might have hit "friendlies." But when I join Lt. Col. Jerry Driscoll, the air officer is updating him, and I learn that's not the case. Two RCT-5 Marines have been seriously wounded by an RPG during a skirmish with an Iraqi infantry patrol. Driscoll and his wingman, Capt. Aaron "Fester" Eckerberg, plot the grid of the pickup zone and the en route checkpoints on their charts, jot down the frequency of the unit waiting for them on the ground, and quickly head for the helos. Though the weather is deteriorating by the minute, neither pilot challenges the wisdom of making the run. A company commander under fire has called for an emergency cas-evac. It's Driscoll's job to pick up the wounded and save their lives by getting them safely back to a hospital. No questions. No complaints.

We stumble through the gathering gloom back to the aircraft. Griff and his camera are aboard Fester's bird, and I strap in with my camera on Driscoll's #12 while he briefs the crew and our two shock-trauma corpsmen on the mission. As we lift off, the crew chief, Gunnery Sgt. Jesse Wills, observes over the intercom, "Nice day for flying, eh, Colonel?"

Driscoll responds, "Ah yes. Red Dragons...real players." As I hang out the right side hatch with my camera, I notice that Capt.

Eckerberg's CH-46, though only seventy-five feet away, is nearly invisible in the dusty haze. We're heading northwest up Highway 1 toward Ad Diwaniyah, but instead of flying at twenty-five to fifty feet at 120 knots, we're at seventy-five feet—and traveling at less than fifty knots. Ahead of us, through Driscoll's windscreen, the ground is barely visible. There is no horizon and everyone aboard is now looking outboard or ahead for power lines, radio towers, light poles, and highway overpasses in hopes that we see them before running into them.

It takes nearly forty minutes to get to the casualties. A lieutenant, commanding the rifle platoon that had called for the cas-evac, does a good job directing us to his location, about 1,500 meters east of the highway. Though we can't see him and he can't see us in the soup, he succeeds in bringing us in by the sound of our rotors flapping around him in the orange muck.

And now, for a few moments, the sandstorm works to our advantage. We have flown past the Marine position, and over the radio, the platoon commander tells us to turn back to the south, but in so doing we fly directly over the enemy force that attacked his platoon an hour ago. As we make our approach, I can hear the distinctive "crack" of AK-47s firing in our direction. But the Iraqis or fedayeen can't see us and are firing wildly. I thank God once again that these guys don't know how to shoot.

Somehow Driscoll finds the zone and we land to find that one of the two casualties—the platoon's Navy medical corpsman, hit by the full force of an RPG—has died without regaining consciousness. The Marines who race aboard our CH-46 gently lower the litter holding his body to the floor of the helicopter and run back out again.

The other casualty, a Marine corporal, has multiple fragment wounds—one of which is a life-threatening piece of shrapnel from an RPG that has penetrated his abdomen. Driscoll orders the wounded corporal to be loaded aboard Eckerberg's aircraft, and then as we launch, he calls DASC on the secure radio to inform that we're headed for the Army shock-trauma hospital set up at the Tallil FARP, some fifty miles to our southeast.

But now the full effects of this sharqi or shamal—or whatever this sandstorm is called—descend upon us. Unable to see the ground from fifty feet, Driscoll brings us down to twenty-five feet and reduces air speed to less than thirty knots. As we arrive back over Route 1 and turn left, we're virtually air-taxiing—the wheels just off the ground, the rotor tips barely visible in front of us. We're making our way slowly down the highway with Eckerberg's helicopter following—we think—some one hundred feet behind. Col. Driscoll says over the intercom, as calmly as if he were out for a Sunday afternoon drive, "Gunny, keep a sharp eye out. I sure don't want to bump into someone coming this way in our lane."

We creep along this way for a half an hour—Wills hanging out the right side door as the helo edges up to overpasses, light poles, and power lines, hovers up over them, then carefully comes back down on the other side of the obstacles. But then Capt. Eckerberg radios that he's developing engine problems. Driscoll tells him to set his bird down on the roadway, and we do so as well.

After a half an hour or so, Eckerberg reports that he thinks he has the problem fixed, and we resume our harrowing low-speed, low-altitude, low-visibility flight. But after a half an hour or so of this nerve-wracking "flying," Eckerberg calls in again and says he's about to lose his left engine and is putting his bird down on the roadway once again. We do the same, and this time Driscoll shuts down, telling Gunnery Sgt. Wills to head back down the highway to see what he can do to fix the problem.

Lt. Col. Driscoll, copilot Capt. Bill Pacatte, the .50-caliber gunner Cpl. Harold Stewart, and our two corpsmen stay with the bird to protect it. I agree to accompany Gunny Wills back to Eckerberg's helo. We each grab an M-16 and some magazines, and I take my GPS and strap on my Camelback water bladder, and then we head out back down the highway, thinking that Eckerberg's broken CH-46 is at most a few hundred yards behind us.

Unfortunately, it's not there. After walking in the orange fog about a mile and finding nothing, we turn around and head back to our helicopter. Neither of us wants to end up like the Army Black Hawk crew or the survivors of the 507th Maintenance convoy—as captives being paraded before the Al Jazeera and Iraqi state-run television cameras.

Later, Griff Jenkins fills in the blanks about what happened aboard Eckerberg's helicopter. He was there and records the events in his own "After Action Report."

✪   GRIFF JENKINS: AFTER ACTION REPORT
    With HMM-268 Cas-Evac Detachment
    Wrigley FARP, Route 1, Vic Euphrates River
    Wednesday, 26 March 2003
    1030 Hours Local

When we lift out of the zone behind Lt. Col. Driscoll's helicopter, everyone aboard knows that our flight to the hospital with this wounded Marine on board is going to be tough. We lose sight of the colonel's bird almost immediately after he took off. Chief Tom Barry and Petty Officer Jason Comeaux, the two shock-trauma Navy medical corpsmen aboard our CH-46, start treating the wounded Marine corporal as soon as he is brought aboard. He's been hit pretty badly by an RPG and has a piece of shrapnel in his gut. The docs say he is in danger of internal bleeding and going into shock. While Capt. Eckerberg and his copilot, 1st Lt. Ryan Sather, fly us through the dirt cloud, the two corpsmen start an IV on the wounded Marine and wrap him up in a shock blanket.

These two medical corpsmen are tough, brave, yet amazingly gentle men. Chief Barry has been in combat before and Comeaux is a pararescue specialist from the Navy-Marine Cold Weather Survival School in Brunswick, Maine. They have just given the wounded Marine some morphine to ease his pain when Capt. Eckerberg has to put the helicopter down on the roadway because of an engine problem.

We have been trying to follow Lt. Col. Driscoll's helicopter back to a field hospital at the nearest FARP, but in this weather, it's impossible to see the other bird. Visibility is down to less than fifty feet and the air is thick with orange dust. As Capt. Eckerberg has the crew chief trying to fix our engine problem, Chief Barry says, "We've only got hours here, we don't have days to get someone with a gut wound into surgery."

When we shut down on the road, all we know is where we were from the GPS fix, and that we can't start our engines. We have no idea how far ahead of us Col. Driscoll's bird is and I can't call on the Iridium sat-phone because the battery in my phone was dead.

About two hours after we shut down we can hear—over the noise of the wind—the sound of gunfire and what the Marines say is mortar or RPG impacts about a kilometer off to the north. From the volume of fire it sounds like a really intense firefight and it seems to be getting closer. To make matters worse, we have no idea where the nearest "friendlies" are. For all we know, the next thing we might see is a group of Iraqis or fedayeen on "technicals"—those pickup trucks with a .50-caliber mounted on the back—roaring down the road behind us.

To protect the helicopter and our wounded corporal, Capt. Eckerberg assumes the role of "fire team" leader and assigns sectors of fire for our two .50-caliber machine guns and the three M-16s we have aboard the aircraft. Magazines and ammo are handed out to our crew chief Sgt. Derrick Dickerson, Cpl. David Chastain, and Lt. Sather and they prepare for the worst. Inside the bird, Chief Barry and "Doc"

Comeaux have me playing the role of nurse for Frank, our badly wounded corporal. While one of the docs stands guard, I help the other change Frank's IV bags, pat his lips with a moistened gauze pad because he is so thirsty, and help him to relieve himself.

By the time it gets dark, Frank's temperature is rising, his pulse and blood pressure are growing steadily weaker, and he's passing blood in his urine. Chief Barry is concerned that we're going to lose him and spends the whole night with him inside the CH-46 as the wind buffets it from side to side. At times it seems as though one of the gusts will literally tip this twelve-ton helicopter over on its side.

So that Chief Barry can stay with Frank, I take his turn on watch—cradling an M-16 instead of the Sony video-cam in my lap as I hunker down behind a small berm just off the road where the damaged helicopter is parked.

I'm not ashamed to say that I'm afraid. With all the dust being whipped through the air, none of us can see even ten feet in front of us—even with NVGs. Periodically through the night there is the sound of gunfire. Some of it seems very close—other firing is farther away. At one point, over the noise of the wind, we hear an artillery barrage hit not too far away. I ask Sgt. Dickerson if it was "ours" or "theirs."

He replies, "It's probably ours... most likely RAP rounds. Sure as hell hope that the 11th Marines know we're out here."

Just after dawn on Tuesday, March 25, a Marine Humvee with a big American flag fastened to its side came creeping down the road. It's a good thing that it wasn't an Iraqi or fedayeen vehicle because we couldn't hear or see it until it almost hit the back of the helicopter. The driver, a Marine lieutenant colonel named Stroehman, commands a special Marine Air Wing support unit that's establishing FARPs behind the RCT-5 route of advance on Baghdad. He and a small detachment had been reconnoitering a location for a FARP just south of our position when the sandstorm hit. He and his men had been "holed up" along Route 1, waiting for the storm to pass.

Lt. Col. Stroehman informs Capt. Eckerberg that enemy patrols have been moving in between the lead elements of RCT 5—where we had picked up Frank, the wounded corporal—and the main body of the regiment, about eight miles to our south. He points out our vulnerability to anyone coming down the highway, and when he learns that we have a severely wounded Marine aboard and cannot "light off" our engines, he comes up with an ingenious solution—towing our helicopter to a safer location where he has established a defensive position.

By late afternoon, using a strap from a large cargo net and his Humvee, Lt. Col. Stroehman finally has our helicopter safely inside his little defensive perimeter and has gotten up on his radio to Lt. Col. Driscoll and the FARP at Tallil to inform them that we are alive, safe, and in need of a cas-evac for our wounded Marine.

Doc Comeaux and Chief Barry discuss loading Frank on Col. Stroehman's Humvee and trying to crawl down Route 1 to the field hospital at Tallil but decide against it since we don't know if the enemy is between here and there and darkness is already settling in again.

Through the night—though we're safer here from the enemy— Frank suffers even more than the rest of us from the sandstorm. Dust cakes around his nostrils, mouth, and eyes. He can't wipe it away or blow his nose because of the IVs flowing into the veins of his arms. Just before morning, there is an enormous electrical display of lightning, thunder, then rain and even hail. The sound of the frozen water beating against the aluminum skin of the helicopter is unnerving.

For a while, I try wearing my gas mask to keep the fine airborne grit from filling my lungs but the filters soon clog with dust and I realize that there's nothing that can be done to keep from being sand-blasted. The docs are now administering some antibiotics to our wounded Marine in hopes that it will reduce the infection that seems to have taken hold in his stomach wounds. But other than morphine, there is little we can do to ease his pain. Throughout the long night, each time the wind buffets the CH-46 we can see him grit his teeth as everyone is pummeled like a load of laundry in an unbalanced spin cycle.

On the morning of March 26, the wind drops a good twenty to twenty-five knots to a strong but steady breeze and we can finally see the glow of the sun—still overcast, but the storm is obviously blowing itself out. As the ceiling lifts and visibility improves slightly, a UH1N comes hovering down the road at about twenty knots, looking for fuel. Lt. Col. Stroehman directs the bird to land next to a fuel truck and tells the pilot, Maj. Tim Kolb, about the plight of our wounded corporal. Maj. Kolb instantly agrees to take him down to Tallil.

We carry Frank to the Huey in the litter on which he had lain since we picked him up more than thirty hours ago. As we slide him off the stretcher and strap him to the midship troop seat, Frank grits his teeth in pain but never makes a sound. He is one very tough Marine.

With the weather clearing and our wounded Marine finally on his way to lifesaving surgery, we can finally take a break. Doc Comeaux and Chief Barry are napping for the first time since we started this cas-evac mission. Then Col. Driscoll's helicopter comes flapping slowly toward us, about thirty feet above the ground.

✪ OPERATION IRAQI FREEDOM SIT REP #16
With HMM-268 Detachment
Pac Bell FARP on Route 1
North of the Euphrates River
Wednesday 26 March 2003
1830 Hours Local

As the weather cleared this morning, one of Jerry Driscoll's persistent radio calls is answered by Lt. Col. Stroehman, the 3rd Marine Air Wing officer responsible for establishing forward arming and refueling points in the trace of the RCT-5 attack. Over a secure voice channel, Stroehman reports that he has towed Capt. Eckerberg's aircraft to a safer location where a FARP—code-named Pac Bell—is being constructed.

As soon as Gunnery Sgt. Pennington has enough sand cleared out of the air intakes, Driscoll fires up the engines and we air-taxi back to where Griff and Fester are grounded with a helicopter that won't start. By the time we arrive, their WIA Marine has been airlifted out aboard a passing UH1N. As soon as we shut down, Pennington heads over to Eckerberg's aircraft to see if he can troubleshoot the problem.

When Chief Barry comes aboard our helo, he has to step around the body of our dead corpsman. His face and upper body are covered with an orange shock blanket and the chief is understandably agitated that the body of one of his medical specialists killed in action more than thirty-five hours ago has yet to be evacuated.

On the other side of the sand berm that serves as the highway median strip, the chief sees something no one else even knows is there—an Army H-60—parked in the sand. It is one of several aircraft forced to land during the height of the sandstorm.

Since Driscoll's bird is going to have to remain here until repairs can be made to Capt. Eckerberg's helicopter, Chief Barry heads over to the H-60 to ask them to take the dead corpsman back to the Tallil field hospital, where there is a graves registration unit, so that procedures to notify next of kin can commence.

He's back in a few minutes. Choking with emotion, he says, "They are doing a 'preflight' on their H-60 but the pilot says he doesn't have room to take the body."

I tell the chief, "Let me take care of this." I walk over the dune to where an obviously exhausted pilot is climbing down from atop his helicopter, having just scooped buckets of sand out of his engine intakes. There's a large red cross on the side of his bird.

Without preamble, I say to the pilot, "We have a dead Navy medical corpsman aboard our helicopter and his body needs to get back to a field hospital. The chief who was just here tells me that you don't have room."

"That's right, I'm overloaded and with all the sand in my engines, I can't haul any more weight."

"What do you mean, you don't have room?" I answer angrily. "That's what this helicopter is for—taking casualties to the rear. That's what the Red Cross on your door is all about." And with that I rudely reach around him and slide back the hatch. Inside, strapped to the seats are cases of water and rations.

I explode. "This is outrageous!" I shout at him. "You're going to carry food and water back to the rear and you won't carry a corpsman who was killed trying to save the life of a Marine?"

Clearly incensed by my offensive words and behavior, the tired young pilot firmly closes the door of his helicopter, turns back to me. Gesturing to the bird, he says, "Look, I've signed for what's in here. I didn't sign for a dead Navy corpsman."

At this point I lose it. More than thirty years ago in Vietnam, a valiant Navy corpsman saved my life. In my anger and exhaustion, I have probably heard the pilot's words as much more derogatory than he meant them. In my fatigue, I am not being reasonable. I grab him by his flight suit and am about to swing at him when his copilot and crew chief jump between us and break up the fracas.

Disgusted, I walk back to our bird, only to discover that Doc Comeaux, the door gunner aboard Griff's bird, and several of Stroehman's men have witnessed the whole episode. A short while after the H-60 takes off—without our dead Navy medical corpsman aboard—some of them come to talk to me about the incident.

They see it as a case of righteous indignation—believing that the H-60 pilot deserved a good thrashing for refusing to take the corpsman's body with him. But having calmed down, I disagree.

I explain. "Set aside whether a former Navy welterweight boxing champion pushing sixty could have prevailed over a man half his age if the altercation had gone the distance. There are really two other issues that matter more: First, I lost my temper—never a good thing to do in any circumstance. Losing your temper always clouds your judgment. In combat that can get good men killed. And second, because I lost my temper, I didn't accomplish the mission."

I add, "My reason for approaching the pilot wasn't to exchange blows with a thirty-year-old. I went to persuade him to evacuate the body of our dead corpsman—and I failed." The H-60 has departed and the body of Navy Hospital Corpsman Third Class Michael Vann Johnson, Jr., is still lying on the ramp of our helicopter.

He is finally taken to the rear about four hours later when a CH-46 from HMM-268 shows up with the repair parts for Fester's broken helicopter. They take the body aboard on the way back to Ali Al Salem Air Base. I regret that it took so long to notify his family in Little Rock, Arkansas, of their terrible loss.

With the new parts installed, and the sandstorm now well past, Griff sticks a camera in Capt. Aaron Eckerberg's exhausted, dirt-streaked face and asks for his thoughts on "The Sandstorm from Hell."

"I'm just happy to be alive" is all he can manage to say.

CHAPTER SEVEN
WHAT QUAGMIRE?

✪ OPERATION IRAQI FREEDOM SIT REP #17
With HMM-268 Detachment
RCT-5 CP, 20 km south of Ad Diwaniyah
Thursday, 27 March 2003
1230 Hours Local

By dawn this morning—the first time we've seen the sun rise in five days—HMM-268 had four replacement helicopters and crews positioned with RCT-5. Joe Dunford's reinforced regiment, with RCT-7 in trace, was on the move up Route 1 toward the Tigris River and Baghdad. Off to our east, despite continued harsh engagements with small groups of foreign fedayeen, Task Force Tarawa and RCT-1 have succeeded in forcing the passage through An Nasiriyah and reopened the offensive up Route 7 toward Al Kut. Farther south, the British have surrounded Basra, secured Iraq's southern oil infrastructure, and liberated the towns along the Shatt al Arab waterway so that it can be swept for mines. Off to the west, the main attack by the Army's V Corps, spearheaded by Maj. Gen. Buford Blount's 3rd Infantry Division, has beaten the Medina division of the

Republican Guard and is now resupplying its armored columns north of Najaf.

From our satellite hookup with FOX News Channel in New York we learn that last night, as the dust storm blew itself out, more than nine hundred paratroopers of the 173rd Airborne Brigade parachuted onto a strategic airfield north of Mosul, setting the stage for the northern offensive that had been derailed when NATO ally Turkey refused to allow the 4th Infantry Division to enter Iraq through Turkish territory. And now, with the air clear for the first time in five days, the sky above us is filled with Marine Cobras, AV-8 Harriers, and Navy and Marine F-18s, flying close air support (CAS) missions for the lead elements of RCT-5 as they close in on Ad Diwaniyah.

During the sandstorm, deep strikes directed by JSTARS and AWACS aircraft had continued, but these close-in missions directed by Marine FACs with units on the ground had all but ceased while we were enveloped in orange dust. This morning they are back with a vengeance, firing TOW and Hellfire missiles from the Cobras and dropping laser-guided bombs on enemy armor and emplacements that threaten the Marine column.

We are only *seven days* into Operation Iraqi Freedom, and almost half the country and nearly all of its resources are in coalition hands. The 485,000-man Iraqi army is being mauled in every confrontation with American and British forces. More than eight thousand Iraqi soldiers have been taken prisoner and tens of thousands more have decided that they are unwilling to die for Saddam and have simply walked away from their defensive positions.

While some Iraqi units, like those at Najaf and An Nasiriyah, fight fiercely, and surrender ground reluctantly when confronted with overwhelming U.S. firepower, many others will engage for a few minutes, and in some cases a few hours, and then the soldiers quickly slip into civilian clothes and join the local population. It's not uncommon for Marines sweeping through a trench line from which they have just taken fire to find the position littered with green uniforms, helmets, gas masks, empty magazine pouches, and black boots. And then, a few moments later, dozens of beardless young men with short, military-style haircuts, garbed in Arab dress, are just standing around with no apparent place to go. Everyone knows that just minutes or hours before, they were wearing the discarded uniforms. Yet stopping to detain these "civilians" will delay the Marines' movement north—and exacerbate an already strained logistics system if trucks have to be diverted from resupply runs to haul EPWs south to the prisoner-of-war camps.

Given that there have been a handful of well-publicized suicide attacks against the Marines and a good deal of "scuttlebutt" about phony surrenders resulting in Marine casualties, it's still amazing to some of my colleagues in the press that there haven't been more "civilian" casualties. In fact, there have been some—most notably during the close fighting in An Nasiriyah, when several carloads of civilians ignored orders to stop at a Marine roadblock or defensive position and were fired upon. That there have been relatively few such incidents is a tribute to the exceptional discipline of these young men. It's apparent to me, if not to all of my media colleagues, that the small-unit NCO leadership—corporals, sergeants, staff sergeants, and gunnery sergeants, the people who make the difference in a firefight—is exceptional.

So too is the compassion that these Marines are showing toward the foe and the Iraqi people. Since crossing the Euphrates, and leaving the trackless southern desert behind, we've been passing by or through increasing numbers of small villages, palm groves, harvested fields, and cultivated farms, many with livestock. Each time we halt for an hour or more, the Marine battalions and companies in RCT-5 and RCT-7 send patrols off to the flanks of the column, which now stretches from just south of Ad Diwaniyah all the way back to the Euphrates. At any moment, now that the weather has improved, thirty or more squad- to platoon-sized combat patrols are deployed off the flanks of the two RCTs moving north up Route 1. Often, if there is no enemy contact, civil affairs, human exploitation teams, and medical personnel accompany these patrols to win some "hearts and minds" by providing limited emergency medical help, humanitarian rations, water, and even small amounts of fuel for tractors and irrigation pumps.

Shortly before 1000 hours, I am accompanying one such patrol into a tiny village about four hundred meters west of the highway. A single RPG had been fired from here at the lead elements of the 2nd Battalion, 5th Marines. It was an incredibly stupid, long-range shot that had detonated harmlessly fifteen meters short of the nearest Marine vehicle. Rather than leveling the eight or ten structures with fire from an Abrams 120mm main gun, the company commander ordered one of his 2nd Tank Battalion M-1s and an AAV to drop off the route and post an overwatch on the column's left flank in case the perpetrator showed himself again. When the RPG shooter moved to take another shot, the tanker, peering through his thermal sights, dropped him with a three-round burst from the Abrams' coaxial mounted machine gun.

The staff sergeant leading the reinforced squad on patrol orders his Marines up and across the field of waist-high wheat between the roadway and the one-story, dun-colored, brick and stucco buildings. As the fifteen Marines spread out and start across the field, the gunners in the tank turret and on the AAV up-gun traverse their weapons left and right searching for targets, prepared to respond in an instant if the Marines moving in the open are fired upon.

When the grunts, sweating in their protective gear and burdened down with weapons and ammo, reach the little hamlet, fire teams conducting tasks to secure the area cover one another as two-man teams run from building to building, disappearing for a moment inside each one, then running out and yelling, "Clear!" There are a few chickens in the courtyard of one house, a half dozen sheep fenced behind another, and two emaciated cows and a few goats behind a wall. But no sign of the human inhabitants until one of the two Cobras dispatched to support this little patrol reports that there is a person on the roof of a building behind us and that several dozen people—apparently civilians, some of them women and children— are behind the gated wall surrounding the largest house at the end of the dirt street.

The staff sergeant orders his Marines to approach the structure cautiously and positions a G-240 machine gun off to one side as a base of fire. With the Cobras snarling overhead, wheeling back and forth over the little hamlet like giant angry hornets, he then dispatchs one fire team to check out the wall while another climbs to the roof of the building where the helicopters report seeing a person.

Within minutes both fire teams report. The one sent up to the roof found the headless corpse of a young male in civilian clothing. A smashed RPG was beside the body. The fire team leader brought back the only document found on the cadaver: a Saudi passport.

The other fire team counted nine adult males, eleven adult females, and nine small children behind the wall of the house at the end of the street. All but one of the men appeared to be well over the age of fifty. In a garage inside the compound the Marines also found a Ford tractor, a Toyota pickup truck, and a Kawasaki motorcycle.

One of the young Marines spoke some Arabic and one of the young women spoke a little broken English. By signs and gestures, she indicates that the tractor and pickup belongs to the head man of the village; that the Kawasaki belonged to the dead "foreigner" on the roof of her house; that they had all been told to gather in this courtyard by that man and two other armed "foreigners" who had arrived early that morning by motorcycle; and that the other two had fled when the shot had killed the fedayeen on the roof.

Once this exposition is finished, the staff sergeant calls back to the tank on the radio that "the village is Alpha Sierra"—meaning "all secure"—and that his patrol is returning. Before heading out of the little cluster of homes, he warns his Marines to stay off the dirt road going out to the main highway, since it could be mined.

As the squad moves back out through the wheat field, the only young male adult in the small community follows us. He carries a small child, a little boy only about four years old who is obviously in pain. One of the fire team leaders gestures to the man to stop following them, but he persists. Finally, the squad's medical corpsman approaches the man and examines the boy. It is obvious to the corpsman that the youngster's left arm is broken. When the corpsman informs the staff sergeant of this, the squad leader allows the man and boy to accompany us.

When we arrive back at the highway, one of the RCT-5 medical officers, a Navy doctor assigned to the 5th Marines, examines the child. One of the human exploitation team translators explains to the father that the child needs to have the bone set and a cast applied.

The Navy doctor and a corpsman administer a mild painkiller, set the broken bone, and apply a fiberglass cast. While all this is being done, the father and the human exploitation team translator carry on a lively conversation. After the father and son leave, the doc asks what was said.

"That man was a soldier until last week," the translator replies. "He deserted from his unit just north of Basra and came back here to his wife and son. His father is the head man in the village. Last night three fedayeen arrived and started pushing people around. This guy hid out on his roof because the word is out that the foreigners are shooting deserters. One of the 'big brave fedayeen' pushed the little kid off the roof and that's how he broke his arm. This morning, when the fedayeen guy on the roof took his RPG potshot at the armor moving up the highway, the tank shot back and killed him. The other two panicked and took off across the fields on their motorcycles. End of story—except that this Iraqi father now says they all owe us big-time and if we ever need anything, just ask. I'll pass it on to the S-2 and the guys from the agency the next time they swing by."

As the translator finishes the story, there is a muffled explosion from the direction of the little village. Instantly, someone yells "Incoming!" but it sounds more like a grenade to me. I stand up and look toward the village, and about 150 meters down the dirt track leading to the cluster of houses there lay what looks like a heap of laundry. Over it hovers a cloud of dust. A couple of Marines start to run toward the scene but are halted by the shouted command, "Stop! Mines!"

It takes more than fifteen minutes for the Marines, the doctor, and his corpsmen, cautiously probing every step of the way, to get to the bodies. I didn't go. I've seen too much fresh death. When they returned the doctor says, with tears in his eyes, "That little boy whose arm I just mended died in his father's arms when the dad stepped on a land mine."

Both the father and his four-year-old son were killed by an Italian land mine planted by a Saudi terrorist fighting to keep Iraqi dictator Saddam Hussein in power. It all seems totally irrational, and it reminds me of the expression that my Marines in Vietnam had used for such deaths. They'd have said the Iraqi father and his son had been "wasted." And they'd have been right.

✪ OPERATION IRAQI FREEDOM SIT REP #18
   With HMLA-267
   Ranging south of Ad Diwaniyah, Hantush, Iraq
   Thursday, 27 March 2003
   2350 Hours Local

A half an hour or so after the bodies of the dead father and son were taken away by their family members, Maj. John Ashby, the XO of HMLA-267, asked if I wanted to go with him on an "admin" flight to bring Brig. Gen. John Kelly, the assistant commander of the 1st Marine Division, over to Qal' at Sukkar, about 110 kilometers east on Route 7, where RCT-1 and elements of Task Force Tarawa were located. Thinking this might be a good opportunity to get some footage of other units, I grabbed my pack and camera out of the CH-46 and jumped aboard the armed UH1N "chase bird" that was accompanying the Huey with the general aboard. Two Cobras lifted with us from the landing zone adjacent to the RCT-5 and 1st Marine Division CPs.

The flight east was uneventful, since we stayed well south of the villages along Route 17, the east-west highway connecting the two prongs of the 1st Marine Division attack. Despite the pronouncements of the armchair admirals and barroom brigadiers pontificating from air-conditioned studios in New York, Washington, and Atlanta, the abysmal weather had slowed the attack north but hadn't stopped it. The lead elements of RCT-1 were less than fifty miles from Al Kut and ready to attack north to force a crossing of the Tigris. And 110 kilometers to the west, RCT-5 and RCT-7 were closed up on Route 1, and the Iraqis couldn't tell whether they would veer left up Route 8 past Babylon or hook a right at Route 27 to cross the Tigris at An Numaniyah. To those of us on the ground, it appeared that the slow but steady movement during the sandstorm had confused not only the Iraqis but the "military analysts" back in the States as well.

As we flew south of Route 17 toward Qal' at Sukkar, the Cobras roamed off to our north. On two occasions they attacked Iraqi tanks and armored vehicles in revetments but took no ground fire in return. Even in the several sizable towns along Route 17, there were no signs of any major Iraqi units that could oppose the Marines using the "hardball" highway as a logistics corridor.

When we landed at Qal' at Sukkar, Gen. Kelly went immediately to meet with Col. Joe Dowdy, the RCT-1 commander. I stayed at the LZ, talking with the pilots and aircrews while the Cobras rearmed and refueled and our UH1N took on fuel. One of the officers in this squadron is the son of one of my closest friends. Capt. Allen Grinalds's father, John, a much respected, retired major general, is now the president of the Citadel, in Charleston, South Carolina. But Allen is already making a reputation of his own as a Cobra pilot. One of the younger officers in the squadron told me "Captain Grinalds is the best instructor I've ever had."

Our "bull session" was interrupted by a call for the Cobras to launch in support of a 1st Marines Company engaged with an Iraqi unit east of Route 7. They took off in a cloud of dust.

Gen. Kelly returned for his flight back to the 1st Marine Division CP. This time he had with him two old friends: Maj. Gen. Ray Smith, USMC (Ret.), and Francis "Bing" West, also a former Marine and an assistant secretary of defense during the Reagan administration. We all served as small unit leaders in Vietnam and I have known and admired both these old warriors for years. Ray is one of the most decorated Marines alive and has a well-deserved reputation as a "warrior's warrior." Bing West was at the Pentagon while I was on the NSC staff at the White House and he is now a bestselling writer.

Kelly, Smith, and West board the lead bird, and we take off to retrace the route west along Route 17, heading back to the 1st Marine Division CP. As we turn into the afternoon sun, I hear in my headset the pilots in the two helicopters discussing whether they should wait for the Cobra escort. When they get the word that it would take at least another hour to get the Cobras back from their mission, rearmed, and refueled, the decision is made to proceed unescorted.

That's not as dangerous as it might seem. These aren't "slicks"—birds without guns. Both UH1Ns have door-mounted, .50-caliber XM2 machine guns, and the one I'm in also has a pod loaded with 2.75-inch rockets and a GAU-17, 7.62mm mini-gun that looks like a Gatling gun hanging out the right side. When we hear that we were returning unescorted, the crew chief says, "No sweat, Colonel. This isn't your father's Oldsmobile! We can take care of ourselves."

But this time, instead of staying over the largely unpopulated terrain south of Route 17, we fly almost right down the hardball at fifty to seventy-five feet, clipping along at ninety to one hundred knots. I have my video camera out on my lap as we follow the bird with Gen. Kelly, Gen. Smith, and Bing West aboard. Unlike the mud huts and single-level structures south of here, these houses are nearly all multistory and they all seem to have electricity. Because we're fifty to a hundred meters behind the lead helicopter, we can spot people running out of their homes to see what's making the racket. Kids come out and wave—and from the back of our bird, the gunner and crew chief wave back.

I'm sitting on a troop seat in the center of the bird, following our course along Route 17 and have just marked our location on my map, "Al Budayr," when I hear through my headphones, "We're taking fire!" I look up from my map to see the lead bird jinking left and right as green tracers just miss the left side of the helicopter. The VIP bird with Kelly, Smith, and West aboard rolls left as its machine gun unleashes a burst almost straight down at the weapon on the ground that had just fired at their helicopter.

By now I've grabbed my camera and am holding it over Maj. Ashby's head, aiming it forward through the windscreen. Through the viewfinder I can see five or six men wearing what look like black pajamas, running out of a two-story building carrying AK-47s. Across the street from the building there is an unmanned ZSU-23mm dual-mount anti-aircraft gun, but none of them run toward it. Instead, they appear transfixed by the lead helicopter screaming directly over their heads.

As the lead helicopter swoops hard left out of our line of fire, Ashby says over the intercom, "Arming rockets. Stand by." His voice is cool as ice, flat, unexcited, as if he were ordering lunch over the phone as he flicks a red switch on the console. Through the viewfinder on the little camera, I can see several of the Iraqis kneel down and fire at the lead bird as it passes over them. They still haven't seen us. But then, just as Ashby tilts our UH1N into a shallow dive from 150 feet, one of the black-clad shooters spots us. As he wheels to aim at our helicopter, I hear Ashby say calmly, "Firing rockets."

On the tape, there is a roar as three of the 2.75-inch rockets ripple out of the pod on the left side of our helicopter. Although I don't recall being startled by the sound, the camera jerks as if I had been and then quickly focuses back on the trajectory of the three deadly missiles. The three rockets Ashby selected are fleschette rounds—each warhead contains thousands of tiny metal darts set to detonate twenty feet from the target. They perform as advertised, and puffs of red smoke from all three erupt over the Iraqis. The videotape shows them being cut down in an instant by the shower of steel. The bird pulls up and hard left, the g-force pushing me back in my seat, the camera pointing off at a crazy angle, and Ashby's voice comes over the intercom: "And they all fall down." No euphoria, no pleasure, no sadness, simply a statement of fact.

When we landed at the 1st Marine Division CP to drop off Gen. Kelly, I intended to grab Ray Smith and Bing West and get an interview on tape of their reactions to being nearly shot down. But I notice as we land that the four CH-46s from HMM-268 that had been there when I left on the Huey several hours before are gone. One of the Marines at the fuel point—another one of the unsung heroes of the war for their tireless work at all hours of the day and night—tells me that the CH-46s had displaced forward with Col. Dunford's command group while I was gone.

Since it is nearly dark, I abandon the effort to track down Smith and West and hike up to Route 1 to hitch a ride forward, knowing that my only hope of getting my tape back to the FOX bureau in Kuwait is to link up with the HMM-268 detachment before they rotate helos in the morning. About two hundred meters up the hardball highway I found a 2nd Battalion, 11th Marines artillery convoy of six 155mm howitzers and about twenty ammunition trucks, interspersed with armed Humvees, LAVs, and four tanks formed up and about to head north on Route 1. The convoy commander, a captain, offers me a ride in his Humvee. Not one to lead from the rear, he's positioned right behind the lead tank. As soon as I strap my pack on the back of his vehicle, we're off in a cloud of dust and diesel smoke, accompanied by the sound of tank treads, screeching and grumbling on their road wheels.

We head up the highway, averaging at least twenty-five kilometers per hour. Between taking and making calls on his encrypted PRC-119 FM radio, the captain informs me that they will be setting up their tubes directly behind the RCT-5 CP, so I shouldn't have any trouble finding the CH-46s with Joe Dunford's command group. As we're riding up the road he notices that I'm jotting notes with my left hand and says I ought to give lessons to Capt. Jason Frei, "A" Battery commander, 1st Battalion, 11th Marines. Frei lost his right hand to an RPG that struck his Humvee when his artillery convoy was ambushed in An Nasiriyah. "That isn't going to happen to us tonight," the captain explains. "We've got you along."

I decide not to tell him I've turned into something of a metal magnet over here. But thankfully, we do make an uneventful forty-kilometer run to the RCT-5 CP at Hantush, on Route 27, northeast of the intersection of Routes 1, 8, and 27, arriving just after 2300. A few hundred meters up the road I find a circle of LVTs and Humvees with "5>" painted on their sides—the distinctive RCT-5 tac mark. The four HMM-268 CH-46s are parked in a field about fifty meters north of the CP. When I climb aboard the lead helicopter, the crew is asleep, but Capt. Dave Roen, one of the pilots, awakens and says, "You aren't going to believe what happened while you were gone."

"What's that?" I respond.

"The war is on hold."

✪ OPERATION IRAQI FREEDOM SIT REP #19
With HMM-268 and RCT-5
Near Hantush, Iraq
Friday, 28 March 2003
2115 Hours Local

As Griff and I hook up our satellite gear in preparation for our regular report on *Hannity & Colmes*, we learn from FOX News Channel that CENTCOM has ordered an "operational pause" for all ground combat units so that supplies of food, water, and ammunition can catch up with units about to make the final push on Baghdad. We're stunned by the information, for there has been no serious shortages of any of these items thus far in the units that I have seen. In fact, for the eight days since the war started, the Marine logisticians back in Kuwait have done an amazing job of pushing all necessary supplies—plus spare parts and the myriad items of equipment needed to keep a military force of this size and complexity on the move day and night. Further, stopping where we are, well within the fan of chemical weapons that can be launched by Saddam's artillery in a last ditch effort to save his capital, seems to add considerable risk to what had thus far been a remarkably successful campaign.

When the sun rises as it's supposed to—clear, without a tinge of sand in the air—I make my way to the RCT-5 CP to scrounge a cup of hot coffee and the latest hot scoop. It turns out that we're not just going to "pause" in place. The new command is "to the rear, march." Topic number one for everyone is a new order: RCT-5 has been directed by CENTCOM to reverse march forty kilometers back down Route 27 to Route 1 and stand in place. While I'm talking with "Hamster," the RCT-5 assistant air officer, Col. Dunford walks out of the CP. He looks not only tired but exasperated as well. I ask him if he can give us an interview. He looks as though he might spit nails, but then softens and says, "Not on camera."

When I ask him to fill me in on what's happening for documentary purposes, he tells me that CENTCOM is concerned that we're inside the "red zone" for chemical attack and that we have to move south until V Corps, which has seen a lot of action at Najaf, can be resupplied with food, water, and ammunition. Using my map, Dunford shows how leaving RCT-5 in place this far north on Route 27 risks compromising the very closely held I-MEF/1st Marine Division deception plan for crossing the Tigris.

Until the "operational pause" had been ordered, I-MEF had planned to deceive the Iraqis into thinking that RCT-5 and RCT-7 were planning to charge straight up Route 1 to Baghdad, while RCT-1 forced a crossing of the Tigris at Al Kut. It was hoped that the elite Baghdad division of the Republican Guard defending Al Kut would be so intent on stopping RCT-1 from crossing the Tigris that the Iraqis would be fixed in place and unable to respond when RCT-5 and RCT-7 made a surprise move up Route 27 to cross the river at An Numaniyah. All of this would be in jeopardy if RCT-5 remained "parked" on Route 27, so the regiment dutifully turned around and rolled back down the hardball to the Route 1/Route 8 interchange.

By mid-afternoon we are back to within a kilometer of where we had been when I had gone on the VIP flight with HMLA-267. The HMM-268 pilots and aircrews have all been briefed on the reason for reversing course and seem to understand. But that's not the case with many others.

For the grunts who gather around our tiny TV set to watch what's being said back in the States and around the world, both the pause and the move to the rear have created consternation. They wonder who it is that's out of supplies when they hear news reports that the Marines have had to stop because they outran their supplies. While we're getting ready to go on the air, a Marine C-130 makes a pass over the highway that they had rolled over yesterday. I turn on my camera and catch the giant, four-engine cargo craft as it lands to disgorge tons of supplies and then pump thousands of gallons of fuel into waiting tank trucks and fuel bladders.

Back in the United States, second-guessing of the Pentagon is well under way. Much of the media back home apparently believe that Operation Iraqi Freedom has run afoul of bad planning. Once again, retired generals are on the air with dire predictions that the war in Iraq could cost up to three thousand American and British deaths. The word "quagmire" is mentioned now as if coalition forces were bogged down in a swamp. Some commentators are comparing the situation to Vietnam.

One of the troopers watching the news on our little TV set asks, "Is that right, Colonel North? You were in Vietnam. Is this what happened there?"

He's clearly too young to have been alive while I was at Khe Sanh or Con Thien or know much about Hue city, where Ray Smith led a rifle company during the Tet offensive of 1968, so I try to explain how different the two wars really are.

"From their safe haven in North Vietnam, the rulers in Hanoi invaded South Vietnam with conventional military forces and simultaneously orchestrated an indigenous insurgency," I tell him. "Other than a bombing campaign, we never seriously threatened Hanoi. That's not the case here in Iraq, where we're taking the fight directly to the despot who has attacked his neighbors and oppressed the Iraqi people for more than three decades. Here we face a conventional indigenous army and some 'guerrillas'—mostly foreign fedayeen on a jihad.

"In Vietnam, the Viet Cong guerrillas were operating as a 'wholly owned subsidiary' of the North Vietnamese. Here, we're being attacked by criminals released from prison just before the war started and by Baathists who want to restore their power and prestige by orchestrating the attacks, along with jihadist foreign fedayeen who are coming here to become 'martyrs.' But none of these groups are coordinating their efforts and activities."

The young Marine nods, seeming to understand the differences.

Iraq isn't the "quagmire" that Vietnam became, at least not for anyone but the Iraqis, who have been leaderless since the beginning of the war. Saddam may have survived thus far, but the Iraqi military is essentially on its own. There is little, if any, command-and-control structure. No one seems to be giving orders to the enemy commanders in the field. And while some Iraqi soldiers fight bravely, there is no evidence of any real coordinated defense—only a series of point-to-point engagements that have hardly slowed the coalition attack.

Quagmire? I don't think so.

▲ Operation Iraqi Freedom Area of Operations

▲ "Baghdad or Bust"—Griff Jenkins and Oliver North standing beside a Humvee we saw often on the way to Baghdad.

▲ Chief Warrant Officer Dale Ferguson, MAG-39 NBC officer, and Sgt. Elwood explain to our audience the benefits of the U.S. military MOPP suit.

▲ A Marine CH-46 Sea Knight ("frog" or "phrog") under repair at a captured Iraqi airfield.

Griff Jenkins

Maj. Carroll Harris, USMC

▲ Communicating with FOX News Channel in New York via satellite phone during the attack on Baghdad.

▲ Griff "Mailbag" Jenkins at work aboard a Red Dragon CH-46 helicopter that's older than he is.

Courtesy FOX News Channel

▲ Geraldine, the 5th Marines "backup" biological and chemical weapons detection system.

▲ Griff Jenkins and Oliver North prepare for a live satellite broadcast from the intersection of Routes 1 & 27, south of Baghdad.

▲ Maj. Gen. Mattis told RCT-5 to "go heavy kinetic all the way to Baghdad." They did.

Griff Jenkins

▲ Sgt. Peter DiMartino manning .50-caliber machine gun aboard an HMM-268 CH-46 on a cas-evac mission.

Griff Jenkins

▲ Dawn near Salman Pak before the battle for Baghdad.

Courtesy FOX News Channel

▲ Towing Fester's and Griff's bird through the MOASS.

Maj. Carroll Harris, USMC

▲ Brave 5th Marines Navy corpsman evacuating a wounded enemy prisoner of war (EPW).

Lt. Col. Jerry Driscoll, USMC

◀ (From left to right) Lt. Col. Jerry Driscoll, Capt. Bill Pacatte, Oliver North, Gunnery Sgt. Jesse Wills, Cpl. Harold Stewart. Taken after the MOASS of "biblical proportions."

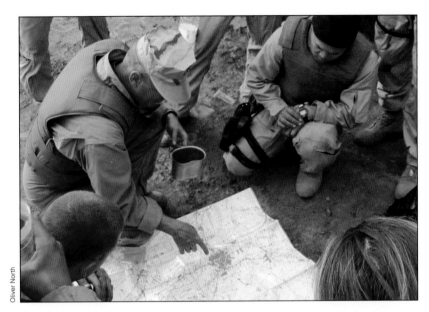

▲ Squadron CO Lt. Col. Jerry Driscoll briefs HMM-268 pilots and flight crews on enemy anti-aircraft positions before leading them into Baghdad. Maj. Don Presto, kneeling, top right, would be awarded the Distinguished Flying Cross for this mission.

▲ (From left to right) Maj. Carroll Harris, Capt. Mike "Gogo" Gogolin, Sgt. Steve Campoy, Cpl. Charlie Campbell, Gunnery Sgt. Dennis Pennington, and Oliver North just before the 10 April 2003 Baghdad mission.

▲ U.S. Navy corpsmen of the I-MEF Cas-Evac Unit saved the lives of more than 150 wounded Marines aboard Red Dragon helicopters.

▲ One of Saddam's many palaces after being captured by U.S. forces. This one is on the Tigris, south of Baghdad.

▲ A Red Dragon CH-46 evacuates a seriously wounded 5th Marines casualty under fire at Saddam's presidential palace in Baghdad on 10 April 2003.

▲ Cpl. Joe Mireles "suppressing the enemy" with his .50-caliber machine gun as his CH-46 lifts off under fire from the palace LZ.

▲ Saddam's Baghdad palace after the 10 April 2003 gunfight.

▲ A Marine HMLA-267 Cobra downed at an Iraqi air force base east of Samarra on 14 April. Miraculously, both pilots survived.

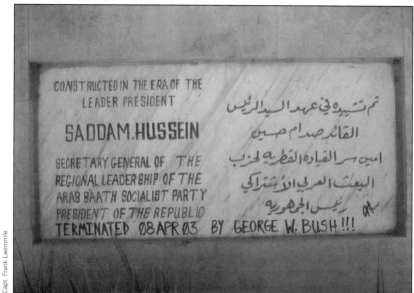

Capt. Frank Laemmle

▲ Monument to Saddam in Baghdad—updated by the U.S. Marines.

Griff Jenkins

▲ One of the many cheering crowds that greeted us as we entered Baghdad, in an example of the often unreported response from the Iraqi people.

▲ Interviewing Col. Don Campbell, CO of 1st Brigade, 4th ID, outside Saddam's palace in Tikrit on 21 April 2003

▲ Lt. Col. Larry "Pepper" Jackson, CO of 3rd Battalion, 66th Armored Regiment, 4th ID, at the captured Iraqi munitions depot south of Bayji on 22 April 2003. The depot holds 300 million tons of ordnance.

▲ Sgt. Maj. James Booker in Ramadi, Iraq, April 2004. He personified the courage, perseverance, and esprit of the "Magnificent Bastards," official nickname of 2nd Battalion, 4th Marines.

▲ Col. "Buck" Connor, CO of 1st Brigade, 1st ID, was ambushed in Ramadi on 14 July 2004. By the end of the gunfight, his U.S. Army Bradley fighting vehicles and the 2nd Battalion, 4th Marines had killed nearly two dozen of the enemy.

▲ Some of the twenty-one enemy combatants detained after the four-hour gunfight on 21 July 2004—another "Wicked Wednesday" in the Sunni Triangle.

▲ Marines of Company E, 2nd Battalion, 4th Marines fire and maneuver against enemy combatants holed up in a building in downtown Ramadi, July 2004.

▲ The venerable .50-caliber machine gun has been an infantryman's best friend since World War I. Mounted on a Humvee like this one, it provides responsive fire that can punch through a masonry wall.

◀ Capt. Mark Carlton, CO of Fox Company, 2nd Battalion, 4th Marines. He had dozens of holes in him from an enemy RPG. It was 125 degrees. He was sweating. He was bleeding. When the battle ended three hours later, he was still leading his Marines.

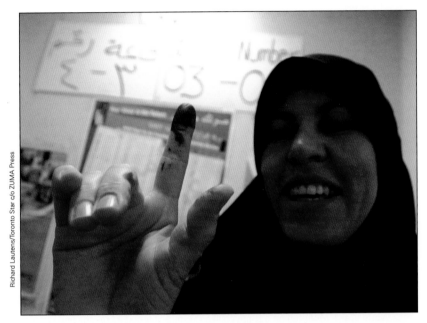

▲ On 30 January 2005, an Iraqi woman proves that the "fire of freedom" is spreading. The terrorists threatened to kill them if they voted. They came anyway—braving intimidation, gunfire, suicide bombers, and mortar attacks—just to cast a ballot.

"By our efforts, we have lit a fire as well—a fire in the minds of men. It warms those who feel its power, it burns those who fight its progress, and one day this untamed fire of freedom will reach the darkest corners of our world."

—George W. Bush, second inaugural address

✪ OPERATION IRAQI FREEDOM SIT REP #20
With HMM-268 and RCT-5
Near Hantush, Iraq
Monday, 31 March 2003
2300 Hours Local

Early this morning we got the word from RCT-5. The so-called "operational pause" is officially over. The 1st Marine Division has resumed
the march on Baghdad. Though we haven't been "advancing" toward
Saddam Hussein's capital, the last four days haven't been devoid of
combat: 3rd Battalion, 4th Marines, part of RCT-7, has been busy
clearing Route 17 of fedayeen like those who had shot at our Hueys
over Al Budayr on March 27. And RCT-5 has had gunfights every day,
most of them engagements against irregular units, small bands of
roving Iraqis who have not surrendered despite the disappearance of
their senior officers, or in other cases, the foreign fedayeen.

Yesterday afternoon, there was a major fight with more than two
hundred of these irregulars near Ad Diwaniyah that continued until
well past nightfall. Earlier today, Griff and I went to interview the
Marines in the unit that had discovered the enemy force. VMU-2 is
one of the squadrons of RPVs that has done a remarkable job of finding the enemy here in the desert. Flown like remote control air planes,
these vehicles currently provide the capability to locate, observe, and
assess enemy targets through the use of a small, high-powered camera that disseminates imagery back to the aircraft control center. This
information can then be passed on to air or ground units to assist forward assault and capture of enemy assets. We videotaped the takeoff
and recovery of several Pioneer UAVs, the less expensive predecessor
to the now-famous, sleek new Predators.

Hurled into the sky from an elevated launch rail by compressed
air, and recovered on a highway, the boom-tailed Pioneers have a GPS

tracking system, cameras, emission detectors, and electronic sensors jammed into their fuselage. And even though each one costs nearly a million dollars, they are all flown under remote control by young enlisted Marines.

When an RPV spots an enemy force, emplacement, or equipment, the VMU-2 can bring artillery fire or strikes from fixed-wing or rotary-wing aircraft to bear on the target in a matter of minutes. The VMU-2 control van also has the ability to transmit the image of what the RPV sees in real time to ground combat unit commanders or print out aerial photos of the area over which the RPV has just flown.

Yesterday afternoon, when one of these Pioneer UAVs spotted a large Iraqi unit massing east of Ad Diwaniyah, the area was first hit with artillery fire and then a half dozen Cobras followed up for several hours after dark. The attack was so devastating that, throughout much of today, small groups of Iraqis have been wandering into RCT-5 positions to surrender.

This morning, in a surreal scene worthy of a *M.A.S.H.* or *Hogan's Heroes* episode, Griff, armed with only a Sony camera, took Iraqi prisoners! We were recording the capture of another group of Iraqis when two young men wearing *thobes* and carrying white flags walked up behind him and surrendered. We quickly summoned Maj. Sara Cope, the CO of the Military Police detachment, and she had them taken into custody. She later told us that they had given themselves up because they were hungry and thirsty—somewhat deflating Griff's claim that they had done so because he looked so tough in his FOX News Channel baseball hat.

❂ ❂ ❂

At 1400 this afternoon, as we were setting up our camera and satellite gear to go live on our network morning show, *FOX & Friends*, the producer called me on my satellite phone to say that the *New York*

Times, the *Washington Post*, and several other newspapers were beating the drum about the Marines being out of food, water, and ammo. I complained that it just wasn't true, but if they liked, I would be glad to put on some Marines to tell the American people how things really were.

New York agreed that would be a good idea—probably thinking that I would interview a general or at least a colonel. Instead, I grabbed a gunnery sergeant and asked him if he could produce two enlisted Marines to stand on either side of me. In an instant, Sgt. Jason Witt was on my left and a young lance corporal was on my right.

Without having time to brief the young Marines on what was happening, I hear Steve, E. D., and Brian talking to me through my earpiece. Their first question is about the Marines having outrun their supplies. I turn to Sgt. Witt and ask, "Have you guys been hungry out here?"

"No, sir," he replies. "We've been well taken care of."

"And how about thirsty?"

"No, sir . . . we're good."

"And ammo?"

The sergeant grins and answers, "Good on ammo, and morale is good, sir." Relishing the chance to send another message as well, Witt goes on to say hello to his wife, Melissa, his parents, and his twin brother back in Tyler, Texas.

And when the lance corporal has his chance, he responds the same way when I put the questions to him.

"The *New York Times* says the Marines are out of food, water, and ammo. Are you hungry?"

"No, sir."

"Are you thirsty?"

"No, sir."

"Are you short on ammo?"

"No, sir."

"Well, what do you need?" I persist.

Without a moment's hesitation, the young Marine replies, "Just send more enemy, sir."

To some, these two leathernecks probably sounded as if they were spouting typical Marine bravado. But in fact they had all been told before they left Kuwait that they were going into the attack "light" on supplies. Marines were instructed that two MRE rations per day, consisting of five thousand calories, were what they would be getting. They were also told, "Potable water will be delivered in bottles, so don't waste it on showers. Ammunition and fuel are the number one priorities for resupply, so don't waste them either. When you can, shut off your engine—and if you find uncontaminated Iraqi diesel fuel, use it."

All of this was accepted by the troops pretty much as "business as usual." Marines who have been in the service for more than a few years like to joke that the official motto of the Marine Corps may be *Semper Fidelis*, but the real slogan is, "The Marines have done so much, with so little, for so long—we now can do anything, with nothing, forever."

Because they knew that they were expected to go farther and faster with less, many Marines came to resent how they were being portrayed by the media. This threatened to undo much of the goodwill accrued by having embedding correspondents directly with the troops. But consternation over the "hungry, thirsty, out of ammo" story was nothing compared with the firestorm created by another member of the U.S. media—this time from Baghdad.

By nightfall on the evening of March 31, word was already spreading among the troops about the comments of Peter Arnett during an interview he had given on Iraqi state television. Arnett was well known for his coverage of the first Gulf War for CNN and for a televised "documentary" piece called "Tailwind," which alleged that U.S. forces had illegally used nerve gas in Vietnam. Fairly or not, Arnett is widely perceived by many in the ranks to be antimilitary. Now he was in Baghdad "reporting" for NBC and *National Geographic*, and apparently apologizing to the Iraqis for the U.S.-led invasion.

Though few of the troops actually saw the broadcast of Arnett being interviewed by an Iraqi in military uniform, almost everyone had heard some of what he had said. "The first U.S. war plan has failed because of Iraqi resistance. Now they are trying to write another war plan. Clearly, the American war planners misjudged the determination of the Iraqi forces."

From what we were picking up on our satellite transceiver, the interview precipitated an uproar back in the United States. Here in Iraq, the troops wonder out loud why, with all our precision-guided munitions, Iraqi state television is still on the air. As for Arnett, they regard his comments to be treasonous, a personal affront, and have taken to describing his lineage in unprintable terms.

CHAPTER EIGHT
OF RIVERS AND RESCUES

✪ OPERATION IRAQI FREEDOM SIT REP #21
HMM-268 Detachment with RCT-5
Hantush, Iraq
Tuesday, 1 April 2003
2045 Hours Local

The "operational pause" is over with a vengeance. Before midnight, the three reinforced battalions of "Fighting Joe" Dunford's RCT-5 were on the move, back up Route 1, to the "right turn" on Route 27, following the hardball highway to Hantush. It's the same path they had taken on March 27—before they'd been turned around and sent back. This attack north has been preceded by a dramatic display of artillery fire from the 11th Marines. Throughout the night, RAP rounds, their orange trajectories arching over our heads like a fireworks display, pounded enemy positions that had been reoccupied when the Marines were told to reverse course for the "pause."

In the race north, I-MEF has left the remnants of at least four Iraqi divisions in its wake, some of them with enough residual strength to make mischief by setting ambushes for Marine resupply convoys—but none of them sufficiently intact to threaten the drive to the Tigris River. Now the Iraqi forces arrayed in front of the Marines are about to feel the full wrath of those who believed they had been wronged by the media and slighted by the decision to make the Army's V Corps the "Main Attack" force on Baghdad.

Though I've not heard a single Marine commander utter a word that could be construed as "interservice rivalry"—most have even praised the cooperation among the Army, Navy, Air Force, and Marines—many of the troops still feel that the USMC just isn't getting enough credit where credit is due. The Marines were the first to deploy, and most have been "in-theater" since December or January. And even the most junior Marines are aware that the Corps has a far higher proportion of its combat power committed in Iraq than any other U.S. service.

With the exception of contingents in Afghanistan and small detachments deployed with Marine Expeditionary Units elsewhere around the world, the Marine Corps has committed all of its tank and light armored vehicle battalions, over half its infantry and artillery, two-thirds of its engineers, all of its bridging equipment, over half of its helicopter assets, and nearly the same proportion of its AV-8 and F/A-18 fixed-wing aircraft to Operation Iraqi Freedom. In all, nearly 66,000 Marines, more than one-third of the entire Marine Corps, are in this fight. And so, when I-MEF was given the order to "get up and go" after the "tactical pause," the Marines were more than ready to do just that.

By dawn this morning, Dunford's RCT-5 CP had moved forward yet again and the helicopters displaced with them. Before noon we were back at the Iraqi "highway" airstrip at Hantush—right where we were when we were told to turn around for the pause.

Beside us on the highway there is a steady rumble as Dunford's one thousand tracked and wheeled vehicles move north up Route 27 headed for the Tigris. Behind us at Ad Diwaniyah, RCT-7 is in a series of running gunfights with fedayeen and Iraqi irregulars. Over the last twenty-four hours, the Iraqis have been lobbing 122mm rockets at the Marines from within the city. Several of these Soviet-era BM-21 rockets have hit in the general vicinity of the RCT-5 CP, causing us to scramble for cover. On two occasions we were ordered to "mask up" for fear that they might be firing chemical warheads. Though these rockets are wildly inaccurate, each one is packed with 140 pounds of high explosives—and no one wants an Iraqi rocketeer to get lucky. The 11th Marines counter-battery fire has been great, but if the RCT-7 infantry can eliminate the shooters inside Ad Diwaniyah, everyone will be safer while traversing Routes 1 and 27.

Enemy resistance as we move up the highway this morning has been sporadic rather than sustained, nothing like the Task Force Tarawa battle for An Nasiriyah. There, dismounted infantry had to battle from block to block and house to house against fedayeen, who had the advantage of sheltering themselves among the civilian population. Here the terrain is open, and aside from small farming villages along the way, RCT-5 is prepping every kilometer, first with fixed-wing air—F/A-18s and AV-8s—then with artillery and mortars, and finally with waves of Cobras under the direction of forward air controllers, the Marine pilots assigned to every battalion.

The battalion commanders are using their own Dragon Eye RPVs—as small as a radio-controlled model airplane, launched from a giant slingshot. The Dragon Eyes are equipped with sensors to pick out targets well before the armored columns approach what could be an ambush. But even with all this high-tech gear, it's still bone-wearying work for the grunts.

RCT-7 dispatched 3rd Battalion, 4th Marines, reinforced by a company of tanks, to enter Ad Diwaniyah and they have been going at it since dawn. Tasked with clearing out the fedayeen and Baathists loyal to Saddam, the dismounted infantry had to resort to exhausting fire team and squad rushes to root out Iraqi militia, snipers, and irregulars. Fighting from trench lines that seemed to have been hastily dug during the "pause," the disconcerted Iraqi defenders fought bravely enough. But they were no match for disciplined, well-trained Marine infantry backed up by armor. The smart ones surrendered; those who didn't died. By early afternoon, enemy resistance inside Ad Diwaniyah had ceased. So had the rocket fire.

Farther up Route 27, Dunford's RCT-5 was driving hard to the north in an effort to capture a bridge over the Tigris. To save fuel, the helicopters were holding at the roadside airstrip, waiting for the C-130s to start cycling in with bladders, pumps, and equipment for a new FARP. Maj. Mike O'Neill, the HMM-268 flight leader, also wanted to rearm his depleted flare and chaff pods because everyone is expecting heavy Iraqi anti-aircraft fire once we reach the Tigris.

I was talking to the commander of a cobbled-together Marine/Seabee/Army Engineer bridge unit when he got a radio call to come up immediately to the RCT-5 Forward CP. He agreed to take me along, jammed into the back of his Humvee along with a Navy senior chief petty officer and an Army first sergeant. We raced up the highway, weaving between tank retrievers, AAVs, and trucks carrying bridge sections, bulldozers, girders, pontoons, boats, and fuel.

From the look of things going up Route 27, the Iraqis clearly did not expect the Marines to be taking this approach to the Tigris. Unlike Route 1, with enemy bunkers at every intersection, flaming fire trenches, bulldozed tank revetments, and sandbagged fighting positions, this two-lane hardball highway was wide open. As we passed by farms and roadside buildings, mothers held their little children and watched. The older youngsters waved. The message was clear: "No Fedayeen Here" might as well have been posted on the walls of their houses. Even with the "pause," and despite the RCT-5 "pullback" of the 27th, the 1st Marine Division deception plan had still worked.

We arrived at Dunford's three-Humvee mobile command post, just as 1st Battalion, 5th Marines (1/5) succeeded in smashing through a dug-in Iraqi infantry company that had been defending the bridge over the twenty-meter-wide Saddam Canal, the last obstacle before reaching the Tigris at An Numaniyah. Despite his fatigue, the normally taciturn Joe Dunford was ecstatic. His approach march had been so swift that the Iraqis hadn't had time to blow the bridge.

The CO of the bridging unit wasn't quite so happy. The entire way up the highway he and his two senior enlisted NCOs—all reservists—had been planning how they were going to "show their stuff" by bridging the canal. But even now, in their disappointment, they began to plan how they would employ their skills the following day when RCT-5 reached the Tigris.

As 1/5 was consolidating its bridgehead on the north side of the Saddam Canal, the four HMM-268 helicopters arrived, their flare and chaff pods were reloaded, and the birds were fully fueled, courtesy of the C-130s that were landing on the roadside airstrip behind us. Griff and I immediately set up the satellite with New York before it became totally dark. The regimental chaplain, Cdr. Frank Holley, let us place our satellite antenna on top of his Humvee and plug into his 24-volt slave, as he had done so many other times to save our skins in time for a report back to the States. But just as we were about to tell the foreign desk at FOX News Channel in New York about the day's success, the Regimental S-3 took me aside and asked that we not announce to the world our location, saying, "It would be best for all of us if the Iraqis didn't know exactly how far we've gotten. We're inside his chemical weapons fan and we don't want him to reinforce the bridge over the Tigris."

It made sense to me, so in the report I prepared for the 3 p.m. (EST) news, I talked only about the success in establishing the FARP some forty kilometers behind us and the RCT-7 success in Ad

Diwaniyah earlier in the day. As it turned out, nobody in New York was much interested in the Marine move toward the Tigris. Unbeknownst to us, there was a much bigger story making news in America.

⊛ OPERATION IRAQI FREEDOM SIT REP #22
   HMM-268 Detachment with RCT-5
   Three Rivers FARP, Vic An Numaniyah, Iraq
   Wednesday, 2 April 2003
   0200 Hours Local

When we dialed into the satellite "catcher" in New York at about 2100 hours local on April 1, I was surprised that the lead story wasn't coming from Rick Leventhal, embedded with 3rd LAR, or Greg Kelly, with the Army's 3rd Infantry Division as they battled their way toward the Karbala Gap southwest of Baghdad. It was coming from CENTCOM, in Qatar. Early in the day, a terse news release had been handed out to journalists at the CENTCOM media center. It left more questions unanswered than it explained:

> April 1, 2003
> Release Number: 03-04-12
> FOR IMMEDIATE RELEASE
>
> U.S. ARMY POW RESCUED—OPERATION IRAQI FREEDOM: Coalition forces have conducted a successful rescue mission of a U.S. Army prisoner of war held captive in Iraq. The soldier has been returned to a Coalition-controlled area. More details will be released as soon as possible.
>
> -30-

That's all anyone wanted to talk about—not Army or Marine forces closing in on Baghdad. Reporters at CENTCOM and Brett

Baier, our FOX News Channel national security correspondent at the Pentagon, reported that the rescued POW was a female American soldier who had been captured by the Iraqis nine days earlier, when the 507th Maintenance Company was ambushed at An Nasiriyah, and that further details would be offered after her family was notified of her safe return. Few of us watching the little satellite television receiver even knew her name: PFC Jessica Lynch.

As Marines gathered around in the darkness to look at our little TV, the report reviewed what had happened that Sunday, the fourth day of the war. Most of us, Marines and embedded media alike, had put the 507th ambush and its tragic consequences behind us in the days since the sandstorm, the "pause," and the renewed offensive. But it hadn't been forgotten back home. Newspaper and newsmagazine writers, as well as some broadcast journalists, had pieced together quite a tale.

While we were preoccupied with the realities around us, all kinds of speculation had floated around about the engagement in which eighteen vehicles of the 507th Maintenance Company, from Fort Bliss, Texas, had become separated from the rest of their convoy. They had taken a wrong turn and fallen prey to fedayeen dressed in civilian clothes, who had unleashed AK-47s, mortars, machine guns, RPGs, and hand grenades at the soft-sided convoy.

Detailed accounts, which we had never seen, described absolute terror and chaos as the Americans tried to escape. The Iraqis had built a barricade in the road using cars and an Iraqi tank to prevent the Americans from getting past them.

Several stories described M/Sgt. Bob Dowdy, the senior NCO among the ambushed Americans, taking charge and jumping from his Humvee and dodging Iraqi bullets to help PFC Lynch and two other soldiers into his vehicle, driven by PFC Lynch's close friend, PFC Lori Piestewa.

According to some narratives, PFC Piestewa had made a valiant effort to drive through the ambush until a rocket-propelled grenade hit the front of her vehicle and it veered into a wrecked truck, killing her, M/Sgt. Dowdy, riding shotgun in the front, and two soldiers in the back of the Humvee.

Some accounts told of PFC Lynch heroically fending off enemy soldiers with an M-16 rifle, expending all of the two hundred rounds issued to her. Yet other stories said her weapon jammed and was useless. Still others said she was seriously injured and unconscious. And as if to prove that no one really knew what had happened, other narratives described both PFCs Piestewa and Lynch fighting valiantly like warriors but then captured and beaten with rifle butts, kicked, and stomped on. Differing versions depicted how PFC Lynch was shot. Others said she was stabbed.

Realizing that my story about FARPs was unlikely to get air time, I left the small crowd of weary Marines huddled around our TV and went to find my old pals from OGA—the "Other Government Agency."

The team chief, "Don," and a dozen of his operators were holed up inside a walled house about fifty meters from Dunford's mobile CP. I was allowed in the gate after convincing the new guy standing guard that, "yes, I really am Ollie North." With the exception of the twelve-inch hole in the wall made by a 25mm bushmaster, and now covered with a piece of cardboard, the place looked nice enough to have belonged to someone important.

Now, after some good-natured ribbing about me always scrounging coffee from them, they tell me what they know about the rescue. According to these guys, the operation was put together very hurriedly on March 31, when an Iraqi in An Nasiriyah told a Marine sergeant from RCT-1 that an American female soldier was being treated for severe injuries in the city's Saddam Hussein General Military Hospital. The information was passed up the line, and CENT-COM had tossed the ball to Task Force 20 (TF-20)—a unit comprising CIA paramilitary personnel, Delta Force operators, and Navy SEALs.

The very secretive TF-20 has been primarily engaged in searching for WMD, seeking out and either "taking out" or bringing in Baath Party leaders, while at the same time looking for scientists working on unconventional weapons for Saddam. Fearing that the wounded POW information might be a ruse to lure U.S. troops into a trap (because so many schools and hospitals have been converted into arsenals by the fedayeen), Special Ops Command put together a "raid plan" by the end of daylight on March 31.

The raid required that the Marines create a diversion several blocks from the hospital while an Army Ranger security cordon was surreptitiously established around the medical facility. Then TF-20 operators would swoop in by helicopter and "take down" the hospital, rescue the American POW or POWs, and extract them before the Iraqis could react.

According to the guys from OGA, at precisely 0100 hours local on April 1, the Marines kicked off "one hell of a firepower demonstration" with troops, tanks, and artillery as the TF-20 operators flew in aboard TF-160 "Nightstalker" Black Hawks at rooftop level to seize the hospital, with AC-130 gunships providing cover. The whole thing apparently "went down" flawlessly.

The lights went out in the hospital as planned, and the Iraqis—disoriented by the Marine fire on the other side of town, the noise of the helicopters, and stun grenades—offered little or no resistance. The rescue team, using NVGs, was able to search the buildings and grounds for other living and deceased Americans. They apparently found PFC Lynch exactly where the source said she was, an unarmed male nurse standing beside her bed.

As it turned out, several Iraqi doctors had wanted to try to turn her over to the Americans, because they were afraid she might die, but were afraid to do so because of the fedayeen. One of the staff led the commandos to the morgue where the bodies of two deceased Americans were located and pointed out where nine more bodies were buried outside. After evacuating Lynch by helicopter, they retrieved the bodies of the other American dead. It was, according to my storyteller, a "perfect op. No American casualties. No Iraqi casualties. Mission accomplished."

"But here's the best part, Colonel," adds one of the agency wise guys. "You got scooped! The Army sent along a combat camera crew and they videotaped the whole thing with a night lens."

I joke that he can shove his scoop where the sun doesn't shine and ask, "Seriously, guys, how much of what you've just told me can I use on the air?"

"Don," my old comrade from years gone by, says, "None of it, till CENTCOM gives the green light. Otherwise, no more coffee."

I bid the OGA boys a good night's sleep and go back to the chaplain's Humvee. The small crowd of Marines watching the poncho-hooded TV has thinned. Fatigue is taking its toll on even the most ardent TV fan. The chaplain is sleeping on top of his vehicle, and Griff is dozing on the hood—my favorite places to bunk down at night because you can't get run over up there. While everyone sleeps, FOX News Channel is playing a tape of Brig. Gen. Vincent Brooks from earlier in the day. "At this point she is safe. She's been retrieved. And some brave souls put their lives on the line to make this happen, loyal to a creed that they know, that they'll never leave a fallen comrade and embarrass their country."

With that, I shut off the TV and set my Iridium pager for 0300 so that I can be halfway awake for *Hannity & Colmes* in an hour. As I doze off, I can hear the sound of armor moving down the road a hundred meters to the west, headed in the direction of the Tigris. Overhead, there is the sound of a predator UAV and, well off in the distance, the rumble of a fixed-wing air strike headed toward Baghdad. My story of how the Marines fooled the Iraqis about the route they had chosen to invade Saddam's capital would have to wait.

✪ OPERATION IRAQI FREEDOM SIT REP #23
  With HMM-268
  North of the Tigris with RCT-5
  Wednesday, 2 April 2003
  2330 Hours Local

By the time we finish our "evening" report on *Hannity & Colmes* it is 0430 local and too late to go back to sleep. Dawn is just an hour away, and Col. Dunford's command group is already stirring. Troops of the 2nd Battalion, 5th Marines (2/5) and 2nd Tank Battalion have been moving for more than two hours, passing through 1st Battalion's lines and headed for the Tigris, just a dozen kilometers north of the Saddam Canal bridgehead that 1/5 seized at last light yesterday. RAP rounds from the artillery are chasing each other across the starlit sky as Griff and I head for a cup of coffee. Gunnery Sgt. Cheramie, Col. Dunford's tough, faithful right arm, almost always has a hot cup available somewhere and I'm in need of one.

As we arrive at the RCT-5 CP—a tent has now been set up to allow the watch officers to plot the course of the attack on their acetate-covered maps—a call comes in for a cas-evac. Two Marines have been wounded by RPG fire. We head back to the birds. A runner from the CP beats us, and by the time we get there, two of the four helos are getting ready to launch. But as we're about to board—me on one helicopter, Griff on the other—one of the crew chiefs informs us that the birds aren't coming back here. "Sir, they're taking the casualties all the way back to the rear," he shouts to us above the sound of the helos spooling up. This means they'll be taken to Kuwait.

The thought of missing the Marines' crossing of the Tigris is inconceivable to me, and so we stay behind. This would be the only cas-evac mission of the entire war that we would miss.

A little over an hour later we are back at the CP when the call comes in from the 2nd Tank Battalion that they had battled their way through An Numaniyah—a city of some seventy-five thousand people—and are firing at Iraqi armor across the Tigris. Col. Dunford, who couldn't have had more than an hour's sleep, is sitting on a folding camp stool with a radio handset pressed against his ear.

The Iraqis caught completely by surprise at the Marine advance up Route 27 have failed to destroy the heavy span over the Tigris at An Numaniyah. Though he has to be exhausted, Dunford is patiently talking to his tank battalion commander as if chatting on the phone with an old friend. No bravado. No tough talk. No BS. Just two warriors who respect each other, knowing the lives of their men hung in the balance if they make the wrong decision.

As the sun crests the horizon on his right, Lt. Col. Mike Oehle, the CO of 2nd Tank Battalion, can see the Iraqis on the far side of the Tigris through the thermal sights of his M-1 tank. The enemy has a handful of T-72s, some BMPs, and dug-in infantry with RPGs. Oehle's unit has already taken some RPG hits coming through the city, but his command is intact, and so is the massive concrete-and-steel span across the muddy Tigris. Incredible as it seems, the Iraqis still have not blown the bridge.

Upstream, commander of the 2nd Battalion, 5th Marines, Lt. Col. Pete Donohue—one of Dunford's so-called Irish Mafia—is thrashing around in the mud with his LAVs and AAVs, looking for an undefended ford where a pontoon span can be put down. Dunford wants the option just in case the bridge at An Numaniyah is unusable by the seventy-two–ton behemoths of Oehle's 2nd Tank Battalion.

Crossing the Tigris on the concrete bridge at An Numaniyah is a terrible risk. The threat of being cut off by a superior force on the other side is very real. So too is the possibility that the Iraqis might have the bridge registered by artillery with high explosives or even chemical weapons. Dunford asks Mike Oehle if he thinks the bridge can be taken. Oehle says, "We can do it."

An hour later, after a brief but furious fight supported by Cobra gunships, the bridge is in American hands and the lead elements of 2nd Tank Battalion have crossed the Tigris. In the battle through An Numaniyah and across the bridge, Oehle has lost just one of his M-1 tanks, and the crew has survived. Still, nearly all his remaining tanks are scarred by RPG hits—deep gouges dug out of the armor plate, and gear strapped to the turrets blackened by fire—yet otherwise unscathed. But Oehle's tankers have also expended hundreds of rounds of main gun ammunition and nearly all of their .50-caliber and 7.62mm. Before he can press on to consolidate the bridgehead, he has to rearm and refuel.

By mid-afternoon, Donahue's 2/5 has secured the second Tigris crossing point some twenty kilometers north of the An Numaniyah bridge, and the combined Marine/Seabee/Army combat engineers— now calling themselves the "bridgemasters"—finally get a chance to deploy the pontoon span they planned to use at the Saddam Canal. By dark, despite having to perform strenuous labor in full MOPP, minus gas masks (which remained on everyone's hips), the Marines have crushed the Baghdad division of the Republican Guard and put down a second span across the Tigris.

But night doesn't mean sleep. Under cover of darkness, Dunford pushes the rest of RCT-5 across the river, along with his log trains, so that every unit will be ready for the final sprint up Route 6 toward Baghdad in the morning. Before anyone rests, he wants his units aligned for the attack up the highway. It is a night full of movement: Humvees, tanks, AAVs, LAVs, trucks—even the helicopters.

Fuel and ammo trucks pull alongside the "combat coils" of armor, while the "wrench turners" do their best to maintain and repair what they can before kicking off again in the attack. Not far up the road, an M-88 tank retriever is pulled up behind an M-1 Abrams tank installing a new engine—the "power pack," they call it—while ammo is being loaded on one side and fuel pumped in from the other.

Fifty kilometers east of RCT-5, along Route 7, RCT-1 has accomplished its mission of making the Iraqis believe that the Marines intend to force a crossing at Al Kut. As night settles in over the Tigris, the regiment is preparing to break contact and race upriver to join RCT-5 and RCT-7 for the final sprint to Saddam's capital. But in none of these units is there a sense of euphoria or elation at what has been accomplished. Everyone is so tired that the historic gravity of the moment simply ebbs away in sweat and fatigue.

✪ OPERATION IRAQI FREEDOM SIT REP #24
   With HMM-268 and RCT-5
   North of the Tigris, Vic Al Aziziyah
   Thursday, 3 April 2003
   2200 Hours Local

The word has come down from the division commander, Maj. Gen. Mattis, directly to Joe Dunford, commanding RCT-5: "Go heavy kinetic all the way to Baghdad." Dunford isn't wasting any time on carrying out the order.

At 0645 hours local, Lt. Col. Jerry Driscoll and two replacement CH-46s arrive at the RCT-5 CP on Route 6. Marine Air Group 39 now has a contingent of four "Phrogs" from HMM-268 and two armed UH1Ns from HMLA-267—along with as many as eight to ten

AH1 Cobras in direct support of the RCT-5 attack. The air controllers have taken to calling this gaggle of helicopters "Dunford's Air Force" and it's getting a workout this morning.

Before dawn, Lt. Col. Sam Mundy's 3rd Battalion, 5th Marines (3/5), supported by a company of LAVs and a company of tanks, kicks off up Route 6 beneath a barrage of artillery. Throughout the night and early dawn, RPVs have traversed the highway, looking for enemy armor and emplacements. When found, they were hit first by the F/A-18 or AV-8 fixed-wing strikes, then artillery. Mundy has kept the Cobras for close-in work—they buzz like pairs of angry wasps up and down the highway, looking for things to shoot at. The closer 3/5 gets to Al Aziziyah, the more they find.

The first call for a cas-evac comes in a little after 0700, Driscoll launches his bird and another one piloted by Maj. Mike O'Neil to pick up three of Mundy's Marines, who have been hit by an Iraqi mortar round. As we fly up the highway, "fire trenches" burning bright orange send plumes of black smoke billowing into the sky. The roadside itself is littered with wrecked Iraqi trucks and armor, some of it still burning. The troops, with their penchant for pithy vernacular, have taken to referring to the wrecked enemy equipment as "roadkill."

Unlike Route 27, which had been all but devoid of defenses, Route 6 has clearly been prepared for a deep defense. On both sides of the hardball highway are interconnected trench lines and numerous fire pits filled with a mixture of kerosene and crude oil. Numerous revetments have been dug with bulldozers, but relatively few contain the tanks or BMP armored personnel carriers for which they have been prepared.

As the CH-46s land on the green smoke that marks the pickup zone, my camera catches a platoon of Marines dismounted from their AAVs, all prone and all pointing outward. Directly on the nose of Driscoll's bird is an M-1, buttoned up, its turret traversing back and forth as the gunner trolls for targets. I can see no other "friendlies" out in front, but off in the distance, perhaps two kilometers away, is the built-up area of Al Aziziyah. Smoke is rising from several multi-story structures. While the litters with the wounded are loaded in the back, an F/A-18 rolls in low and drops an MK-81 one thousand pound bomb. By the time the sound of the concussion reaches us, the jet is already out of sight in the blue sky above.

Even before the fight on Route 6 began, a FARP and Army shock-trauma hospital had been established at the captured airfield south-west of An Numaniyah. We deliver the wounded to the Army doctors, hop to a fuel point about seventy-five meters away, and are on our way back to RCT-5 in less than thirty minutes.

It goes this way for most of the morning: 3rd Battalion pushes up the road a few hundred meters, takes some casualties, we cas-evac them and then return for more. Though it is fraught with some risk (simply flying in a thirty-five-year-old helicopter is risky enough), it is relatively uneventful in comparison with what the troops on the ground are enduring. All that changes with the first mission of the afternoon.

I have just opened an MRE for lunch and the crew chief, Gunnery Sgt. Pennington, and Lt. Col. Driscoll are ribbing me about my penchant for putting Tabasco on everything, when a runner from the RCT-5 air boss breathlessly informs Driscoll that 3/5 has "taken six priority WIA just outside of Aziziyah."

While I gulp down my "Country Captain Chicken" MRE, Driscoll and O'Neil climb into their cockpits, fire up their APUs, and confirm the grid coordinates for the pickup zone. In a matter of minutes both helicopters are airborne, flying up Route 6 at fifty feet and 120 knots, seemingly just clearing the antennas of the vehicles that jam the highway as far as we can see in front of and behind us. To the left and right of the highway, artillery batteries are deployed, the tubes of their 155mm howitzers all pointing northwest—toward the 3/5 fight against the Republican Guard Al Nida division in the outskirts of Al Aziziyah.

As we approach the pickup zone, Driscoll eases back on the air speed as he tries to make radio contact with the unit on the ground with the casualties. Below us, and about two hundred yards to our right, dismounted Marines are doing a fire-and-maneuver action toward a grove of eucalyptus trees. Gunnery Sgt. Pennington peers over his .50-caliber to guide the bird to a safe landing. A hundred meters to our right front, in a field between the highway and the grove of trees, a smoke grenade pops just as Driscoll lifts the nose of the CH-46 to flare for landing. I'm leaning out the right side door of the helicopter with my video camera. Suddenly I see an RPG whizzing toward us from the grove of trees. I'm not supposed to, but instinct takes over and I yell, "RPG, three o'clock, incoming!" into the inter-com mike on my cranial helmet.

The engines screech and the rotor blades sound as if they might break as Driscoll pulls up on the collective, momentarily arresting the helicopter's descent. Gunny Pennington, reaching the doorway, shouts, "Where?" over the din, as the RPG passes beneath us and det-onates against the berm beside the roadway to our left.

The Marines below us, having seen where the RPG came from, open fire in a furious fusillade. A machine gunner with a 240-Golf is hammering away at the tree line, and the up-gun on an AAV off to our right starts popping 40mm grenades into the same area. Pen-nington now decides that there won't be a lot of opportunities to pick up the wounded below us, just forward of the swirling sandstorm being generated by our rotor wash. Leaning out the door, he calmly says to Col. Driscoll, "Straight down, twenty feet, sir."

In the cockpit, Driscoll can't see anything forward or to his side and is totally dependent on Pennington's judgment. His eyes scanning the radar altimeter and attitude indicator, he lowers the twelve-ton helicopter straight down and drops the ramp. As soon as he's on the ground, I can hear him radio his wingman to wave off and slowly head back down the highway. "We'll take all the wounded aboard our bird and catch up on the way to the Army shock-trauma hospital at An Numaniyah," he tells him.

While the AAVs and the dismounted troops on our right keep the enemy in the tree line pinned down, the litter bearers, running hunched over, as Marines do when they are being shot at, bring the three wounded up the ramp and snap the litters into the straps on the left side of the bird. Our two corpsmen, Docs Newsome and Comeaux, are already evaluating them and starting IVs to reduce shock as we lift off. The whole process—from landing to takeoff—has taken less than four minutes.

✪ ✪ ✪

By the time we return from the An Numaniyah FARP, the 2nd Tank Battalion has broken through the Iraqi defenses at Al Aziziyah and Mundy's 3rd Battalion is in the process of aggressively clearing Iraqi defenders from the streets and alleys of the little town alongside the river. Mundy's last task, accomplished just before nightfall, was to push a rifle company across the small bridge over the Tigris. After a sharp pitched battle at the bridge, RCT-5 captured three crossing points over the waterway.

After dark, Dunford decides to move his CP forward, beyond the town Mundy had just secured. Having had enough helicopter adventures for one day, I rode up Route 6 in a Humvee with one of the RCT-5 communications detachments. As we roll through the town and up the highway, the "roadkill" is extraordinary. Through my night-vision goggles I can see dozens of ravaged Iraqi T-55s, BMPs, and BTR-60s littering the edges of the highway. It is clear that the Iraqis had meant to hold Al Aziziyah—but have failed. Most notable is the fact that a good number of the Iraqi tanks have been destroyed, not while facing the oncoming Marines but while heading northwest in retreat toward Baghdad.

Dunford has set up his "jump CP" inside a compound formerly occupied by the local Republican Guard commander. The walls of the buildings are pockmarked by M-1 tank .50-caliber tank fire, and several structures have holes clear through them from main gun rounds. By the time all four of the HMM-268 helicopters land at the new RCT-5 CP, it's after midnight and everyone is totally exhausted. Driscoll, his pilots, and his crew crawl into litters in the back of the 46s to sleep until summoned for another cas-evac.

As Griff and I drag our broadcast gear over to a Humvee to plug into some power so that we can report, the M-1s of 2nd Tank Battalion are being refueled and rearmed on the Route 6 hardball highway, about fifty meters to our southwest. These Abrams tanks are magnificent killing machines. But because they consume a gallon of fuel every two and a half miles or so, they are even thirstier than the Marines who fight from them.

When we come up on the air, Greg Kelly, embedded with 3rd Infantry Division, is reporting on the furious daylong battle to capture Saddam International Airport. The videotape he's fed over his satellite dish back to FOX News Channel in New York is some of the most dramatic combat footage I've ever seen—and I see a lot of it when prepping for each episode of *War Stories*. When we go live for *Hannity & Colmes* at 0330, the starlit sky is once again full of RAP rounds as the 11th Marines' artillery softens up tomorrow's objective, the Tigris River town of Tuwayhah, less than thirty-five kilometers from Baghdad.

CHAPTER NINE
CLOSING IN

Gen. Mattis planned to relaunch the attack up Route 6 before dawn this morning but had to delay it until the RCT-5 "log trains," strung out for miles behind, could catch up to the fast-moving combat elements. I almost bumped into him early this morning as I walked toward the RCT-5 CP, canteen cup in hand, out to beg for a cup of hot coffee. I had been up since doing our 0330 "hit" with *Hannity & Colmes*, but had not yet shaved—something I try to do every day, but only *after* that first cup of coffee, since the canteen cup also serves as a washbasin. Shaving in this war isn't just a matter of hygiene, discipline, or appearance; it could be the difference between life and death, since the military gas mask fits much closer on a clean-shaven face.

Mattis, already clean-shaven despite the early hour, is on his way to his CP, located just a few yards from that of RCT-5, and he looks agitated. For a moment I think he was upset by my hirsute appearance. But when I say, "How about an interview with FOX News Channel, General?" he stops, looks me over, and smiles.

"Aren't you too old for this stuff?" he asks.

"Never too old if you're fit. I'm doing okay!" I reply. "How about we take five minutes and get you on tape for FOX?"

He pauses, then responds, "Not today. I can't do it now. I've got to make some changes. You're doing fine just talking with the troops. Keep up the good work." And with that, he heads on to his CP—two back-to-back LVTC-7s with canvas and a camouflage net thrown over them.

Had I been a little less fatigued, I would have asked the CG (commanding general), "What are you going to change? Will there be a new order of movement? Are we now going straight north, bypassing Baghdad?" (As one rumor has it.) But I wasn't quick enough.

An hour later, when Lt. Col. Jerry Driscoll returns from the CP, he takes me aside and says, "General Mattis is replacing Joe Dowdy as CO of RCT-1."

"Why?" I ask, suddenly realizing that this must be the "change" Mattis had meant. Though I have spent most of the last fifteen days with RCT-5, it seems to me that all the regimental combat teams have been doing an exceptional job. RCT-1 and Task Force Tarawa have seen some of the heaviest action thus far in the war.

"Can't say for sure," Driscoll replies. "Scuttlebutt is that the CG believes Dowdy is burned out. John Toolan, the G-3 Ops, is taking command of RCT-1. Dowdy is going to become the senior Marine on the EP-3."

Serving aboard the EP-3, a flying intelligence-gathering aircraft, as the eyes and ears for the Marines is an extremely important post, but it isn't the same as commanding 6,500 Marines in combat. Considering Dowdy's distinguished record, this would not be something he'd have wanted—no matter how exhausted he was. And for Mattis, changing commanders in the midst of a combat operation had to be a very difficult decision.

This was the kind of event that some could spin into a very negative story, and I decide that both Joe Dowdy and Gen. Mattis deserve better than that. Even though it is after midnight back in the States, I think it was worth trying to get the story up first on FOX, and I head off to locate Griff. I find him asleep on the ramp of a CH-46, his feet hanging over the edge, his head "pillowed" on his backpack, a half-eaten MRE on his chest.

We set out to find a vehicle that is not about to pull out so that we can set up our satellite transmission equipment using its auxiliary power tap. After pleading our case with five or six Humvees and trucks, we finally find a Radio Battalion Humvee that isn't getting lined up for the dash up the road, and we plug in our equipment. When the foreign desk answers in New York, I ask if there is space for a story on a change of command in the 1st Marine Division and quickly learn that the *only* story that matters at the moment was the Army's 3rd Infantry Division action at the Saddam International Airport. And that FOX News Channel is already right in the middle of it.

For the next few hours, as RCT-5 rearms, refuels, and replenishes on Route 6, Griff, the CH-46 crews, and a dozen or so Marines sit in front of our little satellite TV, transfixed by some of the best combat footage and reporting we've seen. Greg Kelly and his field producer/cameraman, Mal James, have been embedded with the 3rd Infantry Division all the way from Kuwait. They have covered the fight at An Najaf and the breakthrough at the Karbala Gap against the Medina division of the Republican Guard. Now Kelly and James are covering, live, the desperate fight to take and hold Saddam International Airport.

Late on April 3, a company-sized unit from 3rd Infantry Division, consisting of fewer than twenty Abrams tanks and Bradley fighting vehicles, had been conducting a "reconnaissance in force" action west of the airport when they seized two intersections on a key approach. Told to hold in place, they had done so against overwhelming odds throughout the night. By dawn on April 4, the small unit had withstood over a dozen assaults by Republican Guard armor and dismounted fedayeen. Kelly's night lens captured much of the action as more than five hundred foreign fighters—charging on foot, in cars, in pickup trucks, and on motorcycles—died trying to take out the U.S. unit.

About the time I call in to New York, Kelly is reporting on an attack by more than twenty Republican Guard T-72 tanks against a small detachment of 3rd Infantry Division Abrams and Bradleys. In minutes, the 25mm chain guns on the Bradleys and the 120mm main guns on the Abrams destroy more than a dozen of the T-72s and so clutter the approach to their position with burning Iraqi armor that the surviving enemy tanks beat a hasty retreat.

Just before noon—0445 back in New York—we have to break down our satellite link because the vehicle we have been using for power has to get in line to move up the highway. As we do so, I tell Griff that we need to have our gear ready to set up again as soon as we are stationary. The footage Kelly and James were feeding from 3rd Infantry Division was too good to miss.

By noon, trucks with food, fuel, ammo, and water have replenished the troops and vehicles of RCT-5 and we are ready to resume the move toward Baghdad on Route 6. With 2nd Tank Battalion leading the attack up the four-lane highway, artillery firing in the distance, Cobra gunships snarling just overhead, and the LAVs heading off to scout the flanks, all one thousand vehicles of RCT-5 begin to move.

From the ramp of Driscoll's CH-46, staged just thirty meters off the hardball highway, I can see Col. Joe Dunford leaning against the hood of his vehicle in the little, three-Humvee command group as the lead element of 2nd Tank Battalion rumbles past. The tank commanders, standing in their turrets, and the gunners in the CAAT Humvees must be able to see him as well—a tall, thin, solitary figure, just a few feet off the road. He's wearing a chemical suit, flak jacket, and helmet just like everyone else, no sign of his rank or position. As I walk toward him, the ground shaking from the weight of the passing vehicles, the air full of dust and diesel smoke, the roar of the engines too loud for speaking, I wonder if any of those passing by him know that this is the man who has just set an astounding arsenal in motion.

When I reach Dunford, I notice that he is simply watching, not gesturing or waving. Ten meters away, Gunnery Sgt. Cheramie is checking his Benelli shotgun to make sure that it's loaded and ready. On the mounts atop the Humvees, the gunners are locking and loading. As I walk up beside the vehicles, Cpl. Moorehead, one of Dunford's command group drivers, sees me and then, gesturing toward the highway, yells, "Awesome."

Not wanting to intrude on Dunford's thoughts, I hang back for a few moments. When he finally turns away from the road and moves toward his vehicle, he notices me standing with Gunny Cheramie and comes over.

"Very impressive, Colonel" was all I could manage.

"Yes," he responds, "It makes you think."

I nod in agreement. "Watching all this go by makes me think of Robert E. Lee's remark to Longstreet at Fredericksburg in 1862: 'It is well that war is so terrible; we would grow too fond of it!'"

Dunford looks at me almost quizzically, and says, "Indeed." Then, taking his seat in the right front of his Humvee, he turns to me and says, "Be careful today." With that, the three vehicles charge up the incline at the edge of the highway and join the column rolling toward Baghdad.

Lt. Col. Driscoll and I go up to the RCT-5 Bravo Command Group CP to listen on the radios for progress reports as the column makes its way up the road. The question on everyone's mind is whether the remnants of the Al Nida division of the Republican Guard, badly mauled already, will put up a fight. Our answer comes in less than a half hour.

At about 1245 hours, the first call for a cas-evac comes in from the lead elements of 2nd Tank Battalion, who have been trying to push into the small industrial city of Tuwayhah. Driscoll plots the grid coordinates for the pickup zone as I look over his shoulder. On his 1:25,000 map, it looks to me as though the pickup zone is right in the middle of an intersection near the outskirts of Tuwayhah. He checks again to confirm the location, verifies the site on the aerial photo taped to a board above the radios, shrugs, and says, "Okay, I'll fly this one."

We walked back to the four CH-46s and he briefs the other flight crews saying that the zone was big enough for only one bird and that he would fly in, and pick up the four casualties and his wingman would loiter behind us while we are on the deck to make sure we get out with the casualties. The DASC promises to send a pair of Cobras for escort if any could be spared.

As soon as we lift off, Gunny Pennington orders the machine guns locked and loaded. As we fly at fifty feet and 110 knots up the highway, my camera records the two corpsmen in the back preparing their gear for the casualties. Cpl. Kendall, the left-side gunner, is crouched and scanning the terrain below. Pennington confirms over the intercom that "Dash Two is seven rotors at five o'clock, level," meaning that Driscoll's wingman was about 140 feet behind, on our right rear at the same altitude.

Holding my camera to shoot through the front canopy, I can see the bright orange of flame trenches on both sides of the road as we fly through billowing black smoke. Wrecked and burning Iraqi T-55s, T-62s, trucks, BMPs, and occasional fuelers are all over the four-lane highway. Some are smoking in the revetments that were so carefully dug in the six months the Iraqis had to prepare their defenses.

Up ahead, columns of smoke are rising above the city. We're now flying over increasing numbers of multistory buildings in what appears to be an industrial area. My camera catches four Cobras, wheeling, diving, and firing—the bright flash and the contrails of Hellfire missiles and five-inch rockets clearly visible. At the rate they are firing, they'll be out of ammunition by the time we arrive at the pickup landing zone. This means we'll have no overhead protection while we're on the ground.

I have jammed the camera's microphone up inside my helmet so that the tape will pick up Driscoll's radio calls to the unit on the ground with the casualties. He's been transmitting, "Iron Horse Alpha, this is Grizzly Two Zero"—the call signs for A Company, 2nd Tank Battalion and for his CH-46 helicopter—but he gets no response. All that can be heard on this frequency is the sound of heavy gunfire, both incoming and outgoing, and a lot of yelling as someone on the ground with a headset mike keyed open shouts orders. It's the sound of a furious firefight, and it seems to be taking place right in front of us.

Driscoll changes frequencies and comes up on a Regimental Tac Net, and now I can hear the unbelievably calm voice of "Fighting Joe" Dunford talking to Lt. Col. Mike Oehle, the 2nd Tank Battalion commander. Neither man seems unduly excited, though the sound of gunfire can be heard in both their transmissions. Oehle reports that he has lost an M-1 to an ATGM—an anti-tank guided missile—either a Russian-supplied Sagger or one provided by our NATO allies, the French.

Driscoll slows his approach—I can see the airspeed indicator drop to forty knots—and he finally makes radio contact with a Humvee at the landing zone. The Marine on the ground advises that they have "popped a smoke" and that the zone is "tight" and "hot." Driscoll's response is a laconic, "Roger, one frog inbound."

We're now flying literally at rooftop level straight down a city street, just clearing the utility poles on both sides. Fixed-wing air strikes, artillery, the Cobras, and fire from the Abrams guns have blasted the buildings on each side of the street. Yet, as we slow to a hover, a black-clad figure leans out a second-story window and points an AK-47 at us. Pennington sees him as I do and says without pre-amble, "Firing the right side fifty."

The noise of the gun opening up just two feet in front of my cam-era is deafening as the shooter disappears amid chunks of flying brick and mortar. Somehow Driscoll manages to put the CH-46 down dead-on in the middle of an intersection. As the ramp at the rear drops down, I can see power lines to our front, our rear, and both sides. All around us are Marines, dismounted from their vehicles, fir-ing into the buildings just twenty to thirty meters on every side. To our right, down the street, an M-1 is slamming .50-caliber rounds into a low-slung building. Directly in front of the CH-46 is another American tank. This one is using its main gun to engage something farther down the street that we can't see. As the dust from our land-ing clears, Marines carrying litters start running in a low crouch for the back of the helicopter from the alleyways and several nearby doorways.

As they make their way toward us, an ambulance comes racing up from our left and skids to a halt in the intersection. We already have four wounded aboard, and it looks as if at least six or seven more are on the ambulance. There's space for only six litters rigged on the bird, because of concern of overloading these old helicopters. Driscoll says, "Let's get everyone possible aboard, so that we don't have to bring in Dash Two if we don't have to."

The corpsmen, ducking rounds that are clearly aimed at them, start to unload the wounded and bring them aboard. Suddenly, an RPG passes in front of the helicopter, exploding in the dirt about fif-teen meters beyond us. The crack of AK-47 rounds is audible over the sound of our engines and the outgoing fire. All this prompts Driscoll to ask over the radio, "How much longer, folks? This is a pretty sporty zone."

Sporty? It strikes me as an interesting way to describe the hottest LZ I've ever been in, and I've been in a bunch. We're downtown, surrounded by multistory buildings and power lines. A whole lot of bad guys have decided to shoot at the biggest target around: a CH-46 parked in their backyard. And Jerry Driscoll calls this "sporty."

Now the unit on the ground calls for help. They don't want their cas-evac helicopter burning in the intersection any more than we do. As Pennington and Kendall work over the second story of the buildings on both sides of the bird, three Humvees race up from the left, machine guns blazing from their roofs. One stays on our left, another takes up a position to our rear, and the third parks in the intersection to our right. As they continue to blast away at our tormentors, a Marine disembarks from the Humvee to our right and crouches down behind the door, prepared to engage any Iraqi or fedayeen crazy enough to show himself. Looking up from the camera viewfinder, I realize that the sentry is Gunnery Sgt. Cheramie. In the front seat of the Humvee is "Grizzly Six," the CO of RCT-5, Col. Joe Dunford.

Dunford had helped load the dead and wounded aboard the ambulance—after fighting off a fedayeen attack—and was escorting the ambulance to our helicopter when he heard over his radio that we were being fired upon in the zone. Knowing that there were far too many casualties for one helicopter, he directed his little command group to surround us. He also ordered Sam Mundy's 3rd Battalion to close up and clear the street behind us so that the second CH-46 could land. Logic would seem to indicate that one helo landing into that "sporty" landing zone was crazy enough—but two of them?

Finally, with eleven casualties aboard our helicopter and ten on the bird behind us, Driscoll gives the word to lift off. The two heavily loaded helicopters lift a few feet off the ground. With power poles and lines just inches away from the blade tips, the helos rotate 180 degrees so that *if* we managed to clear the lines and poles, we'll at least be taking off over "friendlies."

With engines and rotors screaming, the ancient helicopter shudders as Driscoll lifts her straight up between the obstacles, tilts the nose down, and gathers airspeed. Somehow, he clears the power poles, wires, and structures around the zone and delivers the casualties to the hospital. It is, at that point in my life, the hottest helicopter LZ I've ever been in—and over the years I've been in a fair number of "hot" LZs. But as it turned out, the day was just getting started.

By mid-afternoon all four HMM-268 helicopters are shuttling casualties from the engagement in Tuwayhah and another gunfight at Salman Pak—long suspected to be the location of a terrorist training center for the Saddam fedayeen and radicals from other Middle Eastern countries. Like the earlier casualty pickup zones, the Salman Pak LZs are all "urban," meaning that they are mostly intersections of city streets, surrounded by multistory buildings, power lines, and enemy soldiers firing at the birds when they are most vulnerable—while they're getting on the ground and taking off.

In order to get some footage of different runs into the city, I arrange to ride with Maj. Mike O'Neil on a cas-evac run into Salman Pak. But Gunny Pennington pulls rank and comes along as crew chief, saying that he wants to make sure that everything checks out on some fix that's been performed on O'Neil's helicopter.

The flight into the zone is another hair-raising adventure in rooftop terrain avoidance, and Maj. O'Neil drops the bird into a tight little intersection. My camera lens catches the litter-bearers, bending low, racing for the ramp of the bird—and Pennington's .50-caliber hammering at the second story of the building on the right side of the helicopter.

To our left front, the up gun on an AAV pumps a stream of high-explosive rounds into a building as O'Neil lifts off, carefully threading both rotors between the wires that seem only inches from our blade tips.

Then, just as it seemed we were clear, the crack of AK-47 fire comes from a rooftop sniper. Invisible to the troops and armor on the street, the sniper empties his magazine as we fly by.

Bullets hitting the skin of a helicopter sound a lot like someone striking sheet metal with a ball-peen hammer. As we fly through the hail of fire, fuel spurts from the engine area and drains down over the tail ramp. Pennington's response, as he unleashes a burst of .50-caliber fire at the offending Iraqi or fedayeen, is, "Man, they shot my helicopter. Now I'm really pissed."

From the cockpit, Maj. O'Neil, still unflappable, asks, "Everything okay back there?"

Pennington quickly checks with the two corpsmen who have continued attending the wounded as if nothing has happened. He reports, "No other casualties, but it looks like we've got a ruptured fuel line up top."

O'Neil, apparently ignoring the fact that several people have just spent the last ten minutes trying to kill him, replies, "Okay, let's see if we can get some help for these wounded grunts before this thing quits on us."

Most Marine grunts will tell you that the guys who fly helicopters are all a little crazy. First, according to the guys on the ground, the thing they drive around in the sky is sort of like a bumblebee, with a body that seems way too heavy for the little "wings." Second, helicopters have far too many moving parts. Logic dictates that anything with that many pieces is likely to end up in pieces, along with the people it carries. Pilots and air crewmen like the Red Dragons of HMM-268 apparently don't think much of such criticism, since they jump at the chance to fly these ancient contraptions into harm's way, even though tooling around Camp Pendleton in them is dangerous enough.

When we land at the shock-trauma hospital back down Route 6, we're still well within range of Iraqi artillery and rocket fire, but O'Neil says, "Let's shut her down and see how bad the damage is."

Pennington is immediately on the ramp, bathed in jet fuel, looking for the rupture. When he finds where the bullet nicked the fuel line, he takes out his Leatherman tool, pinches the aluminum tube on either side of the rupture, and snips out the damaged length of metal pipe—about the diameter of a soda straw. He looks at it for a few seconds, climbs atop the helicopter, opens the forward rotor nacelle over the cockpit, and snips a length of tubing from the unused heater hidden inside. Climbing back down, he takes the piece of "pipe" he just extracted from the heater and a pair of clamps and repairs the damaged fuel line, all in less than ten minutes. After making sure that the clamps are as tight as he can get them, he puts on his helmet and says over the intercom, "Okay, Major, let's see if we've got this thing fixed. Would you start her up, sir?"

The engine screeches to life and we make an uneventful flight back to the RCT-5 CP. When we land to await the next cas-evac call, I ask Pennington where he had learned to make that repair, adding, "I can't imagine that what you did with that heater fuel line is in the Boeing tech manual."

"No, it's not," Pennington replies with a grin. "But years ago, when I was a corporal, a staff sergeant told a bunch of us youngsters, 'If you ever need a length of fuel line in an emergency, the fuel line for the heater is the same as the ones for the engines.' Turns out he was right."

Marine staff NCOs are said to be the repositories of all the wisdom the Corps has collected since 1775. It's moments like this that make me believe the axiom is true. But I didn't have long to ponder the mysteries of that extraordinary fraternity; Chief Barry now needs us to remove our gear from inside the helicopter. The corpsmen, using five-gallon cans full of water and bleach, are scrubbing the litters, troop seats, and floor. Everything has been soaked with Marine blood. By the time they finish, the sand behind the helicopter is tinged red and there is a small mountain of bloody battle dressings, IV bags and tubes, latex gloves, morphine styrettes, and syringes, as well as boots and pieces of uniforms that the docs cut away while saving lives.

✪ OPERATION IRAQI FREEDOM SIT REP #26
   With RCT-5 and HMM-268
   Route 6, southeast of Baghdad
   Friday, 4 April 2003
   2200 Hours Local

By the end of the day we've evacuated more than three dozen Marine casualties. One of them was a staff sergeant who had walked aboard the helicopter while helping to carry another wounded Marine on a litter. We've been admonished not to show the faces of U.S. casualties, and so my camera catches only his right hand, wrapped in a blood-soaked battle dressing, as he sits down in one of the troop seats.

On the way to the Army shock-trauma hospital, I run out of videotape. We arrive at the hospital, and I help unload the litters so that the most grievously injured will be treated first. The corpsmen tell the "walking wounded" seated in the troop seats to wait. After the last litter case is off the bird, I turn to help the staff sergeant with the wounded hand and notice that he is nearly unconscious. As he tries to stand, I see he has been sitting in a pool of his own blood. I yell for one of the docs, who runs up and opens the staff sergeant's flak jacket. He's been gut shot—some of his intestines are bulging out through the wound. The doc yells, "Keep him awake!" and runs to get a litter team.

As we gently load him on the stretcher, I ask him, "Why didn't you say something?"

He says, "The other guys were hurt worse than I am."

✪ ✪ ✪

This is some of the stiffest fighting thus far in the campaign, but no one here has any doubt about the outcome. It's also clear that increasing numbers of foreign fedayeen are joining the fight. They've cut fire trenches at nearly every intersection, filled them with oil, lit them, and made movement very difficult and dangerous through streets now nearly obscured by thick, black clouds of acrid, choking smoke.

As 2nd Tank Battalion and 3rd Battalion, 5th Marines chew their way through Tuwayhah, increasing numbers of "civilians" straggle out of the town. Many of them are young men with short haircuts wearing clean white thobes and sandals. Everyone knows that they are deserters, but they simply walk on by, having hidden their weapons and shed their uniforms. No one wants to take the time, troops, or trucks necessary to detain them and transport them two hundred miles to the rear.

When we get our satellite equipment up, we learn that, miles behind us, Task Force Tarawa and RCT-1 have accepted the surrender of an estimated 2,500 troops from the Baghdad division of the Republican Guard. The news from New York also informs us that Iraqis are deserting in northern Iraq, and that to discourage others from doing the same, Iraqi commanders and the fedayeen are conducting public executions of any of their troops caught deserting.

By nightfall, RCT-5 has moved through Salman Pak and Tuwayhah, and Sam Mundy's 3/5 has cleared the highway on both sides of Route 6. For Mundy's Marines the afternoon and early evening were a repeat of the action the day before at Al Aziziyah. Dismounted infantry rushed through the built-up area and then beyond that into the farmlands north of the city. It was exhausting for his already tired troops.

Though the Republican Guard regulars cut and ran after 2nd Tanks broke through Tuwayhah, the foreign fedayeen stayed to fight

there and in Salman Pak. For more than five hours and as many kilometers, the 3/5 rifle companies slogged up the rough ground parallel
to the highway, supported by fire from the AAV up-guns on the road.
Together they rooted out Syrian, Jordanian, Saudi, Egyptian, and
Yemeni fighters who weren't just *willing* to die on their jihad—they
wanted to die. Mundy's Marines obliged them. There may be prisoners taken elsewhere, but along this stretch of Route 6, I saw only two
of the fedayeen taken alive—both were badly wounded.

Not all the Iraqis got away. Late in the afternoon, as we landed
next to where the RCT-5 CP would be established for the night, an
Iraqi major general, the chief of staff of the Special Republican Guard,
tried to run a roadblock in his nice white luxury sedan. It was his last
mistake. Griff's camera captured the image—the dead general and his
driver, splayed out on the shoulder of the road beside the car. Inside
the bloody vehicle was the dead general's pet dog, also killed in the
hail of gunfire.

Late that night, a messenger from Mundy's CP brings a sandbag
containing captured documents to the RCT-2 command post. It is full
of foreign passports taken from those who died trying to kill Mundy's
Marines just eighteen kilometers from the outskirts of Baghdad.

✪ OPERATION IRAQI FREEDOM SIT REP #27
    With RCT-5 and HMM-268
    Southeast suburbs of Baghdad
    Saturday, 5 April 2003
    2300 Hours Local

The night does not begin well. At about 2200 hours, I am asleep on
the hood of Chaplain Frank Holley's Humvee when I am awakened
by the sound of incoming Katusha rockets—the big 122mm I
remember so well from Con Thien and Khe Sanh, even after so many

years. In an instant, Marines are yelling, "Incoming!" I'm already face-
down in a little ditch, trying to wriggle into my flak jacket. As the
rockets begin to land nearby, I'm instantly sorry that I left my bor-
rowed helmet on the helicopter.

Then, moments after the rockets impact, the 11th Marines'
155mm batteries across the road behind us are pounding the coordinates where the counter-battery radars and computers tell them the
rockets have come from. In less than ten minutes, the exchange is
over, and I crawl back up on top of the Humvee, so tired that the
flashes on the horizon, the booming concussions, and the ground
trembling with hundreds of coalition air strikes on Baghdad do nothing to disturb four full hours of slumber.

During our 0400 broadcast on *Hannity & Colmes*, the sound of
aircraft flying overhead and the noise of anti-aircraft missiles streaking futilely into the air cause a producer to ask during a commercial
break if we are under attack. I reply with one of the lines the Marines
were using: "That's just some noise from the Baghdad Urban Renewal
Project."

Later, FOX News Channel coverage from the Palestine Hotel
shows a virtual fireworks display, as a strike against one of Saddam's
palaces rocks the central part of the city. Wire service reports claim
CENTCOM suspected that Uday and Qusay Hussein, Saddam's sons,
were inside the complex and consequently hammered the site with all
kinds of munitions. It is also reported that satellite-guided weapons
have been used to destroy the Iraqi air force headquarters in central
Baghdad.

Yet for all of the targets that have been hit, the troops on the
ground know that one target has not been taken out. I hear griping
whenever Griff and I set up our FOX News Channel gear for a feed to
and from the States. The Marines grouse about the fact that Iraqi TV
is still up and running, still blaring out propaganda that encourages

more foreigners to join the fight. When they ask me why the state-run TV and radio haven't been taken off the air, I simply shrug. I don't know either.

While we were flying the cas-evac missions, the Iraqi information minister, Mohammed Saeed al-Sahaf, appeared on Iraqi and Arab TV to announce that Americans were nowhere near Baghdad and certainly none had entered the city. He added that the U.S. forces had been expelled from the former Saddam International Airport, and told the press corps that he would prove it by taking them on a tour of the place. Baghdad Bob then read what he claims is a message from Saddam Hussein, and urged Iraqis and friendly Arabs to step up resistance to the Americans.

Ironically, just as FOX News Channel is showing him telling the Iraqis that the Americans were nowhere near Baghdad, they also put up a split screen showing U.S. Army tanks parked on the lawn of one of Saddam's palaces. And while the Iraqi information minister was busy misinforming his people, Greg Kelly with the 3rd Infantry Division put on a battalion commander from the airport who points out that more than three hundred Iraqi troops were killed defending the place.

✪ ✪ ✪

With the dawn of a new day, we learn that RCT-5, having led the attack all the way to the outskirts of Baghdad, won't be the first group into the city after all. Gen. Mattis has decided he wants a multi-pronged attack here, just as he did for the crossing of the Tigris back at An Numaniyah. RCT-7 will continue to drive north, directly toward the southern suburbs of Baghdad and to the bridges back across the Tigris. RCT-1 will come up on the right of RCT-7 and attack from the east, and RCT-5 will swing all the way around the city to attack across the Diyala River from the northeast. All this means that RCT-5 will have to attack in a new direction.

If Joe Dunford is disappointed, he doesn't show it. He immediately summons his battalion commanders and reorients his forces to
attack northward, parallel to the muddy ditch shown on the map as
the Diyala River. He orders maximum coverage by RPVs and dispatches 1st Light Armored Reconnaissance Battalion's LAVs to find
suitable crossing points where the engineers can throw down bridges
for his one thousand vehicles.

For the rest of the RCT, it's a matter of sitting and waiting, but not
resting. The momentary halt in movement means that much-needed
maintenance will be performed while the infantry patrols out far
enough to keep any lingering fedayeen from dropping mortar rounds
on our heads. Aside from the unremitting air strikes on Baghdad, and
the constant sound of RPVs flying over our heads, it's the quietest
night since the sandstorm.

✪ OPERATION IRAQI FREEDOM SIT REP #28
    With RCT-5 and the Stingers of HMLA-267
    Southeast suburbs of Baghdad
    Sunday, 6 April 2003
    2300 Hours Local

The day begins with a beautiful chapel service. Sam Mundy's sergeant
major has put together a little choir of Marines. They sing with more
fervor and sincerity than most church choirs back in the States. Griff's
camera records a great rendition of "Amazing Grace," sung to the
accompaniment of several artillery barrages in support of the LAVs
as they search for a suitable crossing.

A few minutes after the chaplain finishes, Capt. Shawn Hughes,
one of the pilots from HMLA-267, comes out of the RCT-5 CP and
we walk together to where his armed UH1N is parked next to the
HMM-268 CH-46s. On the way, he tells me that he's heading out to

do a recon of the Diyala River to see if he and his wingman might have better luck finding a crossing point for the increasingly frustrated Col. Joe Dunford. I ask if I can go along and he agrees.

I grab my camera and a single battery out of my kit on the back of the CH-46 and yell to Griff, "I'll be back in an hour or so." The two UH1Ns take off and we head west for the river.

The first thirty minutes or so of the flight are recorded intermittently on the videotape. When we reach the muddy Diyala River, we fly from south to north, noting possible crossing points on the GPS and on a map. There are not many. I notice that there are also relatively few other aircraft in the area—no fixed-wing, no Cobras. Aside from the LAVs, which we left well to our south, there are no friendlies on the ground. But that doesn't strike me as being so bad, since there doesn't seem to be any bad guys down there either.

About a half an hour into the mission, Capt. Hughes receives a call over the radio to check out an Iraqi air base that has supposedly been hit by a coalition air strike just west of the river.

On the map it shows as Khan Bani Saad Air Base. Below the name is the notation *abandoned*. But as we approach the airfield at about seventy-five feet and one hundred knots, the place is anything but abandoned. And if it was targeted by an air strike, they missed.

The runways have several MI-8 aircraft on them—and though not all of them appear flyable, none of the hangars seems to be even scratched by a bomb or a bullet. Through the open doors of one hangar, we see what looks like a fully assembled MI-24 gunship. Yet as we fly straight down the runway, there is no sign of anyone except a few civilian Toyota pickup trucks scurrying down a paved road encircling the perimeter of the field.

But then, as our two Hueys wheel around the far end of the field, all hell breaks loose. Below and to the front of us, men in green uniforms are running from a building and uncovering anti-aircraft machine guns. Others are already taking a bead on us with AK-47s. The flight leader calls out over the radio, "We're taking fire." And indeed we are.

That ball-peen hammer sound is now all around us, hardly affected by the return fire from our GAU-17 mini-gun. S/Sgt. Compton tries to hold his bursts on target, while Hughes is jinking to make our bird harder to hit.

As we whip over a truck loaded with troops, they all open fire, and we realize our lead bird seems to have run into the hail of bullets. The helo begins to spew fuel vapor. On my camera, it looks like something out of one of those old World War II movies, with planes falling out of the sky, trailing streams of smoke as they crash.

Someone says in my headphones, "I'm losing fuel pressure and power. I'm going to try to make it across the Diyala."

Hughes responds with a terse "Roger." And the two birds streak east for the river.

The camera suspended over Captain Hughes's head captures fuel pouring out of the belly of his wingman's helo—instantly vaporizing as it hits the air rushing by. If one of the Huey's anti-aircraft flares goes off right now, or if the bird is hit with a tracer round, it will disappear in a fireball.

When we cross the river, there is no time to find the perfect landing zone. As the two damaged helicopters settle in on a farmer's field next to an irrigation ditch, Hughes is calling out a distress signal.

The TRAP call is heard by an AV-8 flying several miles south. He immediately responds, appearing above us just moments after the two shot up helicopters are on the ground. Hughes tells him that both aircraft have sustained battle damage, but that we have no casualties, yet. He passes on the grid coordinates of the truck that was loading up with Iraqi troops as we flew over the airfield. The AV-8 heads off to hunt after passing our coordinates to Highlander—the LAVs of 1st

Light Armored Reconnaissance Battalion. They are several miles south and headed our way fast.

I fervently hope that they'll hurry. The irrigation ditch reminds me of the final scene in the movie *The Bridges at Toko-Ri*. In that movie, based on James Michener's novel, William Holden and Mickey Rooney, playing Marine pilots, are shot down by Chinese communist troops and killed in an irrigation ditch.

While the crew chief and gunners from both birds struggle, in a shower of jet fuel, to repair the leaks, S/Sgt. Compton does a quick inventory of what we have for defensive weapons—eight Beretta 9mm pistols, three M-16s, a 240-Golf machine gun, and one working .50-caliber. While we're waiting for either the enemy or friendlies to arrive, I volunteer to fix the jammed .50-caliber, telling the Marines, "I've seen the end of this movie and it's not pretty." No one knows what movie I'm talking about.

But it turns out we don't need any of the hardware. The AV-8, acting as a forward air controller, has already engaged the Iraqis who they thought might get to us. After his laser-guided bombs were expended, he stayed around to "illuminate" targets for two Marine F-18s. By the time they all were finished and Highlander's LAVs have rolled up, there are no Iraqis left to come after us.

In the second demonstration of Marine ingenuity in as many days, the gunner mechanics have managed to pull the shot-up fuel pump and remove an armor-piercing 7.62mm slug from it in the process. They then jury-rig the fuel system. After examining the holes in our aircraft, the mechanics determine that no vital parts have been damaged and the bird can limp back to the safety of friendly lines.

As we lift out, Maj. Tim Kolb, flying another HMLA-267 Huey, comes alongside to escort us back to safety. After we land, I learn that he was the HMLA-267 pilot who evacuated the wounded corporal from Capt. Aaron Eckerberg's broken CH-46 after the dust storm from hell. It really is a very small Marine Corps.

By the time I get back to RCT-5, everybody aboard the CH-46 is asleep except Col. Driscoll. As I climb onto one of the litters, he whispers, "You okay?"

"Yes," I reply.

"Good. You're grounded."

CHAPTER TEN
FALLEN IDOLS

✪ OPERATION IRAQI FREEDOM SIT REP #29
With RCT-5
Saddam City, east Baghdad
Tuesday, 8 April 2003
2300 Hours Local

Getting shot up in the UH1N on April 6 didn't really get me "grounded," but I did get a more sympathetic than usual hearing when I asked to go with one of the ground combat units as they entered Baghdad. With the acquiescence of MAG-39 and RCT-5, Griff and I put on our packs, shouldered our cameras and satellite broadcast gear, and joined Sam Mundy's 3rd Battalion, 5th Marines for the move across the Diyala and into the Iraqi capital.

Now that we've finally crossed the river, we're in the midst of the filthiest slum I've ever seen. This is Saddam City. The Iraqi dictator mandated that the Shi'ites who fled to the capital of Iraq had to live in the "planned community" he named after himself. It is a rabbit warren of crumbling, multistory, Soviet-style apartment buildings without running water or functioning sewage systems. It's worse than anything I've ever seen in Calcutta, Haiti, or Bangladesh. The whole place is home to more than a million "internal refugees," teeming with naked children, their stomachs distended from malnutrition. There is raw sewage running in the streets, and piles of trash—some of it smoldering with a stench that is enough to make even Marines who haven't bathed in weeks smell good.

And how we smell is something that's suddenly much more obvious. For the past nineteen days—since D-day—we've all been wearing chemical protective suits: baggy bib overalls and a hooded jacket. The tough, tightly woven, Teflon-treated nylon outer shell is hot, but the activated charcoal lining that protects the skin from chemical or biological agents also absorbs odors. Now that we've entered Baghdad, CENTCOM has advised everyone that Saddam is unlikely to use such weapons in his capital city, so we have shed the suits for the first time in nearly three weeks. We're all much more comfortable wearing field uniforms, but the inevitable consequence of not bathing is now greatly evident.

We're told to keep our gas masks on our hips and keep the chemical suits in our packs just in case this psychotic regime decides to do the unthinkable. Throughout the campaign, chemical weapons have been a threat, and every Marine unit has been on the lookout for any signs of WMD. In every Iraqi military installation we have overrun, the Marines have found large quantities of chemical protective suits, atropine antidote syringes, and Russian, Chinese, Yugoslav, Czech, French, and Jordanian gas masks—even some empty chemical artillery rounds and aircraft dispersal canisters—but they haven't found any of the chemical agents they're designed to hold. Given all the defensive preparations both sides have made in providing chemical protective equipment for their military forces, there's no doubt that both the Iraqis and the coalition forces expected Saddam to use them. What's unclear is where the weapons are now.

What is obvious to all, however, is that if Saddam uses such weapons against the American or British troops, he won't kill many of us—thanks to our protective NBC suits and masks—but he will succeed in killing thousands of Iraqi civilians. Up until now, we've all played it very safe. In addition to the protective gear, every unit has sophisticated, state-of-the-art chemical detection equipment—in some cases even a specialized vehicle for this purpose. And though this apparatus has given us several "false alarms" over the course of the past three weeks, causing us to quickly "mask up," no one suggests that such alerts be ignored. We've all worn our NBC suits, put on our "rubber duckies"—rubber overshoes—when necessary, and kept our rubber gloves handy. But Marines being Marines, they have also taken additional steps, just in case the expensive high-tech equipment doesn't work as advertised. Before leaving Kuwait, almost every unit's NBC NCO bought some chickens and pigeons. The birds, kept in cages on the back of a Humvee, serve as the caged canary in a coal mine—they will succumb to smaller amounts of a chemical agent than humans. Griff, fascinated by what the Marines called their FEWGAD—"fowl early warning gas alarm device"—spent almost an hour "interviewing" Geraldine, one of the RCT-5 chickens. He decided not to videotape the other chicken, nicknamed Kung Pao; he thought the name was too descriptive of the bird's ultimate fate.

Our entry into east Baghdad with RCT-5 is almost anticlimactic, although it hasn't been for other Marine and Army units. After patrolling north along the Diyala River for forty-eight hours searching unsuccessfully for another crossing point, RCT-5, which led the 1st Marine Division the whole way from Kuwait, became the last Marine Regimental Combat Team to enter Saddam's capital. Without a third crossing point, Gen. Mattis decides that RCT-7 will seize a damaged footbridge in the south, just above where the Diyala joins the Tigris, as well as a larger damaged highway bridge farther to the north.

Col. Steve Hummer, commanding RCT-7, gives the task of capturing the southern footbridge to 3rd Battalion, 4th Marines, led by Lt. Col. Brian McCoy. For the northern span, the mission is assigned to Lt. Col. Jim Chartier's 1st Tank Battalion, supported by 3rd Battalion, 7th Marines and the LAVs of 3rd Light Armored Reconnaissance Battalion.

For the first time, the Iraqis have made a serious effort to use obstacles to delay the forces closing in on Baghdad. Until now we have all been amazed that bridges, so essential to moving the thousands of military vehicles in this operation, have been largely intact. But now, as the 1st Marine Division is literally at the gates of the capital, the Iraqis have succeeded in badly damaging all the bridges over the Diyala on the eastern approaches to the city. Mattis is undeterred. Overflights by UAVs and helicopter pilot reports—along with some nighttime patrols by Marine Recon teams—convince him and his engineers that all the spans are repairable. He orders an attack for the following morning.

The attacks on the bridges begin simultaneously early on the morning of April 8 with heavy artillery bombardments. The day is overcast, and for a while it looks as if we're in for a repeat of the MOASS sandstorm of two weeks ago. And though the weather never turned as foul as what we'd experienced on the road north through the desert, the ceiling is low enough to limit close air support to only what the Cobras can deliver.

After a heavy prepfire by the 11th Marines' 155 howitzers and, later on, 81mm mortars, 3rd Battalion, 4th Marines conduct a classic infantry assault across the damaged footbridge. McCoy had brought up a dozen M-1 tanks on the west bank of the river to provide covering fire over the heads of his troops, and the tanks succeed in keeping the Iraqi defenders on the far side of the river pinned down.

As the assault commences, the Iraqis make a futile attempt to halt the Marines' advance. They begin by firing artillery at the Marine vehicles assembled and clearly visible on the east side of the river. The tankers simply button up the hatches on their Abrams and continue firing, though one enemy round hits an AAV not far from McCoy's CP, killing two and wounding four.

The Iraqi fire does nothing to stop or even slow the attack, however. Two companies of Marines force their way across the damaged footbridge using boards and metal engineer planking to span holes in the structure. More than half a dozen intrepid photojournalists— some embedded correspondents, some not—follow McCoy's Marines over the Diyala and into east Baghdad.

Meanwhile, a few kilometers to the north, 1st Tank Battalion, 3/7, and 3rd LAR are forcing a crossing over the larger highway bridge into east Baghdad. Again, the cameras of embedded journalists capture some of the very dramatic close combat at this bridgehead and the subsequent movement into the city. The videotaped footage offers stark testimony to the courage of small-unit leaders who lead the fight as they maneuver into the Iraqi capital. As with the footbridge farther to the south, Marine, Navy Seabee, and Army engineers quickly move in behind the infantry to repair the span under the protection of the armor.

As the Iraqis try to deal with the two RCT-7 bridgeheads, RCT-1 is forcing a third crossing farther north. Col. Toolan's troops use AAVs to traverse both an irrigation canal and then the Diyala. This creates a sufficient diversion for the engineers with RCT-7 to lay down a pontoon span next to the captured footbridge and repair the highway bridge, enabling it to carry the heavy Marine armor into the city. Finally, late in the day, RCT-5 rolls across the Diyala behind RCT-1. As soon as his lead elements are assembled, Dunford drives hard to the north, on the west bank of the Diyala, making a long right hook. He is aiming for a rendezvous with the Army's 3rd Infantry Division along the banks of the Tigris.

Griff and I ride into the city with 3rd Battalion, 5th Marines through streets littered with garbage and lined with people. From the open hatch of an AAV, our cameras record Iraqis waving and cheering. Children, many wearing little more than rags, run beside our armored column, splashing barefoot through puddles of raw sewage, waving and yelling. The sixteen Marines in our vehicle are standing on the troop seats, facing outboard with their weapons at the ready. Behind us, an LAV, its 25mm chain gun traversing ominously, is not threatening enough to keep children from running up beside the large wheeled armored car and asking for food.

The poverty and hunger are so obvious that these battle-hardened Marines reach into their rucksacks, and soon candy, crackers, peanut butter, cheese spread, jelly, and even whole MREs are raining out of the slowly moving vehicles. Fearing that a child will fall beneath the treads or wheels in an effort to retrieve the morsels, someone finally puts a stop to the spontaneous "relief operation" by broadcasting over the tactical net, "Everybody, knock off throwing the food!"

Before nightfall, the city is virtually surrounded. RCT-1 is to our immediate south and RCT-7, coiled up near the junction of the Tigris and Diyala rivers, is prepared to press on into the city with nighttime patrols. Joe Dunford sets up his RCT-5 CP in an abandoned Republican Guard officer housing area, where there's barely room to park the four CH-46s and two UH1Ns among the U.S. vehicles and dozens of abandoned and mostly intact Iraqi army tanks, armored vehicles, and anti-aircraft weapons. For our evening satellite feed, we set up our camera next to a 57mm anti-aircraft gun that still has a round in its breech and crates of ammo beside it, indicating that the Iraqis deserted it quickly. Just down the street from us, a large tire factory is on fire and producing heavy volumes of billowing black smoke.

Once again, we learn more about the course of the war from the FOX News Channel broadcasts originating in New York and Washington than we do from what we can see from our own narrow vantage point. Farther to the west, elements of the Army's 3rd Infantry Division have been conducting "thunder runs"—armored sorties into the city and back out to the area north of the airport. Iraqi command and control has largely broken down. What organized units remain in the city seem to be demoralized by news being broadcast by U.S. Commando Solo aircraft that Saddam and his sons were killed in an air strike yesterday in the Mansour section of Baghdad. Whether they were killed or not, most of the Iraqi civilians that we're seeing seem to believe it—and don't appear to be in mourning.

According to the news, paratroopers of the 173rd Airborne Brigade have linked up with Kurdish *pesh merga* forces in the north and chased the Iraqi army out of Ain Sifni, a strategic town just north of Mosul—not far from ancient Nineveh, made famous by the biblical prophet Jonah. Well to our south, the British have entered Basra after a two-week siege. Strangely absent from the U.S. broadcasts are the retired generals and admirals who just days ago were prognosticating that we faced months of heavy combat and thousands of U.S. casualties before getting to Baghdad.

CENTCOM says that coalition forces are facing "sporadic resistance"—a term that has meaning only to anyone not being shot at. Part of the "sporadic resistance" that we're now experiencing is an occasional mortar round fired from the area just beyond the limit of the Marine advance. Just before dark I go up in one of the HMLA-267 Hueys on a quick hop to see if they can spot the shooter or a forward observer. Flying at about two hundred feet, the two helicopters sweep over crowded streets where civilians are camping out, with small fires, cooking or just staying warm in the cool night air, since the electricity is off in this part of Baghdad. Just outside the Marine lines, the gunner on the right side of our bird spots a man in civilian clothes on the roof of an apartment building. He clearly has an AK-47 and what appears to be a radio. It's logical to assume that this is a forward observer (FO) for the mortar that has been dropping rounds on us. Yesterday, this would have been a no-brainer—with the flick of an arming switch and the squeeze of the trigger on our GAU-17 mini-gun, the FO would have had more holes than a slice of Swiss cheese. But when we crossed the Diyala, the rules of engagement (the ROE) changed. Because of the dense civilian population, the Marine gunners, both in the air and on the ground, have been told to "fire only when fired upon."

On the ground, five hundred yards away, we can see Marine LAVs, who obviously cannot see the guy on the roof. And of course nobody knows what or who else is in the apartment building. It may be hiding a fedayeen platoon, or it may be home to several hundred of the civilians who just hours ago were cheering our arrival.

As we circle the building, trying to make radio contact with the LAV unit on the ground, two USAF F-15 Strike Eagles are running an air strike off to our west over what appears to be the center of Baghdad. As the lead jet pulls up from his run, he's chased by a stream of tracers, and then the arc of a SAM follows him. Even though it's several miles away, and we're peering into the sunset, the missile looks big—an SA3 or 6. It resembles a telephone pole streaking up at the U.S. aircraft. Flares and chaff drop from the lead F-15 as it dives for the rooftops, and his wingman unleashes what looks to be a missile— a HARM, I'm guessing—at the offending Iraqi launcher. The skyline erupts in red where the missile hits, clearly inside the city, and the two aircraft disappear into the clouds.

This whole exchange has taken less than a minute, and I have managed to capture some of it on my camera. The result can only be presumed, but it's very likely three or four Iraqis manning a fire-control console at a surface-to-air missile battery, and possibly ten or twelve other Iraqis loading a ZSU-23-4, are now dead.

While I was distracted by the "air show" off to our west, below us the suspected FO gathers his weapon, picks up his military radio, and disappears into a doorway on the roof. All that the two heavily armed helicopters can do is mark the location with a GPS plot and hope that an infantry patrol will check out the site tonight or tomorrow. The frustration is palpable. The commentary over the intercom is unprintable.

✪ OPERATION IRAQI FREEDOM SIT REP #30
    With RCT-5
    East Baghdad
    Wednesday, 9 April 2003
    2200 Hours Local

It rained on us last night, a cold drizzle that made sleeping on the hood of a Humvee, rolled up in my poncho and poncho liner, particularly uncomfortable. The precipitation forced us to break down our satellite gear; we didn't reestablish communications with New York until after sunrise. The first news of our day is actually the last news from yesterday in the United States. Nearly all of it's bad.

There's one positive story, with some good footage from Rick Leventhal, about the Marines moving across the Diyala into east Baghdad. The next report from Iraq is about an Air Force A-10 Warthog getting shot down yesterday by a French Roland SAM just north of the Saddam International Airport—proving again that not all of the Iraqis have given up. The "big story," as my friend John Gibson would put it, is about a U.S. Army M-1 Abrams tank round that hit the Palestine Hotel, where most of the members of the international press corps—those who chose to be "embedded" with the Iraqi regime—have been living. The tank round reportedly killed two foreign journalists and wounded several, and there is apparently an international uproar.

The Marines who gather around our little TV set to catch up on the news from home absorb all of this. The only story that evinces any response is one about the Baghdad bureau of Al Jazeera having been hit during a U.S. air raid yesterday, killing one of the TV network's reporters. That prompts a Marine staff sergeant to observe, "Now isn't that a damn shame. 'Jihad TV' didn't seem to get that upset when four hijacked planes killed three thousand Americans on nine-eleven." Sympathy for the enemy has never been a strong suit among Marines.

And sitting still isn't one of "Fighting Joe" Dunford's strong suits either. Even before first light he has his battalions preparing to move, completing the "right hook" into the city proper. He wants the Marines of RCT-5 to press on all the way to the Tigris, in the heart of the city, and link up with the Army's 3rd Infantry Division. The company commanders are provided with the grid coordinates to plug into their GPSs. These coordinates are for various high-value targets selected by the OGA teams roaming around the city looking for Baath Party facilities, weapons of mass destruction, and, of course, any surviving regime leaders.

Interestingly enough, nobody here in Iraq seems to have any of the now famous decks of cards depicting the leaders of Saddam's brutal establishment that show up frequently on U.S. TV. The OGA guys, the SEALs, Task Force 20, and the Recon Marines have JPEG images of various wanted Iraqis on their laptops, but there probably aren't a dozen Marine or Army grunts who would recognize Uday or Qusay Hussein if they drove up to a military checkpoint and asked directions. Nonetheless, this morning the leathernecks of RCT-5 are going hunting for whatever members of Saddam's inner circle they can find.

Farther to our south, RCT-7 is moving into the Al Karradah neighborhood of the city, located in the "hook" of the Tigris, with the goal of pushing all the way south to Baghdad University. The sprawling campus occupies much of the terrain at the tip of the peninsula formed by the looping river and is believed to be a bastion for the foreign fedayeen who have flooded into the city since March 20.

On the night of April 8, 3rd Battalion, 7th Marines finds uniforms and documents at the Al Rasheed Medical Center, indicating that American POWs have been held and treated at the facility. Some of the OGA folks believe that the U.S. captives might have been moved to the university. Lt. Col. Chris Conlin, the CO of 1st Battalion, 7th Marines, given the mission of securing the once-respected institution of higher learning, doesn't waste time getting there. When 1/7 arrives, they find the trouble they are looking for—the fedayeen are still there. It takes the rest of the day to dig them out, even though their AK-47s and RPGs are no match for the Marine firepower, training, and discipline. In the end, the foreign fighters and the handful of young Iraqis with them get what they were seeking. They wanted to die for Saddam. The Marines of 1st Battalion, 7th Marines have obliged.

As Conlin is charging onto the university campus with his column of tanks and AAVs, Lt. Col. Brian McCoy's 3rd Battalion, 4th Marines are pushing deeper into the heart of east Baghdad. The reinforced battalion proceeds on this foray as dismounted infantry. Followed by tanks, AAVs, and dozens of armed Humvees, the infantry platoons move slowly, building to building, from the rougher streets of southeast Baghdad into increasingly affluent neighborhoods. As the day wears on, more and more Iraqis come out to greet the Marines with smiles, waves, and other friendly gestures.

By the time they reach Firdus Square, not far from the Palestine Hotel, a large crowd has gathered. Though wary, McCoy's Marines quickly grasp that this is not a hostile mob. In fact, the Iraqis are jubilant. As the Marines approach, the Iraqis shout joyfully and cheer the Americans and their president. "Bush is good," several of them call out. Others cheer, "We love George Bush."

Children soon join the adults, and dozens of them are captured on videotape and film, laughing and shouting happily while running beside the battle-scarred infantrymen. A few youngsters have flowers and hand them to the grinning Marines. Some of the troops take the flowers and place them in the webbing of their battle gear. Others stick them into the camouflage covers of their Kevlar helmets. It confirms the message on leaflets dropped all over the country, what Conway and Mattis have been saying all along: "We've come as liberators, not invaders."

Some individuals are less impressed than the Iraqis. Among those awaiting the Marines at the Palestine Hotel are a handful of sullen antiwar activists from the United States and the United Kingdom. They have come to Baghdad to volunteer as "human shields" for Saddam. One of the protesters, apparently British from the sound of her accent, cries out to the lead tank in the square, "Yankee bastard! Go home!" The Marine doesn't reply, but an Iraqi man tells the woman, "You can go home now. You are not needed here."

Meanwhile, the crowd has decided that Baghdad really is under new management and turns its pent-up fury not on the Americans but on a forty-foot black metal statue of Saddam. After pelting the statue with stones and garbage for a few minutes, several Iraqis enlist the support of the Marines in removing this eyesore from their midst.

With the cameras of the international press recording it all, and some news services broadcasting the event live to the world, Marine Cpl. Edward Chin climbs up the King Kong–sized representation of Saddam and drapes an American flag over its head. The Stars and Stripes cover Saddam's head for a brief moment. Then, after replacing Old Glory with an Iraqi flag, Cpl. Chin helps secure a chain around Saddam's neck and then hooks the end of the chain to the heavy-duty winch cable of an M-88 Tank Retriever.

As the statue pitches forward on its pedestal, the crowd roars its approval and begins clamoring over the fallen idol, attacking it with hammers, stones, and—in an Arab insult—with their shoes. When Saddam's head is detached, the cameras catch children jubilantly beating on it. The symbolism is inescapable: Saddam Hussein has been toppled. The brutal reign of the despot and his Baath Party is finally over.

✪ OPERATION IRAQI FREEDOM SIT REP #31
   With RCT-5 and HMM-268
   Baghdad
   Thursday, 10 April 2003
   2330 Hours Local

Saddam's regime might be finished, but the fighting isn't. While RCT-7 was capturing Baghdad University and ripping down statues, RCT-1 was mopping up resistance in Baghdad's eastern suburbs at the Al Rasheed Air Base. Meanwhile, Joe Dunford's RCT-5 closed in on the presidential palaces along the banks of the Tigris. What had started out this morning as a series of raids into the heart of the city—similar to the Army's "thunder runs" of the last few days—suddenly became a full-scale occupation of the enemy capital.

Having swept around to the northeast side of the city, all of RCT-5 has been busy conducting patrols, both mounted and dismounted, throughout its assigned area of operations. And though extensive stores of munitions are being found, enemy contact has been unusually light for RCT-5 throughout April 9. Early in the afternoon, I go with a squad-sized patrol that encounters several young Iraqis carrying AK-47s. They are relieved of their weapons and briefly detained. Not a shot is fired.

Late that day, Griff and I join up with Lt. Col. Duffy White's 1st Light Armored Reconnaissance Battalion. We've been told that as soon as it turns dark, the LAVs would be going out looking for trouble. We wanted to be there with our cameras if they found it.

Just before sunset we videotape the platoon patrol order, then sit down and eat while we wait for darkness. Sitting on a five-gallon water can, sharing my MRE with Iraqi flies, I can see the large plume of smoke from the oil refinery south of the city. A UAV buzzes over and begins circling the area to our southwest. We hear the sound of American or British jets, well above us. Griff, always looking for the perfect shot, catches the contrails of a B-52 loitering in the upper atmosphere just as the sun dropped below the horizon.

The night patrol by eight LAVs departs RCT-5 lines at about 2100 hours. I hold my camera with its night lens right next to the 25mm Bushmaster turret, hoping that if the gun fires it won't wipe out the camera. But as it turns out, the night lens is useless. The video image on my camera constantly "flares" from green to bright yellow as the patrol encounters an extraordinary number of civilian vehicles moving about with their lights on. Most are Japanese sedans or pickups— many carrying entire families—all apparently attempting to flee the heart of the mostly darkened city.

A little after midnight on April 10, we are poking through a Chaldean Christian neighborhood, complete with churches and cemeteries, when the patrol is ordered to return immediately to the Marine perimeter. When we arrive, we are told that RCT-5 is preparing a raid on the presidential palace complex on the west side of the Tigris and that the operation is to take place as soon as possible. Communications intercepts and an OGA source indicate that a Special Republican Guard unit and numerous fedayeen are inside the palace grounds. Some speculate that the hum of radio traffic coming from the site might mean that Saddam and/or his two evil sons have taken refuge there. If that is the case, "Fighting Joe" Dunford isn't going to miss the chance to capture or kill them.

Dunford chooses Lt. Col. Fred Padilla's 1st Battalion, 5th Marines—reinforced by tanks, AAVs, LAVs, CIA specialists, and a contingent of Delta operators—for the mission. The objective—a series of large palaces and government buildings on the banks of the Tigris, surrounded by a high wall—appears formidable. If well defended, it could require much of Dunford's RCT to search and clear the area. He alerts 2/5 and 3/5 just in case they are needed and asks for immediate UAV overflights of the routes to and over the objective so that his commanders can see what they are up against.

Bounded to the north by the Jamhuriyah bridge and to the south by the 14th of July bridge, the five-kilometer-long presidential complex contains four large residences, including one of the dictator's personal homes, the National Assembly building, apartments for Baath Party and government officials, and a large barracks area for a detachment of the Special Republican Guard. Three of the palaces were extensively damaged by JDAMs and cruise missiles earlier in the war. To prevent collateral damage to a nearby residential area, the southernmost luxurious domicile has been hit with three or four GPS-guided two-thousand pound-concrete inert "bombs" that plunged through the roof and collapsed the interior floors of the palace without the need for high explosives. Somewhere in this maze of buildings, gardens, fig trees, and eucalyptus groves, several hundred Iraqi soldiers and foreign fedayeen are believed to be hiding.

By 0300 hours on April 10, Lt. Col. Padilla's column of tanks, AAVs, LAVs, and Humvees are rumbling, screeching, and grinding south through eleven kilometers of Baghdad's darkened streets, trying to reach the Tigris River bridges and the palace complex before dawn. Padilla rides in an LVTC-7 behind four M-1 tanks; his Company "A" troops jammed into sixteen AAVs, are closely followed by the OGA and Delta Force operators in Humvees and SUVs. The rest of his battalion, a column of more than seventy tanks, AAVs, and Humvees, trails behind for more than two kilometers. The infantry, who will have to seize the objective, are wedged into the AAVs—hatches open, weapons at the ready—peering up at the buildings and at every intersection through their NVGs. Gunners in the tanks use their thermal sights to search for signs of an ambush.

Despite sandbagged emplacements at every overpass, the Route 2 expressway through the city is ominously quiet as the lead tanks of Padilla's task force turn off on the exit for Port Said Street, the best approach to the Jamhuriyah Bridge. Cobras sweeping overhead, scanning the rooftops and palm groves bordering the highway with their infrared scopes, see nothing. Then, just as the lead tanks are crossing the undamaged span over the Tigris, the rear of the 1/5 column comes under heavy RPG and AK-47 fire from the vicinity of the Al Khulafa Mosque as they exit the expressway at Al Thawra Street.

With the rear of his column under attack, and not knowing for sure when the rest of his battalion will be able to close up on him, Padilla makes a bold decision and orders Alpha Company, supported by the four lead tanks, to keep moving and charge the palace complex. After firing two 120mm HEAT rounds into the northwestern gate, the lead tank rotates its turret to the rear and slams through the portal into a hail of RPG and AK-47 fire. Though each Abrams is hit several times by the anti-armor weapons, the four tanks blast their way into the palace grounds and quickly silence all close-in enemy fire with rounds from their main guns and coaxial mounted machine guns. The thermal sights on the tanks give the Marines a tremendous advantage over the Iraqis and fedayeen—a fact that the enemy never seems to grasp. An enemy gunner getting up to his feet to fire an RPG at a tank from three hundred to four hundred meters away stands almost no chance of hitting his target. For the tankers, who can accurately hit well beyond a kilometer, the palace grounds are a "target-rich environment."

Within minutes Padilla has all of Alpha Company's AAVs and the special operators inside the complex. Though he has already taken several wounded, his little force is intact and fighting back. Behind him, Col. Dunford has decided to bring up 2/5 to deal with the problem at the mosque and free up the rest of 1/5 for an assault through the palace complex. Two Marine Cobras from HMLA-267 head off to support the action at the mosque, while two others, growling low over the city, slip down the Tigris to provide overhead fire for the Marines at the palace. Within minutes all four "snakes" are hit by ground fire, though not seriously enough to bring any of them down.

Fifteen kilometers to the north, Griff and I wait with 3/5 and the remaining LAVs for the word to reinforce. We can hear the dull concussions of the furious melee taking place south of us and occasionally see the streak of a Cobra unleashing its rockets. The Marines we are with doze in or on their vehicles, while others on watch stare into the night with NVGs, anticipating an order to join their mates in the battle. But the word to advance never comes. I am sure we are missing the last big gunfight of the war.

I am wrong.

Just about dawn, the sound of a CH-46 APU winding up rouses me as I doze against a Bushmaster turret atop an LAV. I awaken Griff and we jump down and jog over to the nearest bird and ask the crew chief, Cpl. Moreno, where they are going.

"Emergency cas-evac at the palace, sir," he shouts in my ear over the din as the helicopter's main engines light off. I run up to the lead

CH-46, jump aboard, and ask the flight leader, Maj. Don Presto, if Griff and I can ride along. He gives us a thumbs-up, so we hustle back to the LAVs, grab our gear, run back, and pile into the birds.

The two aging helos speed along at one hundred knots just over the rooftops of the city, and our cameras capture the panorama below as Maj. Presto follows Route 2 south toward the palace. As we pass the Al Khulafa Mosque on our right, burning tires in the intersections bordering Al Thawra and Ar Rashid Streets mark the scene where 2/5 was engaged. Both our cameras capture dismounted Marines maneuvering forward of their armored vehicles, firing at dark-clothed figures at close range.

When Maj. Presto reaches Yafa Street, he banks right and brings the two birds over the Tigris just south of the Jamhuriyah bridge and slows to fifty knots. The palace complex is now on our right. Both helicopters drop down until their landing gear is just above the water. Here the river is three to four hundred meters wide and there is a fifteen-foot-high levee, so I'm looking up at the palace complex on our right as we search for the landing zone.

It's now light enough that the NVGs are unnecessary. Off to our right, we can see a skirmish line of Marines, fighting with the water to their backs. The leathernecks are engaging fedayeen inside the structures to their west. Using his call sign, "Spaz," Sean Basco, the Marine F-18 pilot assigned as the air officer with 1/5, tells the helicopters over the secure radio that the only safe landing zone is a small garden surrounded by a low hedge on the east side of the southernmost palace.

The two CH-46s are practically hovering over the river, with the 14th of July bridge five hundred meters in front of us, when Basco pops a smoke grenade. The landing zone is very tight, barely big enough for one helicopter. Presto tells Captains Espinoza and Graham, piloting Dash Two, to land first, and he rotates our bird

ninety degrees to the left, placing our rear wheels on the levee while
the front landing gear hangs out over the Tigris.

The sight of two haze-gray helicopters in such a confined space
must be too much of a temptation for the fedayeen hiding in the
buildings west of the landing zone. Dash Two is no sooner on the
ground than there is a horrific burst of fire from the closest building
to our south. The Marines on the ground respond with a fusillade
that raises the decibel level but does little to stop the enemy fire.

At this point several people inside the bird—myself among
them—are yelling into the intercom, "We're taking fire—three
o'clock!" Cpl. Kendall, manning the .50-caliber machine gun on the
right side of the aircraft, has been searching for the source of the fire.
He spots a dozen black figures on the roof of a building about three
hundred meters to the west and says, "Right side fifty firing." It's not
a request or even an exclamation, it's just a simple declarative statement spoken so calmly I hardly pay any attention, fully engrossed in
videotaping the action going on around us.

Suddenly, the muzzle of the big .50-caliber, about eighteen inches
in front of my lens, erupts with a blast that almost blows out my
eardrums. The videotape shows my reaction. The camera jerks back
and up. There is a spastic pan across the ceiling of the helicopter.
Finally, the lens points back out the hatch and at the roofline, where
Kendall's rounds are impacting our antagonists. Pieces of brick
and mortar fly off the building with puffs of dust as the big armor-
piercing bullets hit home. And through all this, the audio track
records the loud, steady, metallic hammering of a very long string of
fire from the .50-caliber; then another, shorter; and finally a third
burst, just a few rounds.

The barrel of Kendall's .50-caliber is red hot and smoking. Spent
brass shell casings are all over the floor of the helicopter, but the Iraqis
or fedayeen or whoever they were aren't shooting at us any more. The

bird is still half-hovering over the Tigris, and Maj. Don Presto, who hasn't budged an inch through all this, comes up on the intercom and says, "So, Corporal Kendall, did you get some?"

"Yes, sir!" Kendall replies. "I got some."

Dash Two has finished loading eight wounded Marines aboard. Now it's our turn. Presto hovers up a few feet and sideslips into the landing zone as Dash Two lifts off. My camera records our rotor wash flattening the shrubbery, blowing the trees and dust about as we touch down. Once again, litter bearers race for the tail ramp, crouching low, hurrying. Nobody wants this big noisy thing on the ground any longer than necessary. We take eight wounded aboard, and as we lift, there is another furious burst of fire—the unmistakable *crack, crack, crack* of AK-47s.

By the time we have dropped the wounded at the nearest Army shock-trauma hospital, 1/5 has more casualties. We quickly refuel, pick up more ammunition, and head back. The second trip is much like the first—except this time it's full daylight and the birds are clearly visible to anyone who wants to look up and take a pot shot at them.

We go in first this time, and my camera catches a terrible moment. The wounded are loaded very quickly and we take no fire while we're on the ground, but as we start to lift off, an RPG whizzes across in front of the bird, hits in the dirt just behind us, and explodes right in front of two Marines. It looks to me like one of those blown straight up in the air by the blast is Spaz, the air officer. As Don Presto pulls up hard to clear the buildings to our south, somebody says sadly over the intercom, "They'll be on our next lift."

The trip out of the city to the field hospital is another adventure in low-altitude express delivery. We're flying so low and so fast that it seems impossible not to hit something. When we arrive at the Army field hospital, we have to orbit around for a few minutes because the other two HMM-268 helicopters are in the dusty hospital LZ unloading casualties from the battle at the mosque.

By the time we head back for our third lift of the day, the back of our CH-46 looks like a charnel house. Blood-soaked battle dressings, IV bags, latex gloves, pieces of Marine battle gear, and puddles of blood are all over the deck. Each troop seat along the right side of the bird has a pool of blood in it and I suddenly wonder, after all these years, if this is why the nylon webbing is dyed red.

On the way to the palace for our third casualty pickup, two U.S. Air Force A-10s fly the route in front of us, not going much faster than we are. As we're coming down the river I can hear Spaz on the radio talking to the Warthogs, telling them to strafe the 14th of July bridge. A group of fedayeen have run onto the span and are delivering enfilade fire on the Marines surrounding the landing zone. It's probable that the RPG round that just missed our helicopter on the last run has been fired from the bridge. The A-10s do as asked, and this time we take no fire from the bridge as we slide into the zone.

The troops on the ground now have a little SOP worked out as well. While we're landing, on the ground, and taking off—when a helicopter is most vulnerable—the troops around the landing zone unleash volleys of aimed fire at every window and rooftop they can see, pinning down the Iraqis or fedayeen who would otherwise be shooting at us.

Immediately after we land, a Marine with battle dressings on his legs and arms hobbles aboard with the litter bearers. He has dirt and blood all over his face and hands, and his flak jacket is shredded. Since I'm almost out of videotape, I'm helping to load the litters into the straps. The wounded Marine taps me on the shoulder and hands me a piece of cardboard—torn from an MRE case—on which a note has been scrawled in black grease pencil: *Grizzly Six, send more ammo. All DODICs needed urgent. Spaz.*

Translated from Marine jargon into English, the note means, "Col. Dunford [the officer commanding a unit is always known as the "six"], send more ammunition of all types." In short, Padilla's 1st Battalion, 5th Marines has been battling for so long they are running dangerously low on everything: 5.56mm, 7.62mm machine gun ammo, hand grenades, AT-4 rockets, mortar rounds, 40mm grenades for the up guns on the AAVs, 25mm ammo for the chain guns on the LAVs, even .50-caliber and 120mm HE for the tanks.

I take the piece of cardboard and tuck it into my flak jacket and then try to help the wounded Marine into a troop seat, where the docs have been putting the "walking wounded." But he fights me off and says, "I'm not going. I have work to do," and then looks me in the face.

Suddenly he stops, looks at me again, and shouts over the roar of the bird and the gunfire "Ollie North? What are *you* doing here?"

I point to the FOX News Channel patch on my jacket and shout back in jest, "Making a war movie."

The remark reminds him that he has one of those little Kodak disposable cameras in the cargo pocket of his utility trousers. He pulls out the camera, wraps an arm around my shoulders, holds the camera out in front of us with his other bloody paw, yells "Smile!" and snaps a picture of the two of us.

It's one of those weird moments in the midst of horror that make the inhumanity of war just a little bit more human. Before I can force the photographer into a seat, he turns and limps off the helicopter. On the back of his flak jacket is stenciled the name Basco.

The moment is gone the instant we take off. We lift off and make a hard, climbing right turn over the wall separating the palace grounds from the surrounding neighborhood. Two fedayeen with AK-47s are crouched right below us on a rooftop. They are invisible to the troops on the ground but right in the sights of Cpl. Kendall.

This time when he says "Right side fifty firing," I'm ready. The twenty-five or thirty rounds from his machine gun cut them down just as one of them rolls to point his AK-47 at us. They never get a chance.

✪ ✪ ✪

The rest of the day is more of the same. I give the "Need more ammo" note from Basco to "Hamster" at the RCT-5 Bravo Command CP when we stop there between missions. On one of our trips into the zone, one of the birds evacuates Basco, though I don't know which trip or which bird. I was told that he eventually passed out from loss of blood.

Our last cas-evac mission of this very long day is well after dark. Though most of the fedayeen have been killed by then, several stole away from the gunfight with RCT-7 at the university and made their way into the brush along the east side of the river. A Marine sniper with a night scope in the second story of the wrecked palace had been dealing with them handily until the helicopter landing in the zone blocked his line of fire.

While we are picking up the last load of casualties, one of the fedayeen in the bushes across the river decides to open fire across the three hundred meters of open water. Instantly, across the front of our bird, the red beam of a laser target designator can be seen through our NVGs and a voice comes up on the radio, "There's your target."

Cpl. Amanda Hoenes, crouching at the left side .50-caliber and peering through her NVGs out her gunport, says calmly, "I have a target. Left side fifty firing," and opens fire in short, steady, ten-round bursts. The rounds hit right where the laser touched the far bank. The shooting from the far bank stops. An AK-47 is no match for a .50-caliber in the hands of someone who knows how to use it. Amanda Hoenes knows how to use a .50-caliber.

✪ ✪ ✪

Though the palace complex is secured shortly after dark, no one wants to risk moving the helicopters there for the night. So after our last cas-evac mission, we land back where we started the day—at the RCT-5 Bravo CP, up Route 2 in northeast Baghdad. The day has been physically and emotionally exhausting, but sleep evades me. I can't get out of my mind a comment made by one of the young Marines earlier in the day.

On the second or third lift we had taken a young lance corporal who, although wounded in one arm, was helping to load another Marine who was dead or dying. When we arrived at the Army shock-trauma hospital, the facility was so busy they had set up a triage outside, and Don Presto shut the bird down to keep from blowing desert grit on the wounded, who were lying on litters or just sitting on the ground in front of the hospital tents. I aided the wounded lance corporal down the ramp and was about to ease him to the ground, but he insisted that I place him near the litter holding the Marine he had helped load aboard the bird.

The young Marine sat between the handles of the stretcher and cradled the head of the bloody comrade who still had an IV in his arm, the bag of saline fluid suspended from an M-16 jammed into the center of the litter where it folds. I asked the lance corporal if I could get him some water but when he looked up at me, tears were running down his face and he said simply, "He's dying, isn't he, sir?"

"I think he's already gone, son" was all I could manage.

The boy brushed some dirt off the dead man's face and, after a moment, looked back at me as I crouched beside him. Then, through his tears, with wisdom many twice his age never have, the young lance corporal said, "He was my gunny, sir. He was a really good man. He was a hero. Not just for the way he died. He was a hero for the way he lived."

CHAPTER ELEVEN

YOU CAN RUN
BUT YOU CAN'T HIDE

✪ OPERATION IRAQI FREEDOM SIT REP #32
With RCT-5
Downtown, Baghdad, Iraq
Friday, 11 April 2003
2345 Hours Local

The Marines of RCT-5 didn't find Saddam or his sons at the palace, but the fights there and at the mosque were costly. Gunnery Sgt. Jeffrey Bohr was killed, more than fifty were wounded, and four tanks were damaged. The disappointment at not killing or capturing the chief henchmen of the regime was palpable among the Marines and only slightly tempered by the realization that they had killed nearly two hundred fedayeen and Special Republican Guard troops. The handful of prisoners captured, nearly all of them wounded, offered no insight as to why they had fought so hard for the shattered palaces and real estate on the banks of the Tigris. Most Iraqis had chosen to fight to the death, prompting one young sergeant to surmise, "This is what it must have been like fighting the Japs in World War II."

Early this morning, Joe Dunford moved the RCT-5 command post once again. His command group has moved so often since March 20 that one of the officers in the headquarters, who heard me refer to him as "Fighting Joe Dunford," came up to me afterward and said that they were debating changing his nickname to "Moving Joe Dunford" or "Fighting Joe Dun-moved."

We're now in Baghdad's downtown sports complex—once home to the Iraqi National Football Club, their Olympic and World Cup soccer team. Saddam converted the site—a twenty-thousand-seat concrete stadium, modern exercise facility, gymnasium with basketball courts, locker rooms, showers, physical therapy equipment, team offices, and an adjoining school—into a Republican Guard arsenal and anti-aircraft battery. Fighting holes and trenches had been dug in the soccer field and adjoining practice fields, ruining the underground irrigation system. The school and gymnasium had been used to store weapons and ammunition and as quarters for the troops. It's filthy, with cooking utensils, clothing, and personal effects scattered everywhere. Whoever had been living here clearly left in a hurry.

As soon as the gymnasium is thoroughly searched, the Marines set about cleaning the basketball court. Someone puts out the word to find a basketball. Meanwhile, an athletic young trooper climbs up to the scoreboard and, using handmade cardboard signs, tapes the number "0" next to "HOME." Beside "VISITORS" he puts "5,000."

On the streets outside the sports complex, other RCT-5 Marines are patrolling intensively throughout the regiment's sector. While the infantry walks for a change, it seems as though the "wrench turners" are working every armored and wheeled vehicle in the RCT. M-88 tank retrievers are pulling and replacing "power packs" (engines) and transmissions in the M-1s and AAVs. Every truck and Humvee seems to have its hood up. And Marines who were already filthy are now covered in grease and oil up to their armpits.

The regimental sergeant major, a man who walks one step to the right rear of God, seems pleased by all the work that is being done, but is concerned that his Marines are so covered with crud. When one of the engineers reports that the water main to the sports complex is still working, the sergeant major orders the Chemical Decontamination Unit to be brought to the athletic field, which is surrounded by a high brick wall. When the piping for the "Decon Unit"—with its two dozen or so showerheads—is all set up, he has the Marines file through with bars of soap. For the better part of three hours, hundreds of utterly filthy Marines strip off their desert "cammies" and cavort through the warm water.

Just as in the chow line, officers go last. And even though I'm now a civilian, I honor the tradition, regrettably. The water runs out before I have a chance to partake in this simple luxury. As we walk back to Chaplain Frank Holley's Humvee, where our satellite gear is set up, Griff reminds me that he's not an officer and would really have appreciated a shower. In sympathy, I promise not to remove my boots tonight so he won't have to smell my feet when he goes to sleep.

Just before 1400 hours local, FOX News Channel in New York City calls and tells me that we're going to be in the first segment of *FOX & Friends*, and they connect me with Steve Doocy.

Doocy informs me that they want to do a split screen with me in Baghdad and a wounded Marine in Ramstein, Germany, who knows me.

"That's fine, Steve," I reply. "Don't take this the wrong way, but most of the Marines here know me."

"Yeah," says Doocy, "but this one has a picture with you. He's just come out of surgery at the military hospital in Ramstein, Germany, and apparently you were on a helicopter that evacuated him or something. We've just gotten the film from his camera developed and you're in the picture with him."

To me, this sounds about as unusual as the sun coming up in the east. I've posed for photographs with hundreds of soldiers, sailors, airmen, and Marines over here. But a few minutes later we go live, and I see the image of a young Marine on the screen of our little transceiver. He's talking about getting wounded and being taken to an Army shock-trauma hospital, then back to Kuwait and placed on a U.S. Air Force Nightingale and flown to Germany. Then the camera in Ramstein zooms in on the photo. It's the shot Shawn Basco took onboard Don Presto's CH-46 at the palace yesterday!

Basco goes on to say some very flattering things about FOX and our coverage of the war, and some very true things about the courage of the helicopter pilots and aircrews who go into harm's way to rescue the wounded. While he's talking, I send Griff into the CP to retrieve the "send more ammo" note, so I can explain what a hero Basco is. Griff brings it back just in time. I hold it up for the TV audience and explain what it means. And that's when I notice that on the back of the cardboard someone has attached a note: *Capt. Basco deserves the Silver Star.*

He does—and I say so on the air. But it's a definite breach of protocol. The Silver Star is our nation's third-highest award for valor, and in the Marine Corps the determination as to who gets one is made by a board of officers at headquarters back in Washington.

Half an hour later, an old friend on the I-MEF staff seeks me out and comes by to give me some friendly advice: "Be careful about awarding Silver Stars on television. Some people up the line may not like it."

I know he's right, but I can't resist a reply. "So what are they going to do, shave my head and send me to Iraq?"

✪ ✪ ✪

We keep our satellite link set up for most of the day. The news out of New York and Washington is all about the "looting" that's supposedly so rampant here in the city. To get a better sense for how bad it really is, I accompany one of the squad-sized foot patrols that is moving block to block and building to building in this part of the city.

The sergeant leading the patrol has his men well spread out; the Marines have their weapons at the ready as they move down the streets. Most of the shops are shuttered, and there are only a handful of civilians about. Even though we haven't heard a shot fired for some time, the civilian population is practically invisible—a sign that there are probably fedayeen or Baath enforcers still in the area.

As the point man approaches an intersection, one of his mates with a SAW moves up to cover him before he moves out in the open. While he checks out the open space—a natural killing zone—the sergeant orders the others to "take a knee." They all genuflect, fore-fingers extended above the triggers on their M-16s, their thumbs on safeties, ready to fire in an instant. Crouching there with them, my video camera rolling, I can see one man in every fire team scanning the rooftops.

The patrol continues in this fashion for more than an hour, the squad leader constantly toggling his GPS to note his position, in case he has to call for help. Every ten minutes or so he calls a pos-rep (a "position report," meaning his location) back to his company HQ on his PRC-119 radio.

Suddenly, as the patrol approaches an intersection, four young men dressed in black trousers and dirty civilian shirts come running around the corner and nearly collide with the point man. A near cat-astrophe is averted as the Marine yells, "Stop!"

The four youths do as ordered and drop what they are carrying—bags of rice and cans of cooking oil. In an instant they are spread-eagled on the street and searched. No weapons are found, and when they are allowed to get up, the four boys lead the patrol to the place they had stolen their booty—the garage of a tree-shaded house set back from the street. I notice that the two-story residence has an air-conditioning unit, the first one I've seen in Iraq.

Inside the four-car garage is a nearly new Mercedes—along with at least six or seven hundred forty-pound bags of rice, stacks of one-gallon cans of cooking oil, and boxes full of tinned meat. All of the bags and boxes have a large "UN" label stamped on them and a UN emblem. The sergeant is quickly on the radio summoning a HET team and a truck. While they wait, he orders one of the fire team leaders to check out the house.

A Marine uses his Kabar knife to force the door, and four leather-necks cautiously enter. They're back in minutes with the observation, "Nobody home, but nice digs, sar'ent."

That's an understatement. Though not as opulent as one of Saddam's palaces, this is clearly the very comfortable domicile of some-one very highly placed in the Iraqi military, the Baath Party, or both. Persian carpets cover the floors; artwork and tapestries adorn the walls. Blank spots and picture hooks reveal where someone has removed other items—probably photographs. There is still some clothing in the closets, but many drawers are empty or partially empty, indicating that the family who lived here packed quickly but carefully before departing. One room, apparently a home office, has connections for a computer that's been removed. The desk has been sanitized—not even a receipt remains. Behind the desk, a wall safe is open and empty.

Outside, one of the Marines finds a fifty-five-gallon drum full of ashes; it smells of kerosene. A charred shovel lies on the ground beside the "burn barrel." Whoever these people are, they had something to hide and wanted to get out of town before the Americans arrived.

When the three-man HET team arrives in their Humvee and an empty seven-ton truck, they are accompanied by two OGA personnel in an SUV. I go with them back through the garage, the house, and large shed behind the residence. The shed is also full of UN food and relief supplies. After poking around awhile, the OGA fellows decide that there is little left of intelligence value and I ride with them back to the sports complex and the RCT-5 CP.

On the way I ask the CIA team chief if he has seen more of this kind of thing since we arrived in Baghdad. "Hell, yes. That's nothing," he replies. "There are whole warehouses full of UN food, medicine, and relief supplies that the Baath Party was hoarding. Those kids back there weren't 'looting.' They aren't ripping off their neighbors—this isn't like Watts or Detroit when people pillaged just for the hell of it. Those four boys were just trying to get what was supposed to be theirs but that Saddam and his Baath buddies had stolen," he continues, clearly agitated.

As we enter the sports complex perimeter and I get out of his SUV, he finishes his invective. "The UN Oil-for-Food Program was a bad idea right from the beginning. The UN trades food for oil, the Baath Party takes the food and sells it to the Iraqi people, and the people get screwed in the process. The guy who owned that house probably paid for it and everything in it with money he made from Oil-for-Food. Hell, he left a brand new Mercedes behind. Makes you wonder what his other car is," he adds, cooling down.

"Any idea where he might be?" I ask.

"Probably in Damascus or Amman by now," he replies. "But you can bet he's not one of those guys we killed yesterday at the mosque or palace defending Saddam."

✪ OPERATION IRAQI FREEDOM SIT REP #33
   With HMLA-267
   Eastern Iraq
   Saturday, 12 April 2003
   2345 Hours Local

By the time Griff and I bed down on the night of April 11, the immediate area around the RCT-5 HQ at the sports complex is secure. Earlier in the day, while I was out poking around the warehouse/home,
S/Sgt. Riayan Tejeda, of 3rd Battalion, 5th Marines—with whom I
had gone on patrol a few nights earlier—was killed by an Iraqi or
fedayeen sniper. But by dark last night, things in Baghdad are remarkably quiet. Wrapped in my poncho liner on the concrete steps of the
stadium, I can see stars overhead—and the Marine sniper team on
the roof of the school next door. And though there are occasional
bursts of AK-47 fire off in the distance, for the first time since March
20, we don't hear the sound of U.S. or British jets or UAVs overhead.

In the morning, Capt. Allen Grinalds, a Cobra pilot with HMLA-
267, offers to have me ride along on a "hunter-killer" mission. Grinalds was flight leader for two AH1J Cobras and two UH1N Hueys.
They are heading north toward Tikrit, Saddam's hometown, looking
for a fight. It sounds like a way to get some good footage for one of
my FOX News Channel feeds and see some of the country I haven't
yet been over, so I go along. As is so often the case in war, things don't
go as intended.

The original flight plan called for us to fly the route that would be
taken by Task Force Tripoli. This hastily organized unit, comprising
1st, 2nd, and 3rd LAR Battalions, an artillery battalion, an infantry
company, a Marine engineer detachment, and a Navy SEAL team—
all commanded by Brig. Gen. John Kelly, the 1st Marine Division
assistant commander—was to take Tikrit as fast as possible. Task

Force Tripoli had two missions: kill or capture any leaders of the regime who might have taken refuge in the city, and make sure that the Kurds didn't get there first. The CENTCOM staff was justifiably concerned that if Kurdish pesh merga troops got to Tikrit before U.S. forces arrived, there would be a slaughter of biblical proportions. There isn't a Kurdish fighter in Iraq who hasn't lost at least one family member to Saddam's goons. And in this part of the world, retribution is a way of life.

The mission to be "the *firstest* with the *mostest*" in Tikrit fell to I-MEF, even though the Marines had already come farther, faster than anyone else in the war, and farther from water than any Marine force had ever gone before.

Grinalds and his four-bird flight take off and head north for about ten minutes. But shortly after we leave the Baghdad skyline behind, an urgent call comes over the radio diverting the mission to a "high-priority target"—an enemy armor concentration to our east—in the Task Force Tarawa zone of action. As the four helicopters wheel right and head off in the new direction, I fumble with my laminated map to plot the grid. I am astounded—we are being sent more than 150 miles east, to the vicinity of Al Amarah, within sight of the Iranian border.

The Marines of Task Force Tarawa, having fought the bloody battle of An Nasiriyah and then all the way north to An Numiniyah, have spent the last two weeks holding more than 150 kilometers of MSR (main supply route) on Routes 1, 7, and 27, keeping them open for Marine and Army convoys rolling up from Kuwait. Despite being spread thin—and even though some units have suffered combat losses of more than 20 percent—not one convoy has been ambushed by roving bands of fedayeen. Now the exhausted and depleted TF Tarawa is tasked with the "urgent mission" of racing east to Al Amarah because someone at "higher headquarters" perceives a threat from an Iraqi border outpost.

We refuel twice on the way, and just as we finally arrive at the out-skirts of the city, Grinalds receives a radio call canceling the mission. The target has been hit by a fixed-wing air strike.

As it turns out, the whole venture is for naught. When Task Force Tarawa swarms into Al Amarah, they confirm what was apparent to all but those who sent us there: the Iraqis have already fled, leaving mountains of unattended weapons, equipment, ordnance, and armor behind.

As the discouraged pilots fly back to the west, one of the Cobra pilots sees a large enclosure surrounded by guard towers, and a berm topped with barbed wire. On closer inspection it turns out to be a tank park. There are dozens of Iraqi T-72s, T-55s, BMPs, BTRs, and anti-aircraft weapons scattered about the site—far too much to be destroyed by four helicopters carrying 2.75-inch and five-inch rock-ets, Hellfire and TOW missiles, 20mm cannons, and machine guns. But after marking the GPS position of the site, the pilots take out their frustration by destroying the anti-aircraft weapons protecting the facility so that they can't threaten any other aircraft. Then, for good measure, they unleash their TOWs and Hellfires on the armor. As the birds wheel away into the setting sun more than thirty of the Iraqi armored vehicles, AA guns, SAMs, and trucks are blazing.

✪ OPERATION IRAQI FREEDOM SIT REP #34
With 3rd Battalion, 5th Marines
Baghdad, Iraq
Palm Sunday, 13 April 2003
2345 Hours Local

We spent last night on the captured runway at An Numaniyah. This is now a full-fledged Marine airbase—MAG-39 and MAG-13 both have operations and logistics centers here. I had just unrolled my poncho liner beside the skid of the Huey when Lt. Gen. Conway, the I-MEF commander, drove up in a Humvee and invited me to join him for a late-night snack. Since he didn't have room in his vehicle for all twelve of the Huey and Cobra pilots and aircrews, I respectfully declined his hospitality and got my first full night's sleep in weeks.

Shortly after dawn, as I am wolfing down a jambalaya MRE for breakfast, my satellite phone rings and the duty officer at the FOX News Channel foreign desk in New York politely inquires if I could link up with Task Force Tripoli, now on its way to Tikrit. I explain, without going into the details, that I was about seventy-five miles southeast of Baghdad and looking for a ride to link up with RCT-5 and HMM-268.

"Why do you want me to cover Task Force Tripoli?" I ask. "We already have Rick Leventhal and Christian Galdabini with 3rd LAR and they're part of TF Tripoli. They're as good or better than anybody out here. Why can't they cover the attack on Tikrit?"

"Their Humvee broke down," he replies.

"I'll do my best," I say, and sign off. Then I make a frantic dash for the MAG-39 Forward Operations tent. Inside I find Gunnery Sgt. Robert Pequeno, the MAG-39 Ops Chief—who also happens to be the best barber in all of I-MEF—and he snags me a ride in a CH-46 up to RCT-5.

But by the time I arrive back at the Baghdad sports complex, find Griff, pack up our satellite gear, and go into the RCT-5 CP to scrounge another hop north to link up with TF Tripoli, it is too late. All the HMM-268 "frogs" and HMLA-267 Hueys are committed to other missions. Breaking one loose to fly two guys from FOX News Channel up the Tigris to Tikrit just isn't in the cards.

Seeing my disappointment, Joe Dunford suggests that we join up with Sam Mundy's 3rd Battalion, 5th Marines again, because they are headed up that way. We promptly load our gear into two Humvees and head across town, where Mundy's Marines are preparing to roll out of Baghdad and head north. We arrive just in time for a Palm Sunday service being offered by the battalion chaplain.

I've been to hundreds of these church services over the years. "Church" has been the hangar deck of an assault landing ship, a bomb crater at Khe Sanh, an artillery revetment at Con Thien, a jungle-covered hillside in Central America, a bunker in Beirut, a sweltering tent in Kuwait, and countless other venues. None of those are more memorable than this gathering of 250 or more bone-weary, grimy young men, clad in their battle gear, standing, sitting, and kneeling in the dusty courtyard of a former Republican Guard barracks.

The sergeant major has organized a choir, which sings as well as any in a cathedral. The chaplain's words are inspiring and almost prophetic. He uses the Gospel text about Christ entering Jerusalem a week before his terrible death as a lesson for the young Marines gathered for worship. "The crowd's cheers turned to jeers. Jesus didn't live up to their expectations," he said. "Most of the people didn't understand his purpose in being there and turned on him."

It somehow seems as though that is already happening to these Marines. Most of the people here in Iraq welcomed them, showering them with flowers, handing them little handmade American flags, and loving them for having ended Saddam's reign of terror. But back home, as evidenced by the criticism in the media, it seems as though their victorious entry into Baghdad, like Christ's into Jerusalem on Palm Sunday, is widely misunderstood. Complaints in the U.S. press and in Paris about their "failures to prevent Iraqi looting," the destruction of "cultural sites," the "inability to get water and electricity flowing" seem grievously unfair to these boys-turned-men who have fought so hard and sacrificed so much to get this far.

Following the service, Griff and I videotape Mundy's Op Order to his company commanders for the attack north. We'll drive through northern Baghdad, pass through the 3rd Infantry Division's lines, and pick up the route north taken by Task Force Tripoli. The battalion's mission is to drive north through hostile territory for sixty kilometers and search for "high-value leadership targets," look for American POWs, check out a major pharmaceutical plant in Samarra for weapons of mass destruction, secure the nearby airfield, and be ready to reinforce TF Tripoli in Tikrit if needed. Just an average day for a Marine infantry battalion.

✪ OPERATION IRAQI FREEDOM SIT REP #35
   With 3rd Battalion, 5th Marines
   Samarra, 60 km north of Baghdad, Iraq
   Monday, 14 April 2003
   2345 Hours Local

Before retiring for a few hours sleep on April 13 we hooked up our satellite gear and dialed into FOX News Channel center in New York. The first report is great news. The Marines of 3rd LAR—part of Task Force Tripoli—have rescued seven American POWs in Samarra. Five are soldiers from the ill-fated, 507th Maintenance Company ambush of March 23 in An Nasiriyah. The other two are Chief Warrant Officers David Williams and Ronald Young, Jr., the Apache helicopter pilots assigned to the 1st Battalion, 227th Aviation Regiment based in Ft. Hood, Texas, shot down the same day near Karbala.

The POWs had apparently been moved constantly since their capture. They were rescued in Samarra without a shot fired thanks to information provided by an Iraqi—and the quick response of the Marines.

We took this as a sign that the Iraqis are becoming less fearful of Baath and fedayeen reprisals for cooperating with U.S. forces. It also meant that as 3/5 moved north, they would have one less mission to perform.

After a few hours of sleep, we're on the road. I ride with Mundy, his sergeant major, a gunner, and a driver. Griff is in a Humvee behind us with the battalion XO, Maj. Jason Morris. In front of us are two M-1 tanks and two AAVs loaded with infantrymen standing in the open hatches, their weapons at the ready.

The move through Baghdad goes smoother than expected because of a curfew that keeps civilian traffic down to a minimum, and before Tuesday's dawn we're well north of the city, moving at twenty-five to thirty kilometers per hour. By the time the sun comes up over the Tigris, we're surrounded by fields of grain and orchards of fig trees that give off a much nicer fragrance than do our unwashed bodies.

Using a Blue Force Tracker mounted on the Humvee dashboard and his PRC-119 radio, Mundy keeps careful track of the vehicles in the fast-moving convoy. By the time we reach the outskirts of Samarra, some sixty kilometers north of Baghdad, he's fully closed up and well prepared for a fedayeen ambush just after we cross the hydroelectric dam west of the city. He dispatches two tanks and a rifle company mounted in AAVs, supported by a section of Cobras, to deal with the fedayeen, and rolls into the pharmaceutical plant.

The plant is directly across the highway from a reconstruction of the Tower of Babel and a fortress built by Alexander the Great 2,300 years ago. I decide to go get a closer shot of these while the intel officers and the guys from OGA look for any signs that the pharmaceutical facility is being used to manufacture chemical or biological weapons. But as I'm crossing the highway accompanied by a Marine rifleman, a three-Mercedes motorcade pulls up beside me. Armed men in western dress, who look much like the Iranians I used to meet with when I was trying to get American hostages out of dungeons in Beirut, get out of the first and third cars. One of them opens the back door of the middle Mercedes and a tall Shi'ite imam emerges.

I'm wondering how fast and far the young Marine and I can run after the shooting starts when the mullah says in perfect English, "How do you do? Would you please escort me to your general?"

Realizing that this is my "get out of jail free" card, I reply, "Please wait right here and we'll be right back," and the PFC and I head for the pharmaceutical plant's main gate.

Since the closest thing we have to a general at this location is Lt. Col. Sam Mundy, he leaves Maj. Morris in charge and goes to meet with the imam. The imam explains that he has just returned to Iraq from exile in Iran and he wants to help us "get rid of the foreigners."

My Arabic isn't as good as Mundy's, and I think at first that he means he wants to get rid of us, but the imam explains by "foreigners" he means the Syrian, Saudi, Egyptian, Jordanian, Palestinian, and Lebanese fedayeen who have "invaded"—his word, not mine—Iraq. The imam, now joined by a local sheikh, invites Mundy and all of our "soldiers" to come to a feast to celebrate the victory over Saddam.

Sam Mundy is not only a warrior, he's also a diplomat. He explains that all of the "foreigners" have not yet been captured or killed, and that while we very much appreciate the kind invitation, it will have to wait.

After another hour of searching the pharmaceutical plant, Mundy decides he needs more expertise to determine whether the plant was making cough drops or something worse. RCT-5 HQ tells him to remain in Samarra overnight and they will send some experts in the morning.

We've just rolled out of the plant to find a suitable place to bivouac his battalion when an urgent call comes in on Mundy's Iridium phone: a Cobra has gone down at the air base about fifteen kilometers east of Samarra. Mundy quickly organizes his TRAP response unit—two tanks, six AAVs full of troops, and four Humvees—and I tag along as we race out to recover the two pilots before the fedayeen can get to them.

The road to the airfield is lined with well-maintained farms—on which Saddam has hidden tanks, armored vehicles, and even disassembled MiG fighters—all abandoned. The up guns on the AAVs—and even some of the .50-caliber gunners on the Humvees—each take turns putting a few rounds into the Iraqi equipment just to make sure that it won't move or be used again.

When we arrive at the air base and find the wreckage of the Cobra, it looks like a giant piece of aluminum foil balled up and tossed on the desert sands. The helicopter had been attacking anti-aircraft weapons around the airfield when it was blown out of the sky by a secondary explosion from one of the hundreds of ammunition storage revetments spread around the field. If you didn't believe in miracles before seeing this wreckage, you'd have to when you learn that the pilots have survived both the explosion and the crash. Though the Cobra was totally demolished, the pilot suffered only a separated shoulder and his copilot/gunner had minor lacerations after crawling out of the wreckage. It's astounding that these guys were recovered alive.

✪ OPERATION IRAQI FREEDOM SIT REP #36
With 3rd Battalion, 5th Marines
Samarra, Iraq
Tuesday, 15 April 2003
2345 Hours Local

It's well after dark when we finally got back to Samarra, where Maj. Morris has coiled the battalion just outside the city for the night. From our bivouac we can see the city lights about a mile to the west. Power was never lost from the hydroelectric generators up here. Though this is Saddam's neighborhood, the locals don't seem to be in mourning.

At 0430 hours local this morning, Maj. Morris joins me in front of the night lens of our camera for the *Hannity & Colmes* show. In response to a question from Alan Colmes, who is wondering how the negative press is affecting morale, Morris responds, "Well, I'll tell you, sir, we've got a great sense of accomplishment.... It's a real testament to the skill and fighting spirit of the Marines for getting where we have." And then Colmes asks about the announcement from CENTCOM that major combat activities have ceased and that all units are to transition into "security and stability operations." Morris answers, "We're looking forward to this mission, sir. It's going to take us back a little ways. We're not going to be quite as ramped up, but we're ready for it."

When we finish, Morris asks me, "How did I do?"

I respond, poking fun at my favorite liberal, "You did fine. But you don't have to call Alan Colmes 'sir.'"

✪ ✪ ✪

On Wednesday, shortly after dawn, I am sitting on the ramp of an AAV washing my feet and changing my socks—one of those pleasant, solitary rituals that infantry Marines try to practice daily but often don't get to—when Griff comes running up to me with the Iridium satellite phone. "CENTCOM says that the Marines down south have captured 'Abu somebody' you were looking for," he exclaims breathlessly.

"Abu who?" I ask, somewhat irritated that my ablutions are being interrupted.

"I don't know," Griff replies. "Here," he says, handing me the phone, "talk to New York."

The foreign desk had the story right. The name is Abu Abbas, and he was captured last night by Marine and Task Force 20 operators during a raid on the outskirts of Baghdad. Abbas is the Palestinian terrorist who masterminded the October 1985 hijacking of the Italian *Achille Lauro* cruise ship.

When I served as the U.S. government's coordinator for counter-terrorism, I was deeply involved in the effort to capture Abbas and his three fellow terrorists. It was an operation in which those who claimed to be our friends thwarted the United States at every turn.

Egyptian president Hosni Mubarak was the first. He lied to Ronald Reagan, and then tried to facilitate the terrorists' escape.

Abbas, the head of the Palestine Liberation Front, had orchestrated the hijacking of the ship and the cold-blooded murder of Leon Klinghoffer. A sixty-nine-year-old invalid, Klinghoffer was shot while he sat in his wheelchair; his body was then dumped overboard. The Egyptians allowed the ship to sail into Alexandria harbor, where officials dispatched by Mubarak took the terrorists off the ship and hid them while arranging for an EgyptAir DC-9 to secretly fly them out of the country.

President Reagan called Mubarak and told him, "I understand the terrorists are in Egypt. I want them."

Mubarak denied they were still there and claimed that he was sorry and that he didn't know that they killed anyone. Meanwhile, the terrorists were secretly moved to the airport for a flight to Tunis, Tunisia, where Yasser Arafat was quietly preparing a hero's welcome.

With help from the Israeli intelligence services, we confirmed information we had received about the EgyptAir escape aircraft with the terrorists aboard. The plane was then intercepted over the Mediterranean Sea by F-14s from the 6th Fleet and escorted to the NATO base at Sigonella, Sicily.

When the EgyptAir commercial airliner touched down at Sigonella, it was immediately surrounded by a Special Operations unit led by Brig. Gen. Carl Steiner, who boldly opened the aircraft door, faced down the armed guard and terrorists, and took them into custody. As the SEALs prepared to escort the four terrorists to a waiting USAF C-141, they were themselves surrounded by Italian police.

To avoid a "friendly fire" incident with our Italian "allies," Steiner was ordered to turn the Palestinian terrorists over to the police.

Once again, President Reagan was on the phone—this time with Italy's Prime Minister Bettino Craxi, who promised that all four would be tried for hijacking and murder. Craxi lied.

The three "trigger-men" were detained, but Abbas, dressed in the uniform of an airline pilot, was secretly put aboard a Yugoslav airliner and flown to Yugoslavia. From there the PLF terror chieftain flew to Tunisia to meet his old buddy Arafat. A few months later, fearing that the Israelis might be closing in on Abbas, Arafat arranged for him to move to Damascus and from there to Baghdad.

President George W. Bush had named Abbas in a speech last fall as part of his argument for removing Saddam Hussein from power. "Iraq has . . . provided safe haven to Abu Abbas," he said, then added, "And we know that Iraq is continuing to finance terror and gives assistance to groups that use terrorism to undermine Middle East peace."

The PLF faction led by Abbas has been a conduit for the money Saddam provided to the families of Palestinian suicide bombers—it's widely believed that millions of dollars have been provided for this purpose.

In response to the news from FOX News Channel about Abbas's capture, we hook up our satellite transceiver but learn little more other than CENTCOM's refusal to comment on whether Abbas would be detained in Iraq, at some American base, or in another country. Nor would anyone comment on whether Abbas would be tried in the United States for the *Achille Lauro* hijacking and its aftermath.

Later in the day, when someone at the network realizes that I was involved in the initial capture of Abbas, I am asked to recall the event. After nearly two decades, I can still hear President Ronald Reagan's words when he told the nation what had happened: "You can run, but you can't hide."

⊛ OPERATION IRAQI FREEDOM SIT REP #37
   With RCT-5 and HMM-268
   Samarra, Iraq
   Wednesday, 16 April 2003
   1800 Hours Local

We spend the night of the fifteenth and all the next day in the bombed-out shell of a Republican Guard headquarters of some kind. Col. Joe Dunford has brought his Alpha Command Group up and co-located it here with Sam Mundy's CP. And as if he knew what was coming, Lt. Col. Jerry Driscoll flew in here this morning with a section of CH-46s. It seems as though everyone here is aware that the mission is about to change dramatically for all of us. Dunford and Driscoll both have said that they expect the Marines to be pulled back down, south of Baghdad, at any moment.

While most of the organized fighting has stopped, there are still pockets of resistance in the major cities of Iraq, particularly Mosul and Baghdad. Most of the snipings and ambushes seem to be the work of irregulars, the fedayeen, some of the tens of thousands of criminals Saddam released from the prisons just before the start of the war, and, of course, remnants of the regime. These sporadic incidents are being readily put down and the nights are becoming more peaceful.

An interesting and touching moment occurs this morning as Driscoll's helicopters land in a farmer's field. As soon as the engines shut down, the farmer walks out to the helicopter. I expect a complaint for scaring his animals or damaging his crops. But instead I see that the farmer is carrying fresh chicken eggs—one for each crew member.

Gunnery Sgt. Pennington tries to decline, knowing that these eggs might well be all the farmer has. Pennington tries to offer the old man some of the humanitarian rations the Red Dragons carry. But the elderly farmer is adamant and insists that the Marines take the eggs. And so for the first time since leaving Kuwait, we have an omelet, and we eat it while the old man, sitting on his haunches, eats the rice from the U.S. ration package. The smile on his face transcends any language barriers.

After that shared breakfast, Jerry Driscoll and I walk over to the RCT-5 CP so that the pilots, crew chiefs, and corpsmen from the two helicopters can properly initiate Griff as an honorary Red Dragon air crewman. The ritual involves duct-taping Griff to a litter, carrying him to where a set of clippers can be plugged in, and then shaving his head. The mission is accomplished in less than five minutes to the tune of the Marine Hymn—intended to mask the sound of Griff's screams.

While Jenkins is getting his much-needed "trim," Dunford, Driscoll, Mundy, and I are sharing some of Gunny Cheramie's good coffee. We had just gotten around the potential pleasures of a shower, clean clothing, and porcelain toilets when I get a call on my Iridium from the FOX News Channel foreign desk.

"How far is Camp Pennsylvania from where you are?" asks the duty officer in New York.

"About five hundred miles," I reply. "It's in Kuwait. I'm just south of Tikrit. Why?" I ask with a twinge of uncertainty.

"Well, that's where the 4th Infantry Division is forming up," he answers. "Someone at the Pentagon has asked for you to be embedded with them as they move into Iraq."

"Yeah, well, tell 'em I smell real bad and maybe they'll take someone else," I say, hoping that maybe Greg Kelly or Rick Leventhal might have been cleaned up by now.

"Can't," he replies. "They asked for you by name. Besides, the other teams are on the way home."

"Well, that's a stunner" is all I can say, knowing that this isn't going to go down well with Griff, who has a new baby at home. "How long?" I ask, hoping for an answer of a few days.

"Couple of weeks," he says and then hastily adds, "There is some thought that they might find Saddam."

"Okay," I say, "a couple of weeks—but if I'm not home for my daughter's wedding in June, you might as well leave me here, because I'll be safer in Baghdad than in my own kitchen."

CHAPTER TWELVE
YOU'RE IN THE ARMY NOW

✪ OPERATION IRAQI FREEDOM SIT REP #38
With 3rd Battalion, 66th Armored Regiment
4th Infantry Division, U.S. Army
80 km south of Baghdad, Iraq
Saturday, 19 April 2003
0700 Hours Local

It's the road trip from hell. Or maybe this is hell. Griff and I are stuffed into the back seats of two Humvees headed slowly north across the southern desert—part of an enormous 4th Infantry Division convoy, crawling at less than fifteen kilometers per hour deep into Iraq. It's one hundred degrees Fahrenheit in the shade and—you guessed it—there's no shade. The dust kicked up by hundreds of vehicles swirls around us like a self-generated sandstorm. Grit coats everything and it cakes on our clothing where the sweat soaks through. My backside has been numb for at least a day. All feeling has left my feet. I am contemplating cruel forms of torture to inflict on the crazed sadists who work at the FOX News Channel foreign desk. Then I remember—I volunteered.

Early on the morning of April 17, Jerry Driscoll and his wingman flew Griff and me all the way back to Ali Al Salem Air Base in Kuwait—a distance of more than five hundred miles—so that we could "marry up" with our new unit. We headed immediately for the MAG-39 billeting area and threw our filthy clothing into new washing machines and our bodies into the new showers. Both had been installed by the Seabees while we were in Iraq. It was the first real cleansing either of us had in twenty-nine days and it may well be the best shower I've ever taken.

Two hours later we emerged with clean bodies garbed in clean clothing, ready to join the Army. Not knowing where HMM-268 would be when we returned from covering the 4th ID, we made a quick round of "goodbyes," "see-you-laters," and "be carefuls" with the Marines before an Army SUV came by to pick us up.

The trip to Camp Pennsylvania—the TAA for the 4th ID up along the Iraqi-Kuwaiti border—takes less than an hour. We arrive in time for noon chow in the mess tent. After eating our first non-MRE meal in nearly a month, Griff and I go with our new hosts, the 66th Armored Regiment of the 4th Infantry Division, to load our gear aboard the vehicles that will be taking us back into Iraq. About a mile from the tents of the base camp, an enormous three-hundred vehicle convoy is formed up in four long columns of trucks, fuelers, Humvees, and scores of heavy equipment transporters.

Heavy equipment transporters are huge tractor-trailer rigs that have M-1 tanks, Bradley fighting vehicles, and M-113 APCs chained to their low-riding flatbeds. The Army calls them HETs, but in the Marines a HET is a "human exploitation team" that helps collect and interpret intelligence. In the Army, a HET is a rig that is twice as big as any eighteen-wheeler on an interstate highway in the United States. They are used to reduce wear and tear on armored vehicles by hauling heavy equipment from a staging area to a site nearer the battle zone, where the armored vehicles are off-loaded and deployed for combat. The closest thing to these behemoths in the Marines are the tractor-trailers the engineers use to haul bulldozers and bridging equipment.

Maj. Douglas Cox, the convoy commander with whom we'll be riding, is surprised that the U.S. Marine Corps doesn't have any HETs until I explain that the Marines have to haul all their tools of war around on amphibious ships. One of his lieutenants listening to our conversation inquires skeptically, "Then how did the Marines get their tanks, LAVs, and AAVs all the way up to Tikrit?"

"They drove," I answer.

"All the way?" he asks, incredulous.

"All the way from the ships that off-loaded them," I reply, trying not to sound too smug.

The young officer simply shakes his head, knowing that such a journey, even without battle damage, is terribly hard on the equipment. And he's right.

But then I realize that the trip we're about to start isn't going to be a picnic either. Sitting on the hood of Maj. Cox's Humvee, I program my GPS for the route we're going to follow: across the border at Safwan, a left turn up Route 8 to Route 1, around Ad Diwaniyah to pick up Route 8 again, and through Baghdad to a TAA that V Corps has established for the 4th ID at a Republican Guard installation just north of the capital. There, the armor will be off-loaded from the HETs and 4th ID will move tactically to their assigned area of operations north of Samarra.

We'll be rolling right through the battlefields that the 1st Marine Division and the 3rd ID fought over for nearly a month on their way north to Tikrit. On my map it looks to be about five hundred miles. That's a full day's driving on interstate highways in the States. But back home there's a gas station at practically every interchange and we don't have sandstorms, ambushes by roving bands of fedayeen, or 299 other vehicles traveling with us when we pile the family into our

SUV and head to the beach. I tell Major Cox that I don't envy his task. He shrugs and says with a smile, "They're good soldiers and they've been waiting a long time for this."

That's certainly true—on both counts. These are among the best troops in the U.S. Army. Nearly every vehicle in the 4th ID is equipped with a "Blue Force Tracker"—an encrypted, GPS-based, satellite-linked computer system that displays the location of friendly and enemy units on a plasma screen.

This capability alone offers an extraordinary advantage to 4th ID field commanders in responding to calls for reinforcements, resupply, cas-evacs, and fire support in the midst of a gunfight. Every trooper in the division has been trained to use and maintain this gear. And because they are so good, the original war plan for Iraq called for the 4th ID to accomplish one of the most difficult missions in the campaign: offload in Turkey, race east across the country to the Iraqi border, and charge south to Baghdad through some of the toughest terrain in all southwest Asia. At least that was the initial plan for these good soldiers—as Cox accurately described them.

There's also great validity to the major's comment that the men have been waiting a long time for this. The 4th ID, based at Fort Hood, Texas, was one of the first units alerted for Operation Iraqi Freedom. As early as November 2002, the division's operations and logistics officers had completed their war plans and started moving equipment to Galveston and other ports for shipment to the theater of operations. More than twenty commercial oceangoing vessels were contracted to move the 4th ID's combat gear from Texas to the NATO port facility at Iskendurun, Turkey. According to the plan, as soon as the ships arrived the division's troops, carrying only their personal weapons and gear, would be flown to the big NATO air base at Incirlik, Turkey. Then they'd bus to the port, offload the ships, and be on their way to the Iraqi border.

By working around the clock, seven days a week (even through the Christmas holidays), everything the 4th ID would need was mounted out and on its way to Turkey by the second week of January. But then the unthinkable happened: Ankara said no to U.S. plans for moving forces through Turkey. And so, with their gear still at sea and no equipment left on which to train, the soldiers of the 4th ID were told to wait.

At CENTCOM, Turkey's denial of access sent the war planners scrambling for alternatives on how to pressure Baghdad from the north. Without some kind of credible threat from that direction, Saddam would be free to move nearly all his forces south to confront coalition units invading from Kuwait.

Gen. Franks intended all along to use Special Forces teams as Scud hunters in the western desert and to rally the Kurdish enclaves in Iraq's northwestern mountains. But those lightly armed units wouldn't be enough of a threat to Baghdad to make Saddam leave six of his best combat divisions north of Tikrit.

Although the international press had reported widely on Turkey's refusal to allow transit rights to U.S. forces, Gen. Franks decided to use the 4th ID in much the same way as Eisenhower had used Patton to deceive Hitler as to where the allies intended to land on the coast of France during World War II.

In May and June of 1944, while the rest of the allies prepared to land at Normandy, George Patton was ordered to set up bogus headquarters units along the English coast between Margate and Brighton, convincing the German general staff that the allies would take the shortest route across the English Channel and land at Calais. The ruse worked and the Germans held dozens of armored divisions near Calais that could have devastated the allied landings had they been closer to Normandy on June 6, 1944.

In the days before launching Operation Iraqi Freedom, Gen. Franks used the 4th ID the same way. Instead of immediately ordering the

ships from Texas through the Suez Canal when the Turks rejected the
U.S. request for transit, Gen. Franks kept the vessels at anchor off Iskendurun and insisted that the Pentagon continue the pretense of trying to change Ankara's decision. It worked. Saddam held his northern
divisions in place until it was too late for them to counter the 3rd ID
and the 1st Marine Division attacks from the south. Only then did
Gen. Franks order the 4th ID ships to proceed through the Suez
Canal, around the Arabian Peninsula, and into the Persian Gulf.

  By the time the 4th ID troops finally loaded up on planes en route
to Kuwait, Saddam's regime was finished. And though the patience of
the soldiers from Ft. Hood was worn thin by constant alerts, canceled
leaves, and interminable waiting, their delay in getting into the fight
had been an important factor in abbreviating the war's duration.

  Now these very frustrated soldiers are finally heading north—just
as the Marines we rode with for a month get ready to head south.
Though some of these soldiers talk about being "too late for the
action," the older officers and NCOs know better. At a brief stop for
refueling—a sergeant first class who fought in the first Gulf War
admonished one of his young troopers, "Don't think that all the
shooting is over. The toughest part of this war is still ahead."

✪ OPERATION IRAQI FREEDOM SIT REP #39
   With 3rd Battalion, 66th Armored Regiment
   4th Infantry Division, U.S. Army
   10 km north of Tikrit, Iraq
   Easter Sunday, 20 April 2003
   2300 Hours Local

At dawn on Easter Sunday we arrive at the 4th ID TAA, just north of
Baghdad. Six days ago, riding with Sam Mundy and the 3rd Battalion, 5th Marines, we breezed right by this Republican Guard training

center en route to Samarra. Just north of here we passed through the lines of the 3rd ID, which had captured this facility on April 11, the day after Baghdad fell.

Now, after two and a half days of mind-deadening, butt-numbing, day-and-night movement, Griff and I are back to exactly where we were almost a week ago. The enormous convoy pulls into the facility behind Major Cox's Humvee and stops on a five-acre paved parade field. Every building around the periphery is shattered, having been hit by bombs, artillery fire, or both. We have stopped only to refuel at points along the route guarded by dust-covered paratroopers of the 82nd Airborne Division. Now the HETs are finally unloading their armored vehicles and preparing to highball it all the way back to Kuwait to pick up another load of equipment and bring it forward.

Every soldier and vehicle is covered with dirt, as we were during the MOASS dust storm back in March. Those passengers, like me and Griff, who have had to ride in the backseats of Humvees—a space designed by some sadist without knees or feet—are practically anesthetized.

At times during this interminable "road march," I jump out of Maj. Cox's Humvee and jog alongside for a few minutes to prevent a potentially lethal blood clot. The first time I do it, about eight hours into the trip, our driver, SPC Rios, asks me if all Marines do this. "No," I reply, "only the old men over fifty. And if they can't keep up we leave 'em behind."

Rios, a communicator by training, has a keen sense of humor. After having to stop several times so that various vehicles could fix flats caused by all the shrapnel on the highway, he begins referring to the journey as an "Ordeal by Tire."

Now that we're finally inside a friendly perimeter, Maj. Cox stretches to get out the kinks from sitting so long and goes off to find the unit that will take us north. Griff and I wander through row after row of M-1 tanks, Bradley infantry fighting vehicles, trucks, artillery pieces, and Humvees looking for an Easter service. We find one, but not until the chaplain for one of the battalions of the 66th Armored Regiment is already wrapping up a sunrise Resurrection celebration.

By noon we have linked up with Lt. Col. Larry Jackson, commander of the 3rd Battalion, 66th Armored Regiment. The famed 66th won acclaim during World War II when it landed in North Africa in 1942, and fought across Utah Beach at Normandy two and a half years later. Col. Jackson, a tough no-nonsense professional Army warrior, is adamant that the 66th will live up to its legacy.

Before we head out of the TAA, Lt. Col. Jackson briefs us on his battalion's mission: move as fast as possible to occupy and secure a wide swath of terrain northeast of Saddam's hometown of Tikrit; search for weapons of mass destruction; detain or kill any "Iraqi leadership targets"; protect the oil pipeline and refinery at Bayji; restore essential services and law and order for the civilian population, and protect U.S. forces. And, he tells me, "The area around Tikrit, Saddam's ancestral home, is the most likely place in all of Iraq where Hussein and those loyal to him will hold out. If he's there, we aim to get him."

I say, "I hope he does—and that it'll happen soon." Just before our briefing with Lt. Col. Jackson, the FOX News Channel foreign desk paged me and asked why we hadn't been on the air for more than forty-eight hours. As gently as I could, I informed them that the satellite equipment Griff and I carry has to be stationary to use, that we had been moving nonstop for more than forty-eight hours, and that we had still another full day's movement before we'd be able to set up. The desk officer replied, "Well, get up on the air as soon as you can. You're our last 'embed team' in Iraq."

✪ ✪ ✪

Lt. Col. Larry Jackson's column of tanks, Bradleys, Humvees, trucks, and artillery forms up inside the perimeter of the Republican Guard cantonment and when he gives the signal, it moves. Griff and I are riding in a Bradley about a dozen vehicles back from the front of the column. As we exit the gate, the column has to slow down and wheel right to get on the hardball highway headed north to Tikrit. When we do so, there is a burst of AK-47 fire from a crowd milling about in front of a shabby *souk* across the highway, less than a hundred meters from our vehicle. As the call goes out over the tactical net, "Taking fire, nine o'clock!," the gunner for our Bradley's 25mm chain gun wheels the turret around hard to the left and depresses the muzzle, looking for targets through his thermal sights. I grab my camera as several hundred civilians scatter in panic. In the midst of the crowd I can see two AK-47 barrels pointed skyward, moving with the horde. But before anyone can flip an arming switch or squeeze a trigger, another call comes over the radio, "Hold your fire! Keep moving. Close up your vehicles!"

I can't tell who is speaking, but the soldiers do as ordered. No one opens fire and the column continues its movement up the highway. I'm impressed. Green troops with loaded weapons hearing rounds go off or words like "taking fire" can easily overreact—and in this situation, several dozen civilian casualties could have resulted. Remarkably the reaction of these soldiers is what one might expect from troops who have already seen combat. Their training and discipline are already showing—and these guys have just gotten here.

With overhead cover from AH-64 Apache and OH-58 Kiowa helicopters, Jackson's column moves rapidly up the four-lane highway without interference—other than crazy Iraqi civilians who totally ignore all known rules of the road. On several occasions, Marine convoys from RCT-5 and Task Force Tripoli, headed south on the other side of the median, were apparently moving too slow for Iraqis going in the same direction. The Iraqi solution was to cut across the median and proceed south in the northbound lanes at high speed. After several near-death experiences with oncoming Toyotas, SFC Terrigino, the scout platoon's senior NCO, asked for and received permission to replace the Humvee that was leading the expedition with a Bradley. The number of Iraqi "lane jumpers" dropped dramatically.

Just before dark we're south of Tikrit and the column halts for the night. As the armored vehicles pull off the road into an open field to establish a perimeter, SFC Terrigino, now back in his .50-caliber-equipped Humvee, swings by and asks if I want to ride with him while he scouts on ahead. Griff jumps into one of the other scout platoon Humvees, and both vehicles race down the empty highway looking for trouble. As we move, the Blue Force Tracker mounted in front of Terrigino shows the location of our vehicle moving north on the map, blue rectangles depicting the other vehicles in the battalion behind us, and two red icons representing possible Iraqi positions about four kilometers up the highway between us and Tikrit.

"These two symbols are a T-72 and an Iraqi BMP, reported by the helicopters," Terrigino says, pointing to the computer screen. "We're going to find out if they are manned or just some abandoned Iraqi armor left beside the road."

Terrigino halts his little motorized patrol about five hundred meters from the bend in the highway where the Iraqi vehicles were plotted and sends four soldiers up the hill on foot to reconnoiter the position. I put the night lens on my little camera. A half an hour later, the foot patrol reports back by radio: "The vehicles are abandoned. We've marked the exact location on the GPS so EOD [explosive ordnance disposal] can destroy them tomorrow."

With that, we turn around and head back to the perimeter. Lt. Col. Jackson already has a CP tent up. Inside the TOC are computer and radio consoles for operations, logistics, and fire support, with watch officers for each already at their stations. It's very impressive, and far more sophisticated than anything a Marine regiment has—much less a battalion.

When I ask Col. Jackson about it, he says, "Yes . . . we do have some neat stuff. And I think the younger soldiers really get a kick out of it. But I came from an 'analog' Army—much like the Marine unit that you came from—with the old maps, acetate sheets, and grease pencils. Those are still great tools. But I wouldn't want to go to war without the digital equipment that we have now."

✪ OPERATION IRAQI FREEDOM SIT REP #40
   With 3rd Battalion, 66th Armored Regiment
   4th Infantry Division, U.S. Army
   Bayji, Iraq
   Monday, 21 April 2003
   2300 Hours Local

Shortly after dawn this morning, SFC Terrigino and his scout platoon brought me and Griff to Saddam's hometown palace in Tikrit. The opulent mansion is now the headquarters for the 1st Brigade of the 4th Infantry Division. The CO, Col. Don Campbell, took possession of the real estate yesterday from Brig. Gen. John Kelly, USMC, commander of Task Force Tripoli.

This is the third of Saddam's many palaces I've seen, but it's the only undamaged one I've been in. Uday's castle, about a kilometer north, is reduced to rubble, but this one is unscathed. For reasons unknown to anyone here, this particular palace was left off the CENTCOM target list.

Like all of Saddam's residences, this one overlooks some of the most beautiful scenery in all of Iraq. Perched high above the Tigris, it's surrounded by irrigated orchards of fig and eucalyptus trees—and a very high wall topped with razor wire. An enormous swimming pool graces the south side of the ornate, three-story building. Carefully manicured gardens are terraced into the hillside to the east and south. On the west side, there is a six-car garage complete with an armored Mercedes limousine. No one seems to know what really happened to the other five cars, but one Army wag suggests that several Marine sergeants from 1st, 2nd, and 3rd Light Armored Reconnaissance Battalions may be driving back to Kuwait in Mercedes sedans instead of their LAVs.

On the east side, wending its way through the terraces, a road leads down to the Tigris and an empty boathouse. One of the young Army specialists from SFC Terrigino's scout platoon suggests that the exterior of the place has all the accoutrements of a resort, and he's right. No matter where you stand on this property, it's impossible to see any other house or building. There is a feeling of privacy and remoteness.

Yet just out of sight in the surrounding neighborhood, there are homes without electricity, running water, or sewage systems. Saddam had to have been totally oblivious to the suffering of his people as he turned the country's oil profits into his own personal fortune—or he just didn't care.

Inside the edifice are more than seventy rooms, not counting closets still full of clothing and more than a dozen bathrooms with goldplated fixtures. But for all the marble floors, rare hardwood paneling, and high-vaulted ceilings complete with murals, the place is positively tacky. Grotesque, handcrafted statuary and original amateurish paintings depicting Saddam as a Bedouin, an Arab sheikh, a horsemounted warrior, a farmer tending his crops, adorn rooms with furniture that looks as though it was bought at the yard sale of a bordello. The palace even has a movie theater and a modern Sony TV, but the microwave oven in the kitchen has to be at least fifteen years old. Beautiful tapestries cover many walls, and there are cabinets full of Limoges china with gold-leaf trim, but the rug covering the floor in the main dining room is a Romanian polyester knockoff of a Persian. Martha Stewart would not approve.

After our tour of what several soldiers call "the evil prince's haunted castle," we mount up with Terrigino's road warriors and head back up the highway. His mission for the day is to find a permanent laager for Lt. Col. Jackson's battalion in the vicinity of Bayji. The colonel wants a spot where the unit will be relatively safe from roving bands of fedayeen and their "technicals"—the ubiquitous pickup trucks with .50-caliber machine guns mounted in their beds—and still have good access to the main highways that will allow his QRF to get in and out quickly if needed.

By late afternoon, Terrigino has found just such a spot: an abandoned Iraqi military base on a hillside overlooking Bayji and the rail marshaling yard just outside the city. The location has good clear fields of fire in all directions and grass instead of dirt to minimize the amount of dust and mud. Best of all, the location already has a bulldozed berm surrounding it, and unlike the desert south of here, the earth is soft enough to easily dig fighting holes. The scouts conclude that the site must have been a chemical warfare training facility, given the number of gas masks, decontamination equipment, training manuals, and atropine injectors left lying around. But when he calls in to report his find, suggesting as he does so that the watch officer check his location on the TOC's Blue Force Tracker, the sergeant is told that Col. Jackson has selected another site about five hundred meters from the "biggest ammo dump we've ever seen." Terrigino checks the CO's location on his tracker and we mount up and head there.

When we arrive at the new battalion perimeter, Lt. Col. Jackson has again already set up his TOC in the large CP tent. He's just starting a meeting with all his company commanders, and several of them are clearly concerned.

While we were out looking for a suitable place for the battalion bivouac, a helicopter flying overhead spotted an enormous warehouse facility not far from the railroad tracks, and Jackson sent a troop of Bradleys to check it out. Their report stunned everyone. The cavalry commander said that the facility was actually an ordnance depot seven kilometers long by five kilometers wide that contained millions of rounds of every kind of ammunition known to man. Worst of all, it was easily accessible. There were no gates, and no guards, and every inch of barbed wire and chain-link fencing that had once surrounded this place—more than fifteen miles of it—was now gone. The place was wide open to anyone.

Jackson ordered night ambushes to be set on the avenues of approach to the ammo dump. His instructions were, "Do what you have to to keep anyone from getting into this place, because God help us if the fedayeen get their hands on this stuff." As soon as his commanders departed to move their troops into position, Jackson was on the radio with Brigade HQ in Tikrit, advising them on what his troops had found and asking that additional ordnance specialists and engineers report to his unit in the morning.

Shortly after the meeting breaks up, Griff and I go outside to catch some sleep. I grab the hood of SFC Terrigino's Humvee. He will be leading the QRF if it gets called out in the middle of the night to assist one of the ambush units, and I don't want to miss capturing some good footage for FOX News Channel. Before rolling up in my poncho liner, I put the night lens on my camera—just in case.

✪ OPERATION IRAQI FREEDOM SIT REP #41
With 3rd Battalion, 66th Armored Regiment
4th Infantry Division, U.S. Army
Bayji, Iraq
Tuesday, 22 April 2003
2300 Hours Local

I hear the first shots at about 0300 and roll over to see what is going on—mostly listening for how close the firing is and evaluating whether I need to jump off the hood of Terrigino's Humvee and run for a fighting position. The hood of a Humvee is a great place to sleep unless someone is shooting artillery, mortars, or RPGs at your position. Not hearing the *tuk, tuk, tuk* of a mortar, I sit up and carefully put on my boots. I've been using them for a pillow.

High on the hillside I can see an occasional burst of red tracer—ours—from a Bradley or a Humvee-mounted .50-caliber. There is the lighter, faster cough of a 240-Golf machine gun and of course the very high crack of M-16s. The only enemy weapons audible are AK-47s—which means that the bad guys are definitely outgunned in this fight.

By the time I have my boots on and my poncho liner stowed in my backpack, SFC Terrigino has his platoon up and ready to move, their Humvee engines idling. The Bradley crew to our left and the M-1 on our right, both part of the QRF, are also ready to roll. But the word to ride to the rescue never comes. Within twenty minutes, the firing dies down, so I wander over to Col. Jackson's TOC to find out what's happened.

I find him inside on the radio to brigade headquarters reporting a successful ambush of a group of men with several pickup trucks who were trying to enter the ammo depot. He promises that I can go inspect the scene right after first light.

Shortly after dawn, SFC Terrigino and four of his scout platoon Humvees drive up to the ambush site. When we arrive, the platoon commander who triggered the ambush is reviewing with his soldiers what happened. The bodies of fourteen men, nearly all dressed in black, are lying on or near a rutted dirt road that enters the ammo dump from the east. According to the battalion S-2, who has collected identity documents from all or most, only two of the dead were Iraqi. Of the remaining twelve, four are Jordanian, three are Syrian, two are Egyptian, one is a Saudi, and the other two are Lebanese.

The foreigners and their two Iraqi guides had disembarked from two pickup trucks about two hundred meters from the Ammunition Supply Point (ASP) and walked straight up the road into the killing zone of a night-vision-equipped platoon-sized ambush. The carnage was completely one-sided. There were no American casualties.

We spend most of the rest of the day going through the biggest and most dangerously unsafe ammo dump I've ever seen.

According to the engineer officer dispatched by helicopter from Brigade HQ at Tikrit, the site contains more than five hundred ordnance bunkers and revetments and ninety-five steel structures filled to the top with every conceivable type of ammunition and explosive. Dry grass is growing right up to the door of every building and bunker—a major fire hazard.

Most of the ammunition is in very good shape; some of it—the Jordanian artillery rounds, the Italian land mines, and the Saudi small-arms ammunition—appears to be nearly new. In one shed, several hundred green wooden boxes bear the label "Ministry of Procurement, Amman Jordan," with a manufacturer's delivery date of January 2003. In another shed we find cases of surface-to-air missiles: SA-7s, SA-14s, and SA-16s.

The man-portable, shoulder-launched surface-to-air missiles and the tens of thousands of RPGs stored here create the greatest anxiety among the soldiers conducting a quick inventory of the site. These weapons can bring down a military helicopter or commercial jet, and the RPGs can take out a Bradley. Fire enough of them at an M-1 tank and it'll go too.

When one of the brigade engineers has a spare moment, I ask him what he's going to do with all this stuff. His answer is honest. "I don't know. We haven't got enough TNT, Det-Cord, and blasting caps to blow all this. Worse yet, there are probably seventy-five to one hundred sites just like this one elsewhere around the country." And then he echoes Lt. Col. Jackson words: "God help us if the terrorists get their hands on this stuff."

But that may have already happened. As my camera documents, many of the surface-to-air missile and RPG boxes are open and empty.

✪ OPERATION IRAQI FREEDOM SIT REP #42
With 3rd Battalion, 66th Armored Regiment
4th Infantry Division, U.S. Army
Bayji, Iraq
Saturday, 26 April 2003
1200 Hours Local

We spend most of April 23, 24, and 25 with the 3rd Battalion scouts patrolling the area between Tikrit and Bayji. Terrigino's troopers are eager to do what's right, and I continue the practice I started early in the war of letting them tell their own story on the air with FOX News Channel. As often as I can, I put a microphone up to the face of one of these youngsters and have Griff point the camera at him while he tells the American people what he does and how well he does it.

And just like the Marines before them, each time we dial in to FOX News Channel in New York, a crowd of soldiers gathers around our miniature TV set to learn what's happening back home or elsewhere in the war. That's how we learn about the capture of other Iraqi leaders and how well things are going for U.S. forces north of us in Mosul and for the British in Basra.

On Thursday, one of SFC Terrigino's patrols followed a looter from a Republican Guard camp just south of the city back to his home. He had a truck full of sinks, toilets, and plumbing fixtures ripped out of the government facility and was apparently intending to make a new start in the home improvement business. The looter's house was then surrounded by scout platoon Humvees while Terrigino called the MPs and the battalion's intelligence officer. A truck was dispatched to the site and seven Iraqi males were taken into custody. Also taken were the stolen plumbing fixtures and a number of weapons and grenades that the scouts removed from a chicken coop.

Yesterday, a twenty-six-year-old Army 1st Lt., Osbaldo Orozco, became the first Fort Hood soldier to die in Iraq, when his Humvee flipped over while on a patrol. The incident prompted me to go back over to Saddam's palace in Tikrit and chat with Col. Joe Campbell about how he sees things shaping up.

"Our biggest challenge right now is civil affairs," Campbell tells me. "We've got to get the infrastructure up and running again. We're working civil affairs to win the hearts and minds of the Iraqi civilians," he says, and then adds, "American soldiers are here to liberate. And it doesn't matter how long it takes."

But it might well matter how long it takes.

He tells me, "The security of Tikrit and this part of Iraq, the home of Saddam Hussein, makes it especially tough. But our soldiers are up to it. They're conducting aggressive patrolling."

When I ask Col. Campbell what the most difficult aspect of all this is for him, he says, "I think it's tougher now because you don't know who the enemy is. He's dressed like the normal civilian in the city, so you really have to keep your guard up. And you have to be vigilant in terms of how you execute your missions and have to keep your eyes and ears open."

When I return to our lonely outpost in Bayji, I learn from FOX News Channel that Tarik Aziz—Saddam's former deputy prime minister and the only Christian in the Baath Party inner circle—has been captured. As in so many other cases, he was fingered by an Iraqi civilian. The Iraqi people really do hate Saddam's regime.

It's late when we retire. Griff is exhausted, but before he takes off his boots and puts his head down on top of the Humvee next to the one I'll be sleeping on, he calls back to the FOX News Channel bureau in Kuwait to order more videotape—we're almost out. When he finishes, he tosses the Iridium sat-phone to me, reminding me that we have to do a live "hit" with the Friday night edition of *Hannity & Colmes* that, for us, comes before dawn on Saturday morning. I tuck the phone up against my chest, inside my flak jacket, so that its vibration will awaken me when they phone up from New York. That's where it is when the foreign desk calls to tell us, "Come on home." But as welcome as those words are, as is so often the case in this war, it's easier said than done.

⊘ AFTER ACTION REPORT
   Dulles International Airport
   Washington, DC
   Monday, 28 April 2003
   1830 Hours Local

If getting there is half the fun, then arriving home is the other half. It's been that way every time I've come home from war: twice from Vietnam, multiple times from Central America, Grenada, and Beirut. But this return was really special. My wife, Betsy, has contacted all our children and they are there to welcome Griff and me at Dulles Airport. It is the first time in nearly two months that we actually arrive at our intended destination, at the appointed time, and without casualties.

The odyssey didn't start out that way. The H-60 Black Hawk we boarded on the morning of April 26 didn't get anywhere close to Baghdad, our intended next stop. Instead, we landed at Tikrit South, a captured Iraqi air base—and eventually caught another H-60 for the long run down the Tigris to the new Baghdad International Airport. Actually, the only thing "new" about it is the name—"Baghdad" has replaced "Saddam"—but I suppose another new thing is the fact that it is now under U.S. management.

✪ ✪ ✪

The Army pilots drop us at the main terminal, where we off-load our gear and find our way—courtesy of a Civil Affairs unit from the Illinois National Guard, to the Army's V Corps Operations Center, a cluster of interconnected, air-conditioned, sandbagged tents set up on the apron. That's when we learn that it really pays to work for FOX News Channel.

From the reception we receive, one would have thought Griff and I had won the war single-handedly. The officers, senior NCOs, and enlisted troops manning this facility have, it turns out, been glued to FOX News Channel since the war began. They describe in intimate detail reports they have seen on the FOX satellite feed for the past two months, including Greg Kelly's and Rick Leventhal's dramatic reports from the vanguard of the 3rd ID and 3rd LAR as they closed in on Baghdad two weeks ago.

Here there's no need to huddle around a tiny satellite transceiver, as the troops did when we were broadcasting in the field. Hanging from the roof of this insulated tent, in front of rows of computers at the watch station, is a huge plasma-screen TV. And there are Brit

Hume and Tony Snow with news for Sunday morning in the United States.

Griff and I have instant culture shock. We're filthy. Our clothing is grimy from living in the field. Our flak jackets and gas masks have so much dirt ground into them that they are the color of Iraqi sand. The scores of officers and senior NCOs gathered around us are... well, clean. They are all clean-shaven, wearing clean uniforms. Their hands and fingernails are clean. There isn't a gas mask or flak jacket in sight. We smell. They don't—though some may have been wearing aftershave.

After nearly two months in the field, the welcome is, as Griff put it, "awesome." But not so overwhelming that he loses his head. After hearing people ask us, "Is there anything we can do for you?" several dozen times, I am about to suggest a shower when Griff says, "We're trying to get back to Kuwait. Are there any aircraft headed that way?"

There are none going there directly, but an hour later we are aboard a C-130 assigned to Brig. Gen. Gary Harrell's Special Operations Command, headed to CENTCOM "Forward" at Doha, Qatar. Harrell's 5th and 10th Special Forces Groups have waged the war with almost no media visibility, and that's the way they want to keep it. We are admonished that if we wanted a ride to Kuwait, we cannot report who goes with us, what cargo the aircraft carries, or even what model C-130 it is. We put away our cameras and get aboard.

After a brief stop in Qatar to drop off the cargo and passengers we can't report about, we take off for the hour-and-a-half flight to Ali Al Salem Air Base in Kuwait. There we return the gas masks, chemical protective suits, flak jackets, and NVGs I signed for with HMM-268. Then we make a quick round of goodbyes again at MAG-39 and throw our personal gear and broadcast equipment into the back of a Suburban that Gary Gastelu has dispatched from the FOX bureau in Kuwait City.

The Kuwait City we return to is completely transformed from the capital we left two months before. Gone are the air raid wardens at the hotels. The police roadblocks and highway checks at key intersections are absent, as are the sirens wailing their warnings about inbound Iraqi missiles. The people on the street seem genuinely pleased to see Americans.

When we arrive at the FOX News Channel bureau at the Marriott Hotel, we are issued room keys and extra towels and are informed that our flight home, via London, departs the following morning. Two hours later—showered, shaved, fed, but still longing for any kind of cold drink with lots of ice in it—we fall asleep. Twelve hours later we are on our way home to our affectionate families at Dulles Airport.

Our warm welcome obscures three important dynamics that, if we were less fatigued, would be obvious. First, the American people are still, despite the stunning victory in Iraq, deeply divided over the war. Second, though we are home with those who love us, the soldiers, sailors, airmen, and Marines we have covered throughout the campaign are without their families, and will be for a long time to come. But most important, some of those families, instead of gathering in joy to meet their returning warrior, will come together to mourn an irreplaceable loss.

CHAPTER THIRTEEN
AFTERMATH

Though much of the "good news" from Iraq dried up when the embedded news teams came home, there was still plenty of positive information to report from the war-torn country. Unfortunately, many of these stories never got printed or aired or were buried beneath a deluge of criticism, casualty statistics, and negative anecdotes.

The events of Tuesday, July 22 in Mosul, Iraq—a major victory in Operation Iraqi Freedom—is but one example of how quickly a "good news" story can disappear. Since we were already home, the following account was prepared from news reports and information supplied by soldiers, Marines, and OGA personnel who were in Iraq when these events occurred.

✪ AFTER ACTION REPORT
 Al Falah District, Mosul, Iraq
 Tuesday, 22 July 2003
 0955 Hours Local

It has been 122 days since the coalition forces launched Operation Iraqi Freedom. For the past month only occasional skirmishes have interrupted the daily routine in Mosul. There has been an American presence in the al Falah district, an area of Mosul that's shared—not always peacefully—by Sunnis and Kurds.

The looting and revenge-taking by the Kurds eased up when the Kurdish troops retreated in late May, and the relieved locals felt that things were getting back to normal. There's been relative freedom of movement for the Iraqis since then.

Iraqi businessman Nawaf al-Zaidan was especially relieved that the Kurds were gone. As someone close to the Hussein clan, he'd have been one of their targets and probably would have been shot and hung from a lamppost like others in Saddam's regime or the Baath Party. Al-Zaidan's neighbors said that he had obtained lucrative contracts from the regime as part of the Oil-for-Food Program. Al-Zaidan made money from his connections with Saddam's family, and probably didn't even resent having to pay a kickback to them for getting his contracts.

After the Kurds left in May, all was quiet for a while. Then there was some unusual activity at al-Zaidan's house in Mosul. The homeowner told his friends and clan members that he had visitors—female relatives. In his culture, males were not allowed to visit while the women were there. For nearly a month none of his friends or neighbors were invited to his house because his "female relatives" were still visiting.

The truth, however, was that the visitors were not female. Nor were they relatives. After several days of preparations during the last week of June, Nawaf al-Zaidan received important visitors who were going to entrust him with their safety. The visitors were Uday and Qusay Hussein. They arrived June 30, with their bodyguard and Qusay's teenage son Mustafa. The fugitives would stay under the roof of the Mosul businessman until their presence was compromised.

At about 2200 local on July 21, an unidentified Iraqi citizen tipped a young U.S. Army sergeant, an intelligence specialist, that Saddam's evil sons were hiding in Nawaf al-Zaidan's house. The young sergeant's report—at the time only a suspicion—was immediately relayed to Maj. Gen. David Petraeus, commander of the 101st Airborne Division. He in turn directed his deputy, Brig. Gen. Frank Helmick, to develop a plan for capturing or killing the high-value targets said to be hiding in the Mosul residence.

Most think it was al-Zaidan who contacted the Americans about the HVTs living in his villa—no doubt for the $30 million bounty. Everyone knew about the $15 million reward for the death or capture of each of the infamous brothers. No one from the American military confirmed that al-Zaidan tipped them off, but no one seems to doubt that he was the one who betrayed Uday and Qusay.

There is, however, another possibility. The Kurdish families who live in the al Falah district near al-Zaidan's villa are loyal to Jalal Talabani, head of the Patriotic Union of Kurdistan (PUK). These neighbors may have seen Saddam's sons at the villa. According to intelligence sources, someone from the PUK group went to Talabani with the news and he took the information directly to U.S officials in Baghdad. If that's the case, the $30 million bounty went to the PUK.

The Americans used a Predator drone to do surveillance on the villa to determine how many people were inside the compound with the Hussein brothers. The 101st Airborne Division's Second Combat Brigade Team—the "Strike Brigade"—sealed off the neighborhood. Also taking part was the same covert Task Force 20 that handled the rescue of PFC Jessica Lynch. Since that famous rescue, Task Force 20 had been chasing leads on the whereabouts of Saddam and his sons. Planning, reconnaissance, and coordination continued through the night of July 21–22.

By early Tuesday morning, the 101st Airborne Division had armored Bradleys and Humvees at five strategic points around the neighborhood, blocking any traffic coming in or out of the target

building on the corner of a neighborhood street and a major boule-
vard. Troops from the division manning TOW missile-equipped
Humvees went through the neighborhood to clear out civilians.

Meanwhile, twenty operators from Task Force 20 moved out on
foot for the target building. They were quickly in position. They
climbed over a wall and headed for the front entry, going through an
unlocked gate. Nawaf al-Zaidan opened the door for them.

Things began to happen immediately after the Special Forces team
came to the door. They hurriedly escorted al-Zaidan and his wife and
son away into the protective custody of the American military. At the
same time, a bodyguard for the two brothers saw what was happening and, from an upstairs balcony, began to fire at the Special Operations troops and 101st Airborne soldiers down on the street. In the
initial fray, one U.S. soldier was hit by AK-47 fire from the balcony.
Inside, three of the TF-20 special ops team, wounded by gunfire and
grenade fragments, were forced to withdraw.

A few minutes later, Uday and Qusay were urged to surrender by
a translator on a Psy Ops loudspeaker. Qusay must have regretted
their choice in selecting al-Zaidan's house, since it had no interior fortifications or exit tunnels. The brothers and the surviving bodyguard
hastily tried to "fortify" the second floor by using mattresses and bed
frames as a makeshift buttress. But both brothers had to know that
while mattresses might stop a few bullets, the ultimate outcome of
their situation didn't look good.

Uday and Qusay had well-deserved reputations for cruelty: Uday,
the elder sibling, who was partially disabled in a 1996 assassination
attempt, apparently enjoyed raping Iraqi women, torturing and ter-
rorizing members of the Iraqi national soccer team for poor perfor-
mances, and executing those he perceived to be his adversaries or
rivals. Qusay was said to take pleasure in killing political prisoners,
stuffing them into oversized wood chippers, and supervising group

executions. The mass graves being exhumed across the Iraqi coun-
tryside today provide evidence of their lust for wholesale murder as
sport. If anyone can be labeled as truly evil, it would surely be these
two.

By midday, Uday and Qusay Hussein, whose names mean "wolf"
and "snake" respectively in Iraqi Arabic, seemed to have lost any of
the mystique and cunning of their animal namesakes. After being on
the run for more than three months, they were now merely pathetic
caricatures of themselves, cowering in a bathroom outside the bedroom they had shared for the past three weeks.

No one knows if they ever entertained the possibility of surrender. Most of those involved think not. They no doubt feared the
Americans more than any international justice that might be meted
out if they were captured. They were probably willing to take their
chances if the UN took custody of them and tried them as war criminals. There would probably be a chance that they'd get off lightly.

Neither Saddam nor his two sons had made any visible or effective efforts to take command or control of the Iraqi army since the
beginning of the war. The earliest coalition air attacks had decapitated
their control of the troops in the field by destroying their communications. By the time entire regular army units and divisions of the
Republican Guard began to surrender, Saddam and his sons had to
see that there was no hope of waging any kind of credible response to
the American and British invasion.

Since March 20, this family of evildoers seems to have been spending its time and effort evading capture by using the hoard of cash and
jewels they had accumulated to pay for personal protection and even-
tual escape.

Uday is largely credited with having devised the scheme for
recruiting foreigners to fight for his father, and there are reports that
he grew increasingly desperate as the Republican Guard began to

desert. He apparently tried to stiffen the backbone of the regulars by using fedayeen execution squads, but that eventually failed as well, when the executioners themselves began to desert. Things got so bad that even his bodyguards were vacillating over the mission of protecting him. When things began to look really bleak, and the possibility that the Americans might capture them seemed imminent, Uday allegedly had nearly twenty of his bodyguards killed—they knew too much about him and his father's regime and couldn't be trusted not to divulge this information to the Americans should there be a war crimes trial.

Qusay was the head of the Amn Al Khass, Iraq's internal intelligence and security force. But in the end, he must have abdicated this responsibility, because at the house in Mosul, he had none of his special security troops to protect him, his son, or Uday.

Why did they have only one bodyguard? It may have been that the Iraqis could no longer stomach what the two evil brothers were doing to their country. Or perhaps the pair were simply so distrustful of their former troops that they actually felt safer without them. It's said that the reason Saddam didn't launch his air force to attack the invading American and British forces when they were moving north on the highways from Kuwait was that he was deathly afraid that his own pilots would turn on him, bomb his palaces, and try to kill him.

That is probably the same reason the two brothers were cowering in a bathroom on the second floor of a house in Mosul, alone except for a teenage boy and a single bodyguard.

✪ ✪ ✪

Outside the house, Col. Joe Anderson, the American officer in charge of the 101st's "Strike Brigade" assigned to the operation, waited about forty-five minutes for the people inside the house to surrender. When there was no response, he decided to "prep" the place for another attack by Task Force 20. His men opened fire with .50-caliber machine guns and rifle grenades. On the opposite side of the house, several Kiowa helicopter gunships hovered, firing rockets through the windows. The prep continued for nearly an hour. There was occasional gunfire from the house, letting Col. Anderson know that the occupants—at least some of them—were still alive.

About noon, the order was given to Task Force 20 to reenter the building in a second attempt to capture the brothers and bring them out alive. Once again, the special ops team was turned away by gunfire coming from upstairs, from behind the mattresses-and-bed-frame fortifications. The Task Force 20 soldiers fell back once more to consider other options.

Col. Anderson then decided that it was too dangerous to make another forcible entry attempt without additional "prep," so he ordered additional firing into the windows and walls of the building. This time, in addition to the .50-caliber machine guns, grenades, and Kiowa gunship rockets, he ordered that ten TOW and AT-4 missiles be fired as well.

Half an hour later, the TF-20 team made a third try. This time the team entered the house unopposed. Upstairs, they found the bodies of Uday, Qusay, and a bodyguard, crumpled on the floor of the bathroom—all of them dead from multiple wounds. In the bedroom, under a bed, was Qusay's teenage son, also dead, the AK-47 that he had been firing lying beside him. Qusay "The Snake" and Uday "The Wolf" Hussein—ranked number two and three respectively on the Pentagon's "most wanted" list of Iraqis—were dead. U.S. and coalition forces had now captured or eliminated thirty-seven of the fifty-five "most wanted" Iraqis.

It was all over in less than four hours. A search of the home turned up a cache of about $100 million in U.S. dollars and Iraqi currency. Some days later, $30 million of that money—the $15 million bounty on each of the Hussein brothers—was paid to the informant who led the Americans to their hiding place in Mosul.

The fact that Saddam has not yet been found dead or alive has some in CENTCOM convinced that those who know where he is probably already have more than $25 million in cash immediately available to them anyway. That is perhaps Saddam's only insurance policy for the moment—assuming he is still alive.

So the search continues for Saddam. But as one Special Forces soldier put it, "The world's a better place, because Uday and Qusay Hussein are in a place that makes today's 120 degrees in Baghdad feel like a summer breeze."

The success of this operation was quickly obscured by protestations that "U.S. troops used excessive force," and complaints that Uday and Qusay "should have been taken alive for their intelligence value," and then "tried for their crimes." But the fact that the endeavor succeeded is because Iraqi civilians felt safe in cooperating with U.S. authorities—something that was apparently missed or ignored by most commentators. Meanwhile, the young Americans in harm's way in Iraq wonder what it is they have to do to please the critics back home.

CHAPTER FOURTEEN

SNATCHING DEFEAT FROM THE JAWS OF VICTORY

I f pleasing the critics at home is going to be the measure of success for the soldiers, sailors, airmen, Guardsmen, and Marines who fought Operation Iraqi Freedom, they may have to wait a very long time for the accolades they deserve. By October 2003, support for keeping U.S. forces in Iraq was higher among Iraqis than Americans.

Most people I talk to believe that this disparity is the consequence of four factors: the deluge of media reports in the United States that focus only on the bad news; the Blame America First crowd in Hollywood; our "love affair" with the United Nations; and a barrage of hateful, partisan political invective aimed at our commander in chief that has caught military personnel in the crossfire.

Many who are still in Iraq wonder what kind of reception they will receive when they arrive in America. Some of them shudder at the prospect of a "welcome" like the one their fathers got when they returned from Vietnam. One young Marine wrote, "I hope they don't snatch defeat from the jaws of victory, like they did with Vietnam."

He's far too young to remember Vietnam. But he knows the "they" of whom he writes. After just a week back in the United States from spending ten months in Kuwait and Iraq, he concluded, "We won the war. But whether we stay the course to win the peace won't be decided in Baghdad, Basra, or Mosul. That's going to be determined on our television screens, newspapers, and in the corridors of power of Washington. I sure hope we don't leave it up to the media, Hollywood, the UN, or overly ambitious politicians."

With the exception of those cited in the introduction, nearly everyone agrees that embedding broadcast and print reporters in military units was a good idea. But it's not really new. Ernie Pyle, Cyril O'Brien, Jeremiah O'Leary, and Edward R. Morrow were all embedded war correspondents, reporting on the units and individuals with whom they lived during World War II. But they had advantages that many in the news business today lack: they came to the task with open minds and filed their reports with objective editors and news directors.

Part of the problem is in the way contemporary "well-trained journalists" see things around them. Since I'm not a "well-trained journalist," I decided that when I had an option, I would report on things that are interesting to the American people—such as "Who are these folks taking our kids into battle?" So for my first report, as the Marines were making final preparations for war, I filed a profile piece on a Marine gunnery sergeant teaching young Marines how to use the .50-caliber machine gun in combat. As I finished transmitting the piece to FOX News Channel, a well-known and respected reporter for another network, also embedded with a Marine helicopter squadron, sent in a profile piece of his own: "Do U.S. Pilots Use Drugs?" He wanted the American people to know that pilots flying sixteen to twenty hours a day occasionally take Dexedrine for alertness and sleeping pills to help them get necessary rest. That they have been doing so since World War II and with the supervision of medical doctors was somehow irrelevant to his story.

Later, while we were deep in Iraq, a very brave cameraman for CNN complained to me, "I'm shooting the same stuff you are, Colonel, but my stuff isn't getting on the air." I doubt he meant technical difficulties with his satellite transmissions.

Just before we reached Baghdad, another colleague, grousing about the TVs at CENTCOM, V Corps, and I-MEF always being tuned to FOX News Channel, observed, "And you don't even bother to interview the generals who are running this war."

"Right," I replied. "I interview the people who are fighting this war."

There is nothing wrong with interviewing generals or colonels, but there are a whole lot more PFCs and lance corporals than there are generals. In modern war reporting, with live satellite feeds from battlefields, the American people are much more interested in knowing how their kids are doing than whether some grumpy general got enough bran flakes for breakfast. Besides, it's been my experience that officers are so concerned about saying the wrong thing that they won't say anything. A PFC, on the other hand, will offer the unvarnished truth.

Shortly after the capture of Baghdad, my friend and FOX News Channel colleague Brit Hume, managing editor and Washington, D.C., bureau chief, addressed the war coverage in a speech at Hillsdale College. He quoted ABC's Ted Koppel as saying, "I'm very cynical, and I remain very cynical, about the reasons for getting into this war."

"Cynical?" Hume asked. "We journalists pride ourselves, and properly so, on being skeptical. That's our job. But I have always thought a cynic is a bad thing to be. A cynic, as I understand the term, means someone who interprets others' actions as coming from the worst motives. It's a knee-jerk way of thinking. A cynic, it is said, understands the price of everything and the value of nothing. So I don't understand why Ted Koppel would say with such pride and ferocity—he said it more than once—that he is a cynic. But I think he speaks for many in the media, and I think it's a very deep problem."

Addressing the issue of "bad news," Hume acknowledged that "bad stuff tends to be exceptional in our world. Reporters have a natural instinct, therefore, to look for the negative." Pointing to the way that many in the media depicted the foreign fedayeen fighters as a serious threat to coalition forces, he observed, "Only this could explain their belief that the fedayeen—by shooting at our troops' flanks and attacking our supply convoys—posed a serious threat. I remember when that story came out, and I thought to myself that it just didn't seem sensible that the fedayeen were militarily significant. They were riding around in pickup trucks with machine guns, for heaven's sake! And it turned out, contrary to all the stories, that they weren't a serious threat, and that they succeeded only in getting themselves killed by the hundreds."

Unfortunately, there has been no shortage of negative, Bush-bashing newsmen. Today they point to the "never-ending stream of U.S. casualties" and talk of a "quagmire"—first on the heels of the initial operational pause, then in the aftermath of the war. It can only be hoped that their prognostications about the peace are as accurate as their discouraging forecasts before the fighting started.

Chris Matthews of NBC warned that if the United States went to war with Iraq "[It] will join the Bay of Pigs, Vietnam, Desert One, Beirut, and Somalia in the history of military catastrophe." His colleague at NBC, analyst Gen. Barry McCaffrey, predicted that if there were a battle for Baghdad, the U.S. would probably take "a couple to three thousand casualties." As of April 11, the day after the battle for Baghdad, the United States reported 102 troops killed in action.

On March 29, just nine days into the war, the *New York Times* boldly proclaimed, "With every passing day, it is more evident that the allies made two gross military misjudgments in concluding that coalition forces could safely bypass Basra and Nasiriya and that Shi'ite Muslims in southern Iraq would rise up against Saddam Hussein." Coalition forces safely crossed Basra and Nasiriya and the Shi'ite Muslims did rebel. Unfortunately for the *Times*, the CENTCOM war plan didn't call for bypassing either city, nor did the coalition forces expect or receive an "uprising" by any Iraqis.

Seymour Hersh, famous since Vietnam for his "investigative journalism," wrote in the March 31, 2003, edition of the *New Yorker*: "According to a dozen or so military men I spoke to, Rumsfeld simply failed to anticipate the consequences of protracted warfare. He put Army and Marine units in the field with few reserves and an insufficient number of tanks and other armored vehicles.... 'It's a stalemate now,' the former intelligence official told me." One can only wonder who these "military men" were that Mr. Hersh "spoke to." In the aftermath of the victory, most of the media seems to be criticizing Secretary Rumsfeld for not anticipating the consequences of a *short*-duration war.

This is the kind of negative reporting Brit Hume was talking about. Now, in retrospect, Hume's observations are dead on: "The majority of the American media who were in a position to comment upon the progress of the war in the early going, and even after that, got it wrong. They didn't get it just a little wrong. They got it completely wrong." He adds, "This level of imperviousness to reality is remarkable. It is consistent and it continues over time. I think about this phenomenon a lot. I worry and wonder about the fact that so many people can get things so wrong, so badly, so often, so consistently, and so repeatedly. And I think that there are ideas lurking under the surface that help to explain why this happens. In brief, when it comes to the exercise of American power in the world, particularly military power, there seems to be a suspicion among those in the media—indeed, a suspicion bordering on a presumption—of illegitimacy, incompetence, and ineffectiveness."

The problem, of course, is that these wrong assumptions and incorrect "facts" get played prominently in the prime-time newscasts and in the front-page newspaper stories, and become part of the official record. Unfortunately, the record won't show how many Iraqis were treated by Army and Navy doctors, medics, and corpsmen. The record doesn't reflect how Army engineers and Seabees rebuilt water treatment plants, repaired generators, and fixed irrigation systems. And the record doesn't include enough heartwarming stories about the compassion American warriors have for the children of Iraq.

One such warrior is a young Marine officer I know well. Matt Grosz was just a kid when his dad and I served together at Quantico, Virginia, and at Camp Lejeune, North Carolina. Now Matt is a Marine captain, commanding "India" Company, 3rd Battalion, 7th Marines. I saw him in Kuwait just before the war started. His regiment endured some of the toughest fighting of the campaign on the way to the capital. After Baghdad was captured, Matt's unit was sent to Karbala, where he was given the mission of protecting a large suburb of the city. Not content to act simply as an "occupation force," Captain Grosz started a whole range of civic action projects that led to local elections and even the formation of a youth soccer league. His one regret: "The Iraqi kids beat my Marines."

But the media ignored the CENTCOM press release in June on this emblematic success story. When I asked a CENTCOM public affairs officer if the story had been picked up, she replied, "I guess their attitude was 'not enough blood,' so it wasn't important."

According to Hume:

• • •

The attitude of the media in times of war is all the more puzzling when considered in the context of what America has done in the world over the last century—and in particular, what the American military has done. It entered World War I toward the end, tipped the balance, and saved our friends and allies. In World War II, it led the free world to victory against genuinely monstrous evils. After that war, it gave aid and comfort to defeated enemies on a scale never before seen. Considering its actions in Japan alone, the U.S. should go down in history as one of the most benevolent victorious powers in history. Japan owes its economy and democracy to Douglas MacArthur, and to the leaders of the American government who put him there to do what he did.

But it didn't stop with Japan. There was the Marshall Plan. During the entire forty-five-year Cold War, America projected military power over Western Europe and in many far-flung outposts elsewhere, such as South Korea. It protected the people who had been our allies, and many who had been our enemies, from the next great evil, Soviet communism—an evil, I might add, which many in our media refused to recognize as such. Then, upon the victorious end of the Cold War, one of the first things the U.S. did was work feverishly to make sure that the reunification of Germany went forward in a way that would work and be effective.

This is the record. It is available and known to the world. It's not particularly controversial. Yet even within this context, ideas have somehow germinated among those in the media, as when America embarks on something like the Iraq war, there are all kinds of tremulous suspicions and fears about what we might really be doing. How many times have we heard it suggested that we're in Iraq for the oil? Does this make any sense at all? If we are there for the oil, why didn't we keep Kuwait's oil after the Gulf War? The best and simplest explanation is that we're just not that kind of country.

• • •

If the so-called mainstream media has a hard time figuring out what kind of country we are, it must be even more difficult for the entertainment industry. There was a time when Tinseltown regarded entertaining America's families as its primary purpose. Interestingly, during World War II, many of Hollywood's leading actors served in the military—Clark Gable, Mickey Rooney, and Jimmy Stewart, to name a few. For decades actors and actresses such as Bo Derek, Marilyn Monroe, Ann-Margret, Connie Stevens, Jill St. John, and Raquel Welch, joined Bob Hope in freely giving of their time to entertain the troops overseas, as did musicians like Louis Armstrong. Filmmakers like John Ford and stars like John Wayne had no problem making pro-America, pro-military movies.

That's no longer the case. Now Hollywood actors like Robert DeNiro and Gary Sinise, and performers like Wayne Newton, are the exception rather than the rule on a USO tour. Worse still, many of today's actors are activists *against* American foreign policy and use their celebrity status to try and drive a wedge between the commander in chief and the troops he leads. The Dixie Chicks alienated country music fans and many other Americans with comments made by singer Natalie Maines during a performance in London. Maines told the audience, "Just so you know, we're ashamed the president of the United States is from Texas."

Actor-turned-political protester Sean Penn is one of the leading luminaries of this movement. He took out a $56,000 full-page ad for an "open letter" to President Bush in the *Washington Post*, just before the start of the Iraq war, in which he claimed, "bombing is answered by bombing, mutilation by mutilation, killing by killing."

Though Penn hasn't found the time in his very successful career to support our troops with the USO, he was able to embark on a "fact-finding mission" to Baghdad, paid for by the leftist Institute for Public Advocacy, to pursue "a deeper understanding of this frightening conflict." When he returned, Penn accused the Bush administration of "teaching a master class in the manifestation of rage into hatred."

He subsequently sued producer Steve Bing for dropping him from an upcoming film, claiming that his outspoken opposition to the war in Iraq has made him a "blacklist" victim.

Blacklist? Baloney! Hollywood is full of "stars" who agree with Sean Penn. Robert Redford, Julia Roberts, Woody Harrelson, Bill Cosby, the Baldwin brothers, Jessica Lange, Danny Glover, Matt Damon, Kim Basinger, Oliver Stone, and Jane Fonda have all denounced the war and President Bush. Martin Sheen, of *The West Wing*, dismissed Operation Iraqi Freedom as a "personal feud." Barbra Streisand judged it "very, very frightening."

Filmmakers have also jumped on the bandwagon. Robert Altman opined in London that he was "embarrassed to be an American." Michael Moore has announced that his next "documentary," entitled *Fahrenheit 9/11: The Temperature at Which Freedom Burns*, will "show linkages between President George W. Bush and Osama bin Laden." The Disney film subsidiary Miramax will reportedly distribute Mr. Moore's new effort.

Like other members of the Hollywood elite, Moore doesn't limit his visceral political attacks to the films he makes. During monologues in Great Britain, he also rebuked the dead passengers on the four hijacked September 11 aircrafts. According to Yasmin Alibhai-Brown, who writes a column for *The Independent* of London, "Moore went into a rant about how the passengers on the planes on 11 September were 'scaredy-cats' because they were mostly white. 'If the passengers had included black men,' he claimed, 'those killers, with their puny bodies and unimpressive small knives, would have been crushed by the dudes.'"

Perhaps Mr. Moore would like to express those thoughts to Lisa Beamer, whose husband Todd was part of the rebellion aboard American Airlines Flight 93 before the aircraft went down in Somerset County, Pennsylvania, on September 11, denying the terrorists an opportunity to hit their intended target—the White House.

✪ ✪ ✪

Starting in the summer of 2002, our "allies"—the French, the Germans, and most of "Old Europe"—began employing every tactic possible in the United Nations to prevent the use of force in Iraq. Encouraged by massive anti-American protests on the streets of European capitals, President Jacques Chirac of France and Chancellor Gerhard Schroeder of Germany repeatedly urged the United States and Great Britain to delay plans for military action against

Saddam Hussein until UN supersleuth Hans Blix had "completed" his search for weapons of mass destruction in Iraq.

By the autumn of 2002, U.S. frustration with the snail's pace of Blix's mission was dismissed as "saber rattling" in Paris, Berlin, and Brussels and on the UN cocktail party circuit. In 2003, with Saddam gone, the same voices that had earlier preached patience before resorting to arms are now unwilling to wait for a full and careful search for Saddam's weapons of mass destruction. According to the rhetoric coming from the UN, it's curtains for American credibility unless coalition forces immediately find significant stockpiles of nerve agents, biotoxins, and nuclear weapons.

Notwithstanding the UN's unwillingness to help disarm Saddam and notwithstanding the unabated criticism, President Bush again went to the international body asking for its assistance—this time in rebuilding Iraq. Despite a terrorist bombing on August 19, 2003, that destroyed the UN headquarters in Baghdad, killing Sergio Vieira de Mello, a Brazilian national and the head of the UN mission in Baghdad, United Nations officials remain unwilling to help unless they assume absolute control over the effort.

For the UN, it's all about power. Before the war, Secretary-General Kofi Annan insisted that any military effort to oust Saddam without UN permission would lack "the unique legitimacy provided by the United Nations." Now Annan demands that the UN be allowed to exercise control over how U.S. forces and U.S. tax dollars are employed and spent in Iraq. All this belies the abysmal, decade-long record of the UN in the land between the rivers.

As we witnessed in Baghdad, the UN-administered Oil-for-Food Program, established in 1995 to provide the Iraqi people with food and medicine, was totally corrupt. Under UN supervision, Saddam stole billions from the program while UN administrators took tens of millions in "management fees." Hundreds of millions in Iraqi oil revenues are simply unaccounted for—and may be sequestered "in trust" by the UN—although this can't be confirmed because auditors have been denied access to the UN's books on the program. Attempts by various media outlets to scrutinize UN financial records have been routinely rebuffed. The United Nations has no Freedom of Information Act like the one we have in the United States to permit reporters to examine its records and documents.

Despite terror attacks against personnel at its facilities—including the bombing attack in Baghdad on September 22, 2003, that killed twenty-two people—the United Nations refuses to take terrorism seriously, and continues to put terrorist nations on a par with peace-loving democracies. In fact, the Blame America First crowd at the UN steadfastly refuses to even *define* terrorism—perhaps because many UN member nations themselves sponsor terrorism, support it financially, or turn a blind eye to it.

Although the UN has no lack of vocal U.S. critics, the recently retired, amiable, Swedish diplomat Hans Blix is undoubtedly the hero of the moment. As he vacated his posh digs overlooking the East River in New York City, Blix conducted a series of exit interviews and soirees in Manhattan, taking a few parting shots at the "bastards" in the Bush administration. "I have my detractors in Washington," Blix huffed, while claiming indifference. But he also accuses the Bush administration of telling "a lot of fairy tales" about Iraq. His principal complaint: he was right and the Bush administration was wrong about Saddam's weapons of mass destruction. But on the recently discovered mass graves containing the bodies of tens of thousands of Iraqis, he is strangely silent.

✪ ✪ ✪

Hans Blix is not alone in ignoring the mass graves and insinuating that the Bush administration "cooked the books" on intelligence about Saddam's WMD arsenal. He has plenty of help from U.S. politicians who see President Bush as vulnerable on this issue and who seem willing to do whatever it takes to capitalize on what they see as the president's Achilles' heel.

Senator Robert Byrd claims that President Bush is "intent on revising history" and suggests that the administration "bent, stretched, or massaged" intelligence reports "to make Iraq look like an imminent threat to the United States."

Senator Byrd is demanding an "immediate investigation" because "the administration's rhetoric played upon the well-founded fear of the American public about future acts of terrorism," and such statements are "just sound bites based on conjecture."

Conjecture? Perhaps Senator Byrd has forgotten his own words of October 3, 2002: "The last UN inspectors left Iraq in October of 1998. We are confident that Saddam Hussein retains some stockpiles of chemical and biological weapons, and that he has since embarked on a crash course to build up his chemical and biological warfare capability. Intelligence reports also indicate that he is seeking nuclear weapons."

So what's going on here? Senator Byrd receives the same intelligence reports the president gets. Every U.S. senator has access to the information provided by the CIA and kept locked in safes in the guarded chambers of the Senate Select Committee on Intelligence. Senator Byrd, in his own words, concluded in October 2002 that Saddam Hussein had weapons of mass destruction. Something must have happened to change his mind—and he's not alone.

Senator John Kerry, as part of his outreach to antiwar Democrats, is now calling for a "regime change" in the White House, and insists that he is the victim of a "misinformation campaign" orchestrated by President Bush. "He misled every one of us," Kerry now claims. But as late as January 23, 2003, he said, "We need to disarm Saddam Hussein. He is a brutal, murderous dictator, leading an oppressive regime.... He presents a particularly grievous threat because he is so consistently prone to miscalculation.... So the threat of Saddam Hussein with weapons of mass destruction is real."

Even though he now tells supporters of his presidential campaign that he was "misinformed" about Saddam, Senator Kerry had access to the same information as the man he wants to replace in the Oval Office. So do other aspirants for the job—like Senator Joe Lieberman, Congressman Dick Gephardt, and Congressman Dennis Kucinich. Yet they all now maintain that they are opposed to the war against Saddam—or would have been had they simply been told the truth.

Vermont's former governor, Howard Dean, might be excused for making outrageous accusations about President Bush and his motives for unseating Saddam, because the antiwar candidate doesn't have access to the classified information. But that doesn't wash for others.

Before he withdrew from the race, Senator Bob Graham, who touted his membership on the Senate Select Committee on Intelligence as one of his "credentials" for higher office, routinely accused President Bush of exaggerating the threat posed by Saddam. Yet on December 8, 2002, as U.S. and British forces were preparing for war, Senator Graham boldly stated, "We are in possession of what we think to be compelling evidence that Saddam Hussein has—and has had for a number of years—a developing capacity for the production and storage of weapons of mass destruction." If he had that "compelling evidence" in his possession then, where did it go? Did it simply disappear in an effort to punch holes in President Bush's approval ratings?

Congressman Gephardt calls President Bush "a miserable failure." Former senator Carol Moseley Braun says that the United States has no business in Iraq and "We got off on the wrong track." And Senator Ted Kennedy, in one of the most egregious slanders in American political history, charges that Operation Iraqi Freedom "was a fraud cooked up in Texas."

All of these politicians, who are members of the U.S. Congress, were provided with the same information that President Bush received about Saddam Hussein and his regime. Senator Kennedy was so impressed by the intelligence he had seen that on October 4, 2002, he felt compelled to acknowledge, "We have known for many years that Saddam Hussein is seeking and developing weapons of mass destruction." Yet, whatever Kennedy and these others knew then, they apparently don't know now.

✪ ✪ ✪

For the young Americans at risk in Iraq and Afghanistan, the drumbeat of criticism from the media, Hollywood, and the UN is "situation normal." Few of the soldiers, sailors, airmen, Guardsmen, or Marines I talk to expect anything better from the media than the "bad news" stories they are now getting. They regard the reports filed by the embedded media as exceptions and the current coverage to be the rule. None seem surprised by the way the stars of the entertainment industry are aligned—although I did watch some Dixie Chicks CDs being used as sporting clays for target practice with a Benelli combat shotgun. As for the UN, most of these troops remember cheering when the current commander in chief told them to throw away their blue UN berets.

But ask any of the troops now committed—or those awaiting orders to duty on the front lines in the war on terrorism—what they think of the current tenor of American political rhetoric and they'll admit that it is at best confusing and at worst demoralizing. Experienced officers and NCOs feel that an effort is being made to "create a divide" between the military and its commander in chief.

Though they are all in danger, and all want to come home—as they should—they also know that given the choice, it is far better to fight terrorists in Baghdad than in Boston or Baltimore. They also know that Saddam was a real threat and that, despite the naysayers, they are making real progress in Iraq.

If asked, the troops who have been searching for WMD will remind the questioner that Saddam had more than five months to destroy, remove, or hide anything he wanted before U.S. and British troops arrived on his doorstep. They will also point to the terror-bomb jackets, terrorist training manuals, and large numbers of foreign terrorists who were trained at Salman Pak. They will present the tons of chemical protective equipment, atropine injectors, and chemical warfare manuals that they found all over Iraq and ask, "If Saddam didn't have chemical agents, how come his troops had all this gear?"

Unfortunately, we don't know the answer to that question, or many others. We don't know where Osama bin Laden is. We can't find Saddam. All of this points to the desperate need to rebuild a human intelligence collection capability within our intelligence services. And we'd better do it quickly. Not just because politicians vying for higher office are apparently confused by what they knew, when they knew it, and when they conveniently forgot it, but because our future may depend on knowing more about our terrorist adversaries than we do now.

Former CIA director James Woolsey maintains that "the war on terrorism is World War IV—a war we cannot afford to lose." Recently retired Gen. Tommy Franks, who commanded CENTCOM through Operation Enduring Freedom in Afghanistan and then led Operation Iraqi Freedom through to the liberation of Iraq, said on October 10, 2003, that "the war on terrorism is going to go on for a long, long time."

He went on to point out that victory in Iraq is an important step in that war. He's right. Those we face aren't just willing to die for their cause—they *want* to die for their cause. They have been taught to hate, to kill, and to die in trying to kill Americans, Christians, and Jews. They have been promised spiritual rewards for themselves and financial benefits for their families if they succeed in killing themselves the "right way." Transforming Iraq into a secure democracy with a thriving economy will mean one less place where terrorists can be recruited or trained or take refuge.

Yet the president's request for funds to accomplish this transformation is described as "too expensive" by political opponents in our

Congress—and by Europeans, who were rescued twice in the last century by force of American arms and dollars. Some have described the request as "throwing good money after bad."

The current excuse for this defamatory political rhetoric is that it's a "presidential election year." So was 1944. Yet no political opponent of FDR tried to smear the seriously ill chief executive by claiming he wasn't "up to the task." No candidate for any office suggested that Roosevelt couldn't handle the job, because of his increasing frailty. No member of the House or Senate dared claim that it was too expensive to beat Hitler in Germany or Tojo in Japan. And no member of Congress tried to tell the commander in chief where to cross the Rhine or what island to take next in the Pacific.

None of these things happened in the midst of World War II because politicians recognized that any such decisions or actions would be disastrous to the morale of millions of young Americans serving in uniform. We don't have millions of men and women in uniform anymore. Instead, we rely on very sophisticated weapons in the hands of a few more than one million warriors. Some of them fly high-performance fighter aircrafts, helicopters, or transports, or they pilot unmanned aerial vehicles with an armchair controller. Others serve at sea—or under it—waiting for the word to use an awesome arsenal against an adversary. And still others, sweating in twenty-pound flak jackets and four-pound helmets, patrol hot, foul-smelling streets far from home, searching for those who want nothing more than to kill them—and us.

And while they hunt for terrorists, they deserve better than political terrorism from their own countrymen here at home. These men and women of America won an extraordinary victory in Iraq. America's critics shouldn't be allowed to steal it.

CHAPTER FIFTEEN
THE ROCKY ROAD TO DEMOCRACY

✪ OPERATION IRAQI FREEDOM SIT REP #43
Baghdad, Iraq
Saturday, 25 October 2003
1415 Hours Local

B y the time I returned to Iraq in the summer, there were ominous signs that "rebuilding" Iraq was not going to be a simple task. Though Uday and Qusay were gone, Saddam himself was still on the loose, and this fact alone seemed to be inspiring resistance—particularly in the Sunni Triangle. The troops on the ground had become increasingly wary of the civilian population in places like Tikrit, Ramadi, Fallujah, and Baghdad proper. Commanders in these areas privately talked about a new threat—the "marriage of convenience" between former regime elements and foreign jihadists bent on trying to prevent the transition to democracy.

Most of Saddam's army had deserted when the dictatorship collapsed. His soldiers, mostly Shi'ite conscripts and poor Sunnis, simply went home—taking their AK-47s and RPGs with them. Within a matter of weeks, many of them began using those weapons to perpetrate crimes against their fellow Iraqis and in small-scale terror attacks against coalition forces.

Paul Bremer, the Coalition Provisional Authority (CPA), rejected the concept of offering financial incentives to Iraqi army deserters who returned to their barracks with their weapons. Instead, the CPA embarked on a costly and time-consuming effort to completely rebuild Iraq's police, national guard, and security forces. Unbeknownst to any of us who had covered the first phase of the war—and most of those who had fought in it—Operation Iraqi Freedom was about to become a very deadly endeavor.

As the heat of summer beat down on the land between the rivers, the number and scale of the attacks increased dramatically. Several factors contributed to the escalating violence—and growing U.S. casualties:

- First, Iraq's neighbors—Saudi Arabia, Jordan, Syria, and Iran—were either unable or unwilling to stop hundreds of fanatical jihadists, inspired radical Islamic clerics and leaders of terror movements, from crossing into Iraq. Terrorists from these neighboring countries and others from Yemen, Somalia, Sudan, Egypt, Lebanon, Afghanistan, and Chechnya flooded into Iraq to join the jihad. By autumn 2003, they were effectively integrated into scores of disparate but deadly "cells" throughout the Sunni Triangle and incorporated into a significant number of Shi'ite communities.

- Second, senior members of Saddam's now outlawed Baath Party had succeeded in fleeing to Syria with tens of millions in stolen funds. From there, they launched an organized effort to convince the Sunni minority in Iraq that Saddam was going to make a "comeback." Messengers from Syria told Sunni sheikhs and imams that unless the Sunnis fought back against American-imposed democracy, they would soon be repressed by the Shi'ite majority.

● Third, Iraq's abandoned ammunition depots, munitions storage facilities, and arms depositories provided a treasure trove of weapons and explosives for arming opponents and building improvised explosive devices (IEDs).

On my first trip to Iraq, I had been with Lt. Col. "Pepper" Jackson's 3rd Battalion, 66th Armored Regiment when they had captured Bayji and its enormous munitions depot. Now his battalion was providing security for USA Environmental—the contractor charged with the destruction of the site's *300 million tons* of ordnance. Their goal: to haul 100 tons per day out into the desert and destroy it in earth-shaking, ear-shattering controlled detonations. From more than a mile away, one such blast knocked my camera off its tripod.

The work is difficult and dangerous. One of the EOD experts who had also worked in Kosovo, Ukraine, and Afghanistan said, "This is the most militarized place on the planet. At this rate, just cleaning up Bayji will take us five years. But it's worth it. Once we've blown it up, the 'bad guys' can't use it to kill anyone else."

He's right. In the hands of suicidal terrorists bent on killing "infidels," a stolen automobile or truck heavily loaded with explosives is a guided bomb, nearly as deadly as the Japanese kamikaze pilots of World War II.

On 19 August 2003, a suicide terrorist driving an explosives-laden truck destroyed the UN headquarters building in Baghdad, killing twenty-four and wounding another hundred. Within weeks, the UN closed its offices in Iraq and fled the country. By October 2003, when the last UN officials departed, IEDs had become the number-one cause of casualties in Iraq.

✪ OPERATION IRAQI FREEDOM SIT REP #44
   4th ID HQ
   Tikrit, Iraq
   Saturday, 13 December 2003
   1730 Hours Local

Each time I visited the headquarters of the 4th ID in Tikrit, General Ray Odierno—the division commander—or one of his subordinates would remind me that they had made it their mission to capture or kill Saddam Hussein. Though reports at the time suggested that the deposed dictator could be hiding anywhere from the suburbs of Baghdad to the outskirts of Damascus, the 4th ID soldiers were convinced that Saddam was still hiding out in the vicinity of his hometown.

Odierno is a tough, tall, lean soldier. He had borne the frustration of getting his division into the fight with considerable grace—a quality that would be sorely tested when his own son was grievously wounded.

On one occasion he took me into the G-2 spaces at his headquarters, where his intelligence staff explained the painstaking effort they were making to track down and double-check every piece of information that had been gleaned about Saddam. I made the observation that this was impressive work and inquired as to how much help the CIA was in this endeavor. A captain working nearby chuckled and replied, "CIA? We don't get much of anything that's useful from them. So we set this up just like we would in the NYPD, where I'm a homicide detective when I'm not wearing this uniform."

The 4th ID staff had set up a system for meticulously double-checking every informant debrief and insisted on carefully interrogating every captured terrorist. All of Saddam's many relatives in the region were quietly reminded that there was a $25 million reward for the information leading to the capture of the dictator.

As we left that afternoon, I wished Odierno a happy Thanksgiving. He thanked me and wished me the same, but added, "If you leave now, you'll miss the capture."

I replied, "How soon?"

"He's here. I know he is," Odierno replied. "He's been right around here all along. It's just a matter of days before we find him."

I should have stayed—because on 13 December, they did.

As Ray Odierno predicted, it turned out to be a tip from a relative of one of Saddam's guards that led to the former dictator's capture. Armed with the information, 600 U.S. Army soldiers went to investigate a farm outside the hamlet of Ad Daw, just beyond the outskirts of Tikrit. There they found the former despot, bearded and filthy, cowering with a sidearm and $750,000 in U.S. currency in a hand-dug "rat-hole." The man who had urged his followers to "fight to the death" put up no resistance and begged his captors not to shoot him.

The troops were euphoric. SPC Michael Tillery, of the 4th Battalion, 42nd Field Artillery Regiment from Alexandria, Virginia, who participated in the raid, said, "All the work has paid off and that one step is finally over—finding Saddam." Video of the tyrant being examined for lice by a U.S. Army doctor flashed around the world.

Unfortunately, jubilation at the capture was not universal. European critics decried the "humiliation" of videotaping a "former head of state" being examined in such an "inhumane" way. Others speculated that Saddam would now be tortured to divulge the whereabouts of his weapons of mass destruction.

In the United States, Howard Dean, a candidate for the Democratic presidential nomination, declared, "The capture of Saddam has not made America safer."

Yet in the month after Hussein's capture, attacks against coalition forces in Iraq dropped 22 percent. U.S. military officers said that the decline in attacks was proof that Saddam's capture dampened resistance to the American presence in Iraq.

Howard Dean wasn't the only one with a peculiar perception of Iraqi reality. Democratic senator Ted Kennedy of Massachusetts charged that the war was a lie "cooked up" in Texas. And just two days after Paul Bremer proclaimed, "We got him," Representative Jim McDermott of Washington accused President Bush of manipulating Saddam's capture for political purposes. McDermott told a Seattle radio audience that U.S. troops could have captured Saddam "a long time ago if they wanted."

Clinton-era secretary of state Madeleine Albright seemed to follow the same line of reasoning. She asserted to Morton Kondracke of FOX News: "Do you suppose that the Bush administration has Osama bin Laden hidden away somewhere and will bring him out before the election?"

Media coverage of Saddam's capture has been as surreal as the conspiracy theorists' conjectures. After watching jubilant Iraqis celebrating Saddam's capture, ABC anchor Peter Jennings saw only sadness and morosely concluded, "There's not a good deal for Iraqis to be happy about at the moment." Jennings added that life for Iraqi citizens is "very chaotic...beset by violence...[and] not as stable for them as it was when Saddam Hussein was in power."

The anchors and talking heads pondered Saddam's situation. CBS's Leslie Stahl taunted Defense Secretary Don Rumsfeld about torturing Saddam. "Would we deprive him of sleep? Would we make it very cold where he is, or very hot? Are there any restrictions on the way we treat him to get him to cooperate more than he has been?"

NBC's Katie Couric said Saddam's capture was only "symbolic." She'd be proved hopelessly wrong less than twenty-four hours later, as the 1st Armored Division, acting on intelligence secured during Saddam's capture, rounded up three former Iraqi generals suspected of supporting the terrorist resistance in Iraq.

In keeping with the mainstream media's axiom that no good deed shall go unpunished, CBS's Dan Rather described the Iraqi people as worse off than they had been under Saddam. Introducing a report by Kimberly Dozier in Baghdad, Rather proclaimed that the "result is a population fearful, frustrated, angry, and heavily armed."

Dozier went on to report, "Day or night, these are some of the most dangerous streets on Earth. Desperation drives murder and theft. Iraqis have traded fear of the despot for fear of their fellow man, and U.S. troops seem powerless to protect them."

Newsweek compared Defense Secretary Don Rumsfeld to "Baghdad Bob" for saying that things were not as bad as the press painted them. *New York Times* reporter Richard Bernstein described President Bush as "a gun-slinging cowboy knocking over international treaties and bent on controlling the world's oil, if not the entire world."

All of this twisted, mind-numbing negativism overlooked Saddam's horrific record:

1. Responsibility for two wars and the deaths of hundreds of thousands
2. Raping, torturing, robbing, starving and murdering his own people
3. Using weapons of mass destruction against his neighbors and countrymen
4. Attempting to assassinate an American president
5. Training and supporting Hamas, Islamic Jihad, Hizballah, Muslim Brotherhood, and Abu Nidal terrorists who killed Americans

Even the most committed followers of Osama bin Laden have to wonder if their bearded leader who wants *them* to die for *his* cause would ignominiously surrender—like Saddam did—to save his own skin, or appeal to the mercy of the International Criminal Court to avoid a death sentence.

Finally, the loopy leftist rhetoric in the aftermath of Saddam's capture ignored the extraordinary courage, training, persistence, and discipline of the American soldiers who pursued and caught the Butcher of Baghdad. It's too bad, because they deserve a lot more credit than they are getting.

✪ ✪ ✪

During our second trip to northern Iraq, an incident occurred that convinced me Griff Jenkins could no longer serve as my combat cameraman and field producer. It was just after dark in Bayji and we were doing a live feed to Tony Snow's Sunday morning broadcast on FOX News Channel when an enemy mortar round impacted about twenty yards away. Though we were unscathed, the concussion of the explosion was enough to knock our little satellite transponder off the top of a nearby Humvee. Viewers saw a flash and then nothing but fuzz on their screens.

Griff quickly reset the satellite equipment and reestablished the link with Washington. Within minutes, we were back on the air and it was clear that no one had been hurt. But afterward, it occurred to me that for Griff's wife, Kathleen, and little daughter, Madeline, those had to be several very anxious minutes. He had already come through some very close calls during Operation Iraqi Freedom. Several times I'd had to consider how I was going to explain to them how their husband and father had been killed.

It's always hard to break up a team—particularly a good one. Griff had been my producer and friend on radio and then TV for more than five years. He is a gifted photographer and cameraman. Technically, he is without peer. When I told him that I wanted him to take a producer position that was opening at the FOX News bureau in Washington, he strenuously objected to being reassigned. But I was equally unwilling to keep putting him at risk on frequent trips into combat zones. Thankfully, the management at FOX agreed and Griff became the producer for Tony Snow's radio show.

The entire episode was a learning experience for me. I had led Marines in combat—and I've spent a considerable time part of my life with and around warriors. Over the years, I'd written painful "next of kin" letters and met with anguished family members when those I'd served with were killed in training or combat.

It's hard enough to have to send such a missive to the families of soldiers, sailors, airmen, or Marines who are slain serving their county in uniform. But it's quite another to contemplate having to deliver such a message to the mother of a young child whose civilian father got killed *covering* the combatants.

I resolved that in the future, my field producers and cameramen would have to be either bachelors or those whose children were grown, and that's the way it has been since. Though we now show up in places like Iraq and Afghanistan like a troup of "grumpy old men," at least my conscience is a little less burdened.

✪ OPERATION IRAQI FREEDOM SIT REP #45
2nd Battalion, 4th Marines, 1st Marine Division
Ramadi, Iraq
Friday, 16 April 2004
1130 Hours Local

Last week was the bloodiest week in Iraq in over a year. U.S. Marines and soldiers have been heavily engaged in Fallujah and Ramadi by heavy gunfire and RPG attacks while searching for the terrorists who killed and desecrated the bodies of four American contractors in Fallujah on 31 March. In Najaf, U.S. Army and Marine units are trying to quell an uprising of radical Shi'ites led by Sheik Muqtada al-Sadr, a fanatical cleric. So far this month, twenty-one U.S. Marines have been killed and sixty-five more have been wounded.

And while Christian Galdabini—my new cameraman—and I cover the "Magnificent Bastards" here in Ramadi and the units surrounding Fallujah, we're being treated to news reports of Senator Ted Kennedy unleashing a verbal carpet-bombing on the president of the United States. Kennedy, whose own integrity and judgment have been called into question on numerous occasions throughout his career, used a forum at the Brookings Institution, a liberal Washington think tank, to charge the Bush administration with "creat(ing) the largest credibility gap since Richard Nixon." Kennedy accused the president of breaking "the basic bond of trust with the American people," and said that Iraq is "George Bush's Vietnam."

Senator Robert Byrd of West Virginia also equated Iraq with Vietnam: "Surely, I am not the only one who hears echoes of Vietnam in this development. Surely this administration recognizes that increasing the U.S. troop presence in Iraq will only suck us deeper, deeper into the maelstrom, into the quicksand of violence that has become the hallmark of that unfortunate, miserable country."

What is truly unfortunate is that those hearing this pessimistic rhetoric are the radical terrorists who are emboldened by it. But also listening are the young American fighting men we are with, and it's disheartening to those who are able to see the news—either on our little satellite transceiver or on television monitors in some of the larger mess halls and recreation facilities around the country.

✪ ✪ ✪

Before arriving here, the Marines we are with spent months in predeployment training at Camp Pendleton in California. They had permitted us to cover their specialized training for operating in and around civilian populations—and now we rejoined them to document how they put the tactics, techniques and procedures they mastered into practice. Lt. Col. Paul Kennedy, the battalion commander, in an on-camera interview, described the fighting as "tough."

This week during a prime-time White House news conference, President Bush used the same word to describe the recent fighting in Ramadi and Fallujah. It *is* tough—war always is. During my first forty hours on the ground this time, anti-Iraqi forces haven't stopped shooting at the Marines, making it more difficult to get around.

But it's also evident that the troops we're with—from the 1st Marine Division out of Camp Pendleton, California, and the Army's 1st Brigade from Fort Riley, Kansas—are indeed "performing brilliantly," as the president said in his remarks. But the troops we interview express it somewhat differently. "The fighting has been intense, but we've been kicking butt everywhere we go," said a Marine sergeant when we put him on the air.

Lt. Col. Kennedy makes it clear that he knows his mission. He tells his company commanders to "hunt down" the terrorists who are infiltrating the provincial capital and reminds them that their enemy "can't stand up to a Marine unit in a gunfight. They aren't as well trained, lack fire discipline, and aren't in shape. If you have to . . . send out invitations. Watch out for the IEDs and when they show themselves, shoot straight. Use only the force you need to eliminate the threat. Avoid civilian casualties and keep your comms up. And remember the Division motto: 'No greater friend—no worse enemy.' Let them figure out which one they want you to be."

Shortly after arriving in Ramadi, his young Marines had suffered six killed and eighteen wounded. But this morning's firefight produces four enemy dead, nine detainees, and sixteen weapons captured—and two wounded Marines. Among the enemy dead and captured were foreign terrorists and a handful of local Baathist loyalists.

One of those detained in the operation was a young Iraqi who had been wounded in an earlier engagement with U.S. troops. He had been treated in a hospital and was recuperating in the home of a "friend" when U.S. Marines, with the cooperation of Iraqis in the neighborhood, knocked on the door and took him into custody.

"One more terrorist off the street and one less bad guy who, later on, could have injured a Marine, sailor, or soldier," was how the squad leader put it.

Many of these Marines and Navy medical corpsmen are on a second tour in Iraq. More than a few were only home for five or six months before they turned around, put on their flak jackets and helmets, and returned to Iraq. I asked one, a Marine corporal who had enlisted the day after the September 11, 2001, attacks, why he had volunteered to come back. His answer: "Because we have a job to do that we didn't finish the first time. In this war on terror, you don't want to play any more 'home games.' We need to play 'on the road'—and beat them here." Unfortunately, these aren't sentiments anyone is likely to see in the mainstream media.

✪ OPERATION IRAQI FREEDOM SIT REP #46
1st Marine Division
Ramadi, Iraq
Friday, 23 April 2004
1400 Hours Local

The Marines here in Ramadi are continuing a 200-year-old tradition in the United States Marine Corps—fighting terrorists. The Corps' history of such confrontations dates back to 1804, when Marine 1st Lt. Presley O'Bannon led his men to defeat the Barbary Pirates.

During an early morning ceremony, 1st Lt. David Dobb was among twenty U.S. Marines who received the Purple Heart for wounds sustained in recent combat. Since arriving "in-country," 116 Marines in this battalion have received the Purple Heart, and yet over seventy of them have decided to stay in Iraq rather than return home, even though, by consequence of their wounds, they can do so.

I asked 1st Lt. Dobb, who sustained injuries to his hand, why so many of these young men decided to stick it out even though they'd been hurt. "This is what these Marines signed up to do," he told me, "and we're going to see this mission through until the job's done the way it is supposed to be."

Sergeant Kenneth Conde, a squad leader with the 2nd Battalion, 4th Marines, was leading his unit in a nighttime raid this week when insurgents tried to ambush his platoon. In the intense gunfight that ensued, Conde was hit in the shoulder. His corpsman quickly treated him and he stayed in the fight. By the time it was over, they had killed six terrorists and collected a pile of enemy weapons and ordnance. Conde's grievous wounds were a free ticket home, yet he decided to stay with the battalion. I asked him why. "There's no other choice for a sergeant in the Marine Corps," Conde explained. "You have to lead your Marines."

It's this kind of courage that makes me wonder what some in our media are thinking. A few weeks ago, Andy Rooney, a syndicated newspaper columnist and commentator for CBS News's *60 Minutes*, wrote a column titled, "Our Soldiers in Iraq Aren't Heroes." Rooney is part of a team of "journalists" at CBS News who have gone out of their way to protest U.S. policies in Iraq and the War on Terror.

Rooney, who to my knowledge hasn't been to Iraq, wrote, "You can be sure our soldiers in Iraq are not all brave heroes gladly risking their lives for us sitting comfortably back here at home."

Not heroes, Andy? Meet Lance Cpl. Conyers, a member of Fox Company, 2nd Battalion, 4th Marines. On 6 April, Conyers was on patrol with his squad when they were ambushed. "I was out in front at an unlucky moment and took a round to the chest," Conyers told me, "then one ricocheted off the light pole next to me and hit me in the leg." The corpsman rushed to Conyers's side and treated him, and Conyers stayed in the fight.

In his column, Rooney insists that our troops "want to come home," and says if he had the chance to interrogate our guys in uniform to prove his point, he'd ask them, "If you could have a medal or a trip home, which would you take?"

Which do you think Conyers chose, Andy? The bullet Conyers took in the chest was fired from an AK-47. It struck inches from his heart and could have killed him. But because of the plate of armor he was wearing—armor that critics claim either doesn't exist, or if it did, it wouldn't work—Conyers is alive. The wound Conyers received to his leg, a "through and through" wound, was his ticket home. But did Conyers take it? Of course not. Of the wound, he told me, "That won't keep me down." He said he owes it to his squad to "continue on and fight."

Lance Cpl. Conyers is just one of hundreds of Marines and soldiers who, while fighting to defend the American public and liberate the Iraqi people, have been shot, hit, wounded, and treated, only to stay on the battlefield with their units instead of going home. These are remarkable young Americans.

Rooney complains in his column, "We don't learn much about what our soldiers in Iraq are thinking or doing." Well, Andy, now you know—they're fighting heroically. Want to know more?

They go on patrol—wearing twenty-five-pound flak jackets and six-pound helmets. They carry another thirty to forty pounds of weapons and ammunition. On longer missions they carry up to seventy pounds on their backs. By day, they're America's diplomats—canvassing neighborhoods to befriend the local Iraqis, conducting intelligence operations, and bringing supplies and gifts to Iraqi families and children. By night, they use the intelligence they gather from Iraqis who want the terrorists out of their neighborhoods and conduct raids to root them out of their hiding places.

And they're having a great deal of success. Second Lt. Tim Mayer told me, "When we first got here, things were a little challenging. But every day, the situation seems to get a little better. We're getting weapons and IEDs turned in by the local people, and they are happier that we are here."

A lot of the Marines who are here now were also here for the first semester of the war. Many, including those in Conyers's unit, which was in Okinawa this time last year, have been away from home and their families for the better part of eighteen months over the last two years. Their motivation and morale remain high. But to Andy Rooney, these courageous young Americans "are victims, not heroes."

✪ OPERATION IRAQI FREEDOM SIT REP #47
Ramadi, Iraq
Tuesday, 11 May 2004
1400 Hours Local

A video was posted on a militant Islamic website today. The grisly tape shows the beheading of Nicholas Berg, a U.S. civilian whose body was found near Baghdad three days ago.

Just about a week or so ago, CBS News showed some other videotaped footage on its *60 Minutes* television show. It was part of a report on abuse of Iraqi detainees at the Abu Ghraib prison by U.S. soldiers. It's pretty obvious that things were not what they should have been at Abu Ghraib. But those responsible will be held accountable, and rightfully so. However, those acts are an aberration compared to the thousands of acts of kindness that U.S. troops are showing to the Iraqi people daily. And as bad as the Abu Ghraib misdeeds were, they pale by comparison with the brutal atrocities being perpetrated by the terrorists here in Iraq.

Bush administration officials rightly condemned the repugnant behavior at Abu Ghraib. The president called it "abhorrent," and Secretary of Defense Don Rumsfeld said it was "totally unacceptable and un-American." The Pentagon announced that those responsible would be court-martialed. But that isn't enough for the press and the president's political opponents in an election year.

Sadly, the drumbeat over Abu Ghraib is having an adverse effect on morale. Tens of thousands of soldiers and Marines who have served honorably in Iraq now wonder if their service will be tainted in the minds of their countrymen by the shameful behavior of a dozen or so miscreants.

Over the past two years, I've spent months in the field with U.S. forces in Iraq, Afghanistan, and throughout the Middle East. During the march to Baghdad in April 2003, I saw hundreds of Iraqis taken prisoner—many of whom turned themselves in to American forces, knowing they would fare much better in U.S. custody than in Saddam's army. They were all treated humanely.

In battle, I watched a Marine risk his life to rescue a wounded Iraqi woman. Troops in the units with which I was embedded treated the Iraqi people with dignity and respect. U.S. forces have played soccer with the kids and built schools with supplies sent by the American public. I've seen Marines give their last MREs to hungry Iraqi children.

I've also seen *why* these troops are in Iraq. I've looked into Saddam's mass graves—a site that makes you sick to your stomach. I saw the evidence of atrocities committed by Saddam, Uday, and Qusay—tapes showing innocent Iraqis having their tongues cut out, or being blindfolded, bound, and marched off the edge of two- and three-story buildings. I saw Iraqi schools turned into ammunition depots and mosques used as bunkers.

U.S. forces are hard at work in their daily efforts to free Iraq and pave the way for their coming democracy and free elections. And just yesterday, American forces destroyed the Baghdad headquarters of rebel Shi'ite Muqtada al-Sadr and killed eighteen of his high-level cohorts during an overnight firefight.

There is no doubt that crimes were committed at Abu Ghraib. But if Abu Ghraib becomes the story that Americans most remember about this war, that would be a crime too.

✪ OPERATION IRAQI FREEDOM SIT REP #48
    Baghdad, Iraq
    Thursday, 19 June 2004
    0950 Hours Local

Eleven days ago, the United Nations Security Council unanimously approved Resolution 1546. Sponsored by the U.S. and Britain, the resolution is intended to end the formal occupation of Iraq on 30 June and transfer "full sovereignty" to an interim Iraqi government. This temporary authority—composed of people selected by Iraqis, not Americans, Britons, or the United Nations—will in turn arrange for nationwide elections in January 2005. The resolution also authorizes a continuation of the U.S.-led multinational force for Iraq until a constitutionally elected government takes power, expected by early 2006, or if the Iraqi government requests it.

But Americans are an impatient lot. We're used to movies on demand, fast food from drive-thru windows, express oil changes, and high speed Internet service. Americans want it when we want it—and we want it now!

Our eagerness for instant results has served as a stimulus to the U.S. economy, inspired scientific progress, and promoted advances in technology. We now build homes and commercial structures in days and weeks that used to take months and even years.

But when it comes to constructing institutions of democracy, the desire for immediate outcomes is a vice rather than a virtue. When interim Iraqi president Ghazi al-Yawer visited the United States, he thanked the American people for the sacrifices we've made in liberating his country and offered assurances that, despite the difficulties, things are on track for a real democratic government in Baghdad. There is, of course, one pre-condition—the transition to democracy will only work as long as the U.S.-led coalition continues to stay the course.

Therein lies the rub—staying the course. According to recent public opinion surveys, a majority of both the American people and the population of Iraq have lost patience with our efforts to bring democracy to Baghdad. Fifteen months after the fall of Saddam's statue in Firdus Square, and six months after he was dragged from a rat-hole, most Iraqis and most Americans want U.S. troops out—*now*.

Set aside the fact that both U.S. and Iraqi polls sampled public opinion in the aftermath of the Abu Ghraib prison fiasco and its attendant tidal wave of negative publicity. As long as Abu Ghraib remains the focal point of a hostile media, it is unlikely that public perception of recognizing the progress in Iraq will improve.

In addition to Abu Ghraib, the media is focused on the perceived increasing violence of the jihadists. Secretary of Defense Don Rumsfeld answered a salvo of press-conference queries based on the premise "that because the violence is escalating," shouldn't we "cut our losses?"

Such a course of action is unthinkable. In the months after the terrorist attacks of September 11, President George W. Bush warned that the War on Terror would be a long, tough fight. Marines and soldiers on the ground in Iraq acknowledge that the violence is likely to increase, right through the establishment of a new Iraqi government. They see the rash of terror attacks on Iraqi civilians and leadership targets as a sign of increasing desperation by foreign terrorists, tribal sheiks and imams who will lose power once a democratic regime is installed in Baghdad.

Progress in Iraq was never going to be immediate. The global War on Terror was never going to be won in Afghanistan alone. Don

Rumsfeld referred to it as a "long hard slog." That's the kind of message Franklin Delano Roosevelt repeated time and again during our last war of national survival—World War II. It's the kind of message that Lyndon Johnson failed to deliver during Vietnam.

But the war on jihadist terror in Iraq isn't Vietnam. We survived fatigue and failure in Vietnam. We won't survive failure in this war. Unless we want our children to live in constant fear of Islamic radicals bringing down buildings on their heads, there has to be a democratic outcome in Iraq. That's why the president's words at MacDill Air Force Base on 16 June were so important. "With each step forward on the path to self-government and self-reliance," Bush said, "the terrorists will grow more desperate and more violent. They see Iraqis taking their country back. They see freedom taking root. The killers know they have no future in a free Iraq. They want America to abandon the mission and to break our word. So they're attacking our soldiers and free Iraqis. They're doing everything in their power to prevent the full transition to democracy."

President Bush added, "We can expect more attacks in the coming few weeks . . . more car bombs, more 'suiciders,' more attempts on the lives of Iraqi officials. But our coalition is standing firm. New Iraq's leaders are not intimidated. I will not yield, and neither will the leaders of Iraq."

The troops out here are hoping that the American people in the fast lane have the patience not to yield either.

✪ OPERATION IRAQI FREEDOM SIT REP #49
   Ramadi, Iraq
   Saturday, 23 July 2004
   1500 Hours Local

"There was about a half-mile stretch of the main road in town that instantly became a battlefield as we moved through it," explained Maj.

Mike Wylie, the executive officer of 2nd Battalion, 4th Marines. Wylie was describing the genesis of a truly violent clash on "Wicked Wednesday" here in Ramadi, the provincial capital that lies about seventy miles west of Baghdad.

Marines and soldiers were on patrol, making their way through town in 120-degree mid-afternoon heat, when insurgents set off an IED in an attempted ambush on the Marine convoy. The IED exploded beside the vehicle that was carrying our FOX News cameraman, Mal James, who jumped out of the Humvee to capture some of the most dramatic war footage since the major hostilities of sixteen months ago.

The ensuing battle, involving more than 600 soldiers and Marines, lasted well over four hours and raged over ten city blocks in the vicinity of the government center. During the battle, twenty-five insurgents were killed, seventeen more wounded, and another twenty-five taken off the streets and into custody. Fourteen Marines sustained only minor injuries during the clash.

The IED—and its deadly cousin, the VBIED (Vehicular-Borne Improvised Explosive Device) or car bomb—is now the preferred form of attack against coalition forces and the new Iraqi government. They are used in every way conceivable—in vehicles, hidden in trash cans beside the road, even placed in dead animals. The enemy no longer wants to face soldiers and Marines head-to-head, as evidenced by the lopsided outcome of Wednesday's firefight.

One evening earlier in the week, just after 2100 hours, the Marines responded when Iraqi police called in a suspected VBIED. The Iraqi officers pulled up to a vehicle parked in the middle of a six-lane highway, inspected it, and quickly realized it was a car bomb. Though the Iraqi police are training to deal with IEDs, they don't yet have the kind of equipment that the Marines do to neutralize them. So the Marine Explosive Ordinance Disposal Team was dispatched with a security force from Weapons Company.

While the engineers and EOD specialists attached to the Weapons Company prepared to deploy a robot to detonate the bomb, insurgent mortars attacked us. Since speed was now a necessity, the Marines decided instead to use a TOW, a wire-guided anti-tank missile, to destroy the VBIED. Mal James's camera caught the dramatic effect of Sgt. Jeremiah Randall, the TOW section leader, firing his weapon and eliminating the IED before it had the chance to do any harm.

Here in Ramadi, the Iraqi national police and national guard are now out in force. It's noticeable how much they have progressed since I was here in April. They now patrol streets, guard checkpoints, and search neighborhoods, helping to root out terrorists. As one Marine put it, "The Iraqi police realize it is up to them to provide safety and security for their fellow citizens," so it gives them incentive.

When I interviewed Gen. Michael Hagee, the commandant of the Marine Corps, during his visit to Ramadi, he acknowledged the complexity of the task—as well as the progress. In speaking of his Marines, he said their job "is difficult. But, are they making a difference? Are they helping the Iraqis to help themselves? Absolutely. And, if you call that winning, then we probably are."

❂ OPERATION IRAQI FREEDOM SIT REP #50
   Ramadi, Iraq
   Thursday, 18 August 2004
   1925 Hours Local

There is little doubt that the violence is escalating as the U.S. and Iraqi elections approach. An insurgent missile killed six Iraqis and wounded twenty-one others in Mosul today. In a central Baghdad neighborhood, a mortar round killed seven and injured another forty-seven.

Here in Ramadi, an Iraqi male suspected of hijacking vehicles to be used for car bombings was hauled into police headquarters. We were granted unprecedented access to watch and listen while the chief of police interrogated the suspect, who confessed to hijacking two cars and four trucks. Without coercion or humiliation, he also confessed to being "a soldier of God" and of killing a police officer.

Yesterday we were embedded with the Marine Weapons Company when an IED was detonated beside the convoy nearly killing the 2nd Brigade commander, Col. "Buck" Conner. Staff Sgt. Michael Drake, a Weapons Company platoon sergeant, described the attack this way: "We received a call while we were at the hospital with the battalion commander that the brigade commander had been hit by an IED and was taking fire, and they were forced to respond. We hurried to their location, became engaged behind the mall, and took heavy fire for over four hours."

In fact, it was an amazing demonstration of Marine and Army firepower. Though they had Cobra gunships and two fixed-wing aircraft overhead, the close urban streets had to be secured building by building, using firepower from Marine infantrymen, armored Humvees, and a platoon of Army Bradley fighting vehicles. When it was over, twelve enemy combatants were dead, four were wounded, and fifteen others were detained. During the fight, eleven Marines were wounded—including Cpt. Mark Carlton, the Fox Company commander, who suffered dozens of shrapnel holes in his body from an enemy RPG.

In the aftermath of the battle I asked Lt. J. D. Stevens, who has been here since March, if democracy could work. His response: "If given enough time, yes."

That's the key. Democracy in Iraq is taking root, but it won't be built overnight.

✪ OPERATION IRAQI FREEDOM SIT REP #51
Fallujah, Iraq
Friday, 17 December 2004
2200 Hours Local

"It's stuff you hear about in boot camp, about World War II and Tarawa Marines who won the Medal of Honor," said Lance Cpl. Rob Rogers of the 1st Battalion, 3rd Marines in the aftermath of the seven-day battle for Fallujah. Rogers was describing the actions of his fellow Marine Sgt. Rafael Peralta, a Mexican immigrant who enlisted in the Marine Corps the day he received his green card.

Most Americans haven't heard about Rafael Peralta. With few exceptions, most of our mainstream media haven't bothered to write about him. The next time you log onto the Internet, do a Google search on Rafael Peralta. As of this writing, the Internet's most used search engine will provide you with only forty-nine citations from news sources that have bothered to write about this heroic young man.

Then, just for laughs, do a Google search on Pablo Paredes. *Hundreds* of media outlets have written about him. The wire services have blasted his story to thousands of newspapers. Television and radio debate programs gladly provide the public with talking heads who can speak eloquently on the actions of Pablo Paredes.

You see, Pablo Paredes, a Navy petty officer third class, did something the liberal elites consider "heroic" and the media consider "newsworthy." He defied a military order. Last week, Paredes refused to board his ship bound for Iraq along with 5,000 other sailors and Marines. He showed up on the pier wearing a black t-shirt that read, "Like a Cabinet member, I resign."

We know this because Paredes had the courtesy and forethought to notify the local media that he would commit an act of cowardice the following day. Perhaps he hoped to follow the lead of another famous war protester who went on to become a U.S. senator and his party's presidential nominee by throwing away his military medals.

Paredes stopped short of trashing his military ID in front of the cameras because he said he didn't want to be charged with the destruction of government property. The media, we are promised, will continue to follow this story intently.

But it's a shame that the media focus on such cynical acts of cowardice when they could tell stories about *real* heroes like Peralta, who "saved the life of my son and every Marine in that room," according to Garry Morrison, the father of a Marine in Peralta's unit—Lance Cpl. Adam Morrison.

On the morning of 15 November 2004, the men of 1st Battalion, 3rd Marines awoke before sunrise and continued what they'd been doing for seven days previously—cleansing the city of Fallujah of terrorists, house by house.

At the fourth house they encountered that morning, the Marines kicked in the door and "cleared" the front rooms, but then noticed a locked door off to the side that required inspection. Peralta threw open the closed door, but behind it were three terrorists with AK-47s. Peralta was hit in the head and chest with multiple shots at close range.

Peralta's fellow Marines had to step over his body to continue the shootout with the terrorists. As the firefight raged on, a "yellow, foreign-made, oval-shaped grenade," as Lance Cpl. Travis Kaemmerer described it, rolled into the room where they were all standing and came to a stop near Peralta's body.

But Sgt. Rafael Peralta wasn't dead—yet. This twenty-five-year-old immigrant, who enlisted in the Marines as soon as he was eligible, and who volunteered for front line duty in Fallujah, had just saved the lives of his buddies by taking the first bullets from that room full of terrorists. But he still had one last act of heroism in him.

Peralta was the polar opposite of Paredes, the petty officer who turned his back on his shipmates and mocked his commander in chief. Peralta was proud to serve his adopted country. On his bedroom walls in his parents' home hung only three items—a copy of the United States Constitution, the Bill of Rights, and his boot camp graduation certificate. Before he set out for Fallujah, Sgt. Rafael Peralta wrote to his fourteen-year-old brother, "Be proud of me, bro... and be proud of being an American."

Not only can Peralta's family be proud of him, but his fellow Marines are alive because of him. As Peralta lay near death on the floor of a Fallujah terrorist hideout, he spotted that yellow grenade, which had rolled across the floor next to his near-lifeless body. He realized that when it detonated it would take out the rest of his squad.

To save his fellow Marines, Peralta reached out, grabbed the grenade, and tucked it under his abdomen, where it exploded.

"Most of the Marines in the house were in the immediate area of the grenade," Lance Cpl. Kaemmerer said sadly. "We will never forget the second chance at life that Sgt. Peralta gave us." Each of the Marines in that house knows that Sgt. Peralta is a *real hero*.

Unfortunately, unlike Paredes, Peralta got little media coverage. He's unlikely to have books written about him or movies made about his extraordinarily selfless sacrifice. He may receive the Medal of Honor. And if he does, that Medal of Honor is likely to be displayed next to the only items that hung on his bedroom wall—the Constitution, Bill of Rights, and his boot camp graduation certificate.

Yes, there are still heroes in America, and Sgt. Rafael Peralta was one of them. It's just too bad that the media continually fails to recognize them.

✪ OPERATION IRAQI FREEDOM SIT REP #52
Baghdad, Iraq
Thursday, 3 February 2005
1030 Hours Local

It's now happened twice in less than four months, though it is more rare than an eclipse of the sun, a shooting star, or a volcanic eruption. It ought to be celebrated as a magnificent, historic event, but it isn't.

I'm referring to the Sunday, 30 January 2005, Iraqi election. Like the October election in Afghanistan before it, it signifies the birth of a new democracy. Both elections mark the first vote of a long-oppressed people, yet the media presents them as dangerous events.

For months, the so-called mainstream media has struggled to depict the Iraqi elections as a fools' errand foisted on the people of Iraq by George W. Bush. When I was in London last week, the BBC and many European newspapers were predicting an "invalid out-come" because "the Sunni population is boycotting the vote."

Last Tuesday, Senate opponents of the president's Iraq policy lined up behind Robert Byrd and Teddy Kennedy to declare Iraq to be "a quagmire . . . a total failure."

And despite a pre-election poll of 33,000 Iraqis by the Arabic paper *Asharq Al-Awsat*, in which 72.4 percent said they intended to vote—the U.S. media continue to denigrate the process. "Is a 50 or 60 percent turnout enough?" reporters skeptically asked the White House, State Department, and every U.S. and Iraqi official they could find in Baghdad. But when 60 percent of American voters went to the polls in November, it was considered a "historic" turnout. You just can't please the press.

But all of this misses the point. Iraqis came out in unprecedented numbers, despite nine suicide bombers and insurgents firing mor-tars in Election Day attacks. Iraqis voted for members of provincial parliaments and a 270-member National Assembly, which will write Iraq's constitution. Sunday's election was the first multi-party election in more than fifty years—and the first in the entire 5,000-year history of Mesopotamia where every man and woman, regardless of tribe, religion, or ethnic origin, was allowed to cast a ballot.

Even Arab television outlets, like Al Jazeera, documented this "grand moment in Iraqi history," as the president said in his news conference. Sunday's election was an instant success and a remarkable accomplishment—first because the terrorists tried so hard to stop it and failed; second, because more than 17,000 candidates were willing to put their lives on the line, vying for 270 seats in the first freely elected National Assembly in the long history of Mesopotamia; and finally, because so many Iraqi women braved bombs, bullets, threats, and intimidation to go to the polls.

Watching the Iraqis proudly hold up thumbs dipped in ink as evidence that they had voted brought tears even to the eyes of cynics in Europe and the doubters in America.

It was the same last October, when whole Afghani families walked miles, skirting minefields and defying threats from Taliban thugs, just to vote. There, it was Moqadasa Sidiqi, a nineteen-year-old woman, who cast the first ballot in Afghanistan's history. *A woman cast the first ballot!*

Here in Iraq, the "feminine factor" is also going to be profoundly important to the country's future—far more so than whether the voter is a Sunni or a Shi'ite. By law, one-third of the new National Assembly must be women. Women are about to transform Iraq, just as they are transforming Afghanistan.

Last summer I interviewed the elected governor of Al Anbar province, Iraq's largest, in the heart of the Sunni Triangle. Months before this momentous election, he told me: "Women voting will change everything. No woman who carries a child for nine months wants that child to grow up to be a suicide terrorist. They want the politicians to give their children something to live for, not die for— and we will have to do it."

Most secular and religious leaders in Iraq echo that judgment— it's only the radical few who want to turn the country back to the Middle Ages. The National Assembly elected on Sunday will not only name a president, two deputy presidents, a prime minister, and a cabinet, but will also produce a new constitution by 15 August 2005. That constitution will then be submitted to a popular referendum—a second free election by mid-October. This new Iraqi constitution will become the law of the land if affirmed by a majority of the voters nationwide. Approval of the constitution will yield yet a third free election on 15 December 2005, to elect a new government.

All of this seems to have escaped the attention of the president's critics in our media—as did the television ads produced by pro-democracy organizations to encourage Iraqi turnout. In one, an elderly man is confronted on the street by a group of masked, armed thugs. The man is soon joined by a handful of his neighbors, then more, until the mass of people greatly outnumber the terrorists, who set off running from the crowd of ordinary, unarmed, but courageous Iraqis.

The voiceover says: "On January 30, we meet our destiny and our duty. We are not alone, and we are not afraid. Our strength is in our unity; together we will work, and together prevail." No ad like this could have possibly run under Saddam's rule.

The terrorist in chief in Iraq, Abu Musab Al-Zarqawi, in a statement showing just how desperate the insurgents were to prevent democracy from taking root, condemned the elections. "We have declared a fierce war on this evil principle of democracy and those who follow this wrong ideology." He went on to brand anyone who took part as an "infidel."

President Bush, in his second inaugural address, said, "By our efforts, we have lit a fire as well—a fire in the minds of men. It warms those who feel its power, it burns those who fight its progress, and one day this untamed fire of freedom will reach the darkest corners of our world."

As if to validate both his remarks and the power of the Iraqi ballots, the television cameras panned to a touching, powerful scene in the balcony as the president delivered his State of the Union address on 2 February. Standing next to Laura Bush was Sofia Taleb al-Suhail, an Iraqi woman who had just voted, and behind her, Janet and Bill Norwood, the parents of Marine Corps Sgt. Byron Norwood of Pflugerville, Texas, who was killed during the assault on Fallujah. Mr. and Mrs. Norwood stood to enthusiastic and sustained applause. The applause became thunderous when Sofia reached over and hugged Janet. That woman-to-woman connection told much more eloquently than any pundit's analysis just what the Iraqi story is all about.

It was an ember from the fire that President Bush said is blazing in Iraq. And, God willing, may it soon spread to some of those other dark corners of the Middle East.

✪ OPERATION IRAQI FREEDOM SIT REP #53
Washington, DC
Friday, 11 March 2005
2245 Hours Local

Ever since U.S. troops first went to Afghanistan in October 2001, our supposedly more experienced "betters" in Europe and the "prudent potentates of the press" have warned us that U.S. military action against an Islamic nation was dangerous. They said that attacking Muslims would cause the "Arab street" to rise up and crush us. This

theme was widely replayed in the buildup to Operation Iraqi Freedom—and has been reiterated many times in the aftermath of Saddam Hussein's capture.

Since his second inaugural address, President Bush has repeatedly
been castigated for his "naiveté" on one hand and for his "aggressive
arrogance" on the other. Why? Because he boldly tells those who suf-
fer tyranny that the United States "will not ignore your oppression or
excuse your oppressors. When you stand for your liberty, we will
stand with you."

Yet, despite the carping critics—and the carnage caused by those
who would rather die than see freedom flourish—any objective
observer has to conclude that George W. Bush is right. "The call of
freedom" does indeed come "to every mind and every soul." Even in
the Middle East freedom is indeed on the march—even down the
"Arab street."

It was evident last October in Afghanistan, in the ballots cast by
Palestinians in early January and in late January on the ink-stained
fingers of Iraqi men and women, raised in proud defiance against
murderous thugs who would return them to brutal bondage.

Whether the America-haters and Bush-bashers want to acknowledge it or not, the "call of freedom" is genuine. And it's now being
heard in places where American "influence" has long been deemed by
the "experts" to be minimal, at best. Here are examples:

● In December, hundreds of thousands of Ukrainians peacefully
  protested to force a new election when a rigged vote installed
  Vladimir Putin's handpicked presidential candidate. As a result,
  reformist Viktor Yushchenko governs today in Kiev. The Bush
  administration needed to do little more than lend its voice to the
  calls for a free and fair election.

- Last week, in long-suffering Syrian-occupied Lebanon, tens of thousands unarmed Christian and Muslim civilians protested the assassination of former prime minister Rafik Hariri, forcing the resignation of Syria's puppet government in Beirut. In the aftermath, the new Iraqi government—and even the French—joined our call for the Syrians to withdraw their forces from Lebanon and deport the residue of Saddam's regime hiding there.

- Though they have yet to fully comply, the Syrians have arrested and turned over the former dictator's half-brother, Sabawi Ibrahim al Hassan. And to ensure that those in Damascus who support terror don't get the idea that this is sufficient, President Bush has since told them to "get your troops and your secret services out of Lebanon, and give democracy a chance."

- In Cairo, Hosni Mubarak, never known to be a friend of liberty or democratic institutions, has announced that opposition candidates will be allowed to run for office in the upcoming Egyptian elections. Mubarak has been the only presidential "candidate" since taking power in 1981. While questions remain about who will be "allowed" to run, a taste of liberty in a democratic election may ignite the "fire of freedom" among the people of the Nile.

- And now, even the royal family in Riyadh, Saudi Arabia, seems to be getting the message, though the recent Saudi "municipal elections" were more show than substance—the elected councilors wield little power. The ruling House of Saud appoints as many councilors as were elected and only men can vote—yet the taste of democracy has intensified the call on the "Arab street" for *real* elections.

Last week, the Saudi kingdom's foreign minister Prince Saud al-Faisal, speaking the heretofore unthinkable, said that in future elections women "may" have the right to vote. Unfortunately, he then added, "We know we want to reform, we know we want to modernize, but for God's sake leave us alone."

And therein lies the first problem: The prince doesn't get it. It's not just President Bush's promise, "When you stand for your liberty we will stand with you," that is at work in Saudi Arabia. It's really a quest for freedom that's sweeping down the "Arab street," right past minarets preaching repression and hatred for all things Western.

But Saud al-Faisal isn't alone in misunderstanding what freedom really means—and from whence it springs. Last week, when President Bush confronted Vladimir Putin about Russia's freedom of the press, Putin shot back with: "We didn't criticize you when you fired those reporters at CBS." Apparently Putin or his advisers believe that a U.S. president has that power.

Thus the second problem: Saud al-Faisal and Putin apparently believe that holding an election is enough. It's not. As we have learned from the "election" of Hugo Chavez in Venezuela, there's much more to freedom than casting a ballot. Liberty also means a free press; freedom to worship—or not; the rule of law where justice is tempered with mercy; freedom from fear—of government, criminals, or outsiders, and the freedom to come and go, to speak politically, and to work and create wealth.

All of this—and more—is what freedom is all about. Elections are not the end of the process, just the beginning. That's what's wrong with the argument being waged by some in Congress to start withdrawing American forces from Iraq now that there has been an election. Whether it's the "Arab street," or elsewhere, liberty doesn't march to the beat of a cadence—it arrives to the sound of many drummers, and impatience is never the friend of freedom.

GLOSSARY

AAV: Assault Amphibious Vehicle
   Carries eighteen to twenty Marines from ship to shore; serves as ground troop transport. Armament: .50-caliber machine gun and 40mm automatic grenade launcher. *See also* **LVT.**

ABM: Anti-Ballistic Missile

AGM: Air-to-Ground Missile

AK-47: Russian- or Chinese-made automatic rifle.

Amn Al Khass: Iraq's internal intelligence and security service; also known as SSS, Special Security Services.

APC: Armored Personnel Carrier

APU: Auxiliary Power Unit

ASP: Ammunition Supply Point

ATGM: Anti-Tank Guided Missile

AWACS: Airborne Warning and Control System (U.S. Air Force)

BMP: A Soviet-made, tracked, infantry fighting vehicle. Carries up to eight troops and is normally armed with a 73mm or a 30mm cannon and ATGMs.

Bn: Battalion

CAAT: Combined Anti-Armor Team
   Consists of several Humvees equipped with TOW and Javelin ATGMs, .50-caliber machine guns, and grenade launchers.

CAS: Close Air Support

cas-evac: casualty evacuation

CENTCOM: Central Command (Also USCENTCOM)
U.S. Central Command, one of nine U.S. unified military commands; headquartered at McDill Air Force Base, Tampa, Florida. During Operation Iraqi Freedom, CENTCOM maintained a forward headquarters in Doha, Qatar.

CG: Commanding General

CO: Commanding Officer

CP: Command Post

DASC: Direct Air Support Center
Provides a direct communications link between Marine air and ground units.

EGBU-28: Enhanced Guided Bomb Unit
More accurate version of the "bunker buster" that uses GPS for guidance. *See also* **GBU.**

EOD: Explosive Ordnance Disposal

EP-3: Lockheed EP-3E Aries II aircraft, designed specifically for Signals Intelligence (SIGINT) collection. The aircraft operates with a five-person flight crew and as many as twenty intelligence specialists.

EPW: Enemy Prisoner of War

FAC: Forward Air Controller
Provides direction and control for aircraft firing or dropping ordnance in support of ground troops.

FARP: Forward Arming and Refueling Point

FO: Forward Observer
Provides fire direction and control for artillery or mortars.

Frag Order: Fragmentary order
An abbreviated operations order that a commander uses to inform troops of information they need to carry out an assigned mission.

G-3: Operations and training function for a military command of brigade or higher. *See also* **S-3.**

GBU: Guided Bomb Unit
E.g., GBU-15, an unpowered, glide weapon used to destroy high-value enemy targets; the GBU-37 "bunker buster" is a five-thousand-pound laser-guided conventional explosive with a 4,400-pound penetrating warhead. The operator

illuminates a target with a laser designator and then the munition is guided to a spot of laser energy reflected from the target.

GOSP: Gas-Oil Separation Plant

GPS: Global Positioning System

Gunny: Slang for Marine gunnery sergeant.

HARM: High-Speed Anti-Radiation Missile
An air-to-ground missile, specifically the AGM-88 HARM.

HEAT: High Explosive Anti-Tank
Armor-piercing, anti-tank ammunition.

HET: (U.S. Army) Heavy Equipment Transporter

HET: (U.S. Marines) Human Exploitation Team
Helps collect and interpret intelligence.

HMLA: Marine Light Attack Helicopter Squadron
Flies AH1J Cobras and armed UH1N "Hueys."

HMM: Marine Medium Helicopter Squadron
Flies CH-46 "Sea Knight" helicopters.

HUMINT: Human intelligence—as contrasted with electronic, satellite, or other intelligence gathering.

HVT: High-Value Target

ICM: Improved Conventional Munitions

ID: In the context of a military unit, *Infantry Division*. Also an abbreviation for identification.

IED: Improvised Explosive Device

IFB: Interruptible Feedback Line
Allows a television producer, director, talent, and others to communicate with each other during a program; usually through an earpiece.

IFF: Identification Friend or Foe

I-MEF: 1st Marine Expeditionary Force

JDAM: Joint Direct Attack Munition
An unpowered, GPS-guided, one-thousand or two-thousand pound, glide bomb.

Jihaz Haneen: Clandestine Baath intelligence and security organization.

JSTARS: Joint Surveillance Target Attack Radar System

LAR: Light Armored Reconnaissance Battalion
Marine unit equipped with LAVs for rapid ground reconnaissance forward and on the flanks of a larger force.

LAV: Light Armored Vehicle
LAV-25, wheeled light armored vehicle employed by Marine LAR Battalion. Carries six troops; armament: 25mm chain gun.

LVT: Landing Vehicle, Tracked; *See also* **AAV**.

LVTC: Landing Vehicle, Tracked, Command
An LVT equipped with communications equipment and configured so that a commander can use an LVTC-7 as his command. Armament: .50-caliber machine gun.

LZ: Landing Zone

MAG: Marine Air Group

MAW: Marine Aircraft Wing
The 3rd MAW served as the Air Combat Element of 1st Marine Expeditionary Force.

MAWTS: Marine Aviation Weapons and Tactics Squadron

MEU: Marine Expeditionary Unit
The smallest air-ground task force, consisting of a reinforced infantry battalion, a composite helicopter squadron, and a logistics support element.

MIA: Missing In Action

MOPP: Mission Oriented Protective Posture
Designation for the protective suit, mask, and other equipment worn to shield troops from nuclear, chemical, and biological weapons. *See also* **NBC suit.**

MP: Military Police

MPS: Maritime Prepositioning Ship
Large "roll-on roll-off" vessels full of military equipment, weapons, and ammunition; strategically placed to expedite the deployment of U.S. military units.

MRE: Meal, Ready-to-Eat

Mukhabarat: The foreign intelligence service of Iraq

NBC suit: Nuclear, biological, and chemical protective gear

NCO: Non-commissioned officer in the military services

NOK: Next of Kin

NVG: Night-Vision Goggles

OGA: Other Government Agency
Euphemism for CIA or other intelligence service personnel operating in Iraq, Afghanistan, and other places.

Overwatch: A base of fire from heavy weapons in support of a maneuver

PAO: Public Affairs Officer

PAX: U.S. military abbreviation for *passengers*, usually in an aircraft. Also "packs."

PFC: Private First Class

POW: Prisoner of War

QRF: Quick Reaction Force

RAP: Rocket-Assisted Projectiles

RCT: Regimental Combat Team

Rein.: Reinforced

ROE: Rules of Engagement

RPG: Rocket-Propelled Grenade

RPV: Remotely Piloted Vehicle
Radio controlled aircraft used to conduct reconnaissance and/or intelligence collection. *See also* **UAV.**

S-1: Staff officer that performs administrative record-keeping and personnel function for a battalion or regiment.

S-2: Staff officer that performs intelligence and counter-intelligence function for a battalion or regiment.

S-3: Staff officer performing operations plans and training functions for a battalion or regiment.

S-4: Staff officer who performs logistics, maintenance, and supply function for a battalion or regiment.

SAM: Surface-to-Air Missile

SAW: Squad Automatic Weapon
Carried by one member of each Marine infantry fire team.

SERE: Survival, Escape, Resistance, and Evasion
Plan followed in the event a pilot or other Armed Forces member is down or lost behind enemy lines.

sharqi: Iraqi sandstorm

Sit Rep: situation report

SOP: Standard Operating Procedure

TAA: Tactical Assembly Area

TF: Task Force

TOC: Tactical Operations Center

TOT: Time on Target

TOW: Tube-launched, Optically tracked, Wire-guided
Is the primary anti-tank missile used by the U.S. Marine Corps and the U.S. Army.

UAV: Unmanned Aerial Vehicle
Reconnaissance aircraft operated by remote radio control and/or GPS.

UN: United Nations

UNSCOM: UN Special Commission
The organization appointed by the UN to seek weapons of mass destruction in Iraq.

V Corps: U.S. Army forward-deployed headquarters for two divisions, a corps support command, and nine separate brigades totaling approximately 41,000 soldiers.

VBIED: Vehicular-Borne Improvised Explosive Device

VMU-2: Marine Unmanned Aerial Vehicle Squadron Two
Operated RPVs over the battlefield for the Regimental Combat teams. *See also* **UAV.**

WIA: Wounded In Action

WMD: Weapons of Mass Destruction

XO: Executive Officer

INDEX